Futurizing the Jews

Futurizing the Jews

ALTERNATIVE FUTURES FOR MEANINGFUL JEWISH EXISTENCE IN THE 21ST CENTURY

Tsvi Bisk and Moshe Dror

Foreword by Gad Yaacobi
Former Israeli Ambassador to the United Nations
and Cabinet Minister

Westport, Connecticut
London

Library of Congress Cataloging-in-Publication Data

Bisk, Tsvi, 1943–
  Futurizing the Jews : alternative futures for meaningful Jewish existence in the 21st century /
Tsvi Bisk and Moshe Dror ; foreword by Gad Yaacobi.
    p. cm.
  Includes bibliographical references and index.
  ISBN 0–275–96908–8 (alk. paper)
  1. Judaism—Forecasting. 2. Israel—Forecasting. 3. Twenty-first century—Forecasts. 4.
Jews—History. 5. Zionism—History. 6. Arab-Israeli conflict. I. Dror, Moshe, 1934– II. Title.
DS102.95.B58 2003
909′.04924083—dc21   2003042067

British Library Cataloguing in Publication Data is available.

Library of Congress Catalog Card Number: 2003042067
ISBN: 0–275–96908–8

First published in 2003

Praeger Publishers, 88 Post Road West, Westport, CT 06881
An imprint of Greenwood Publishing Group, Inc.
www.praeger.com

Printed in the United States of America

The paper used in this book complies with the
Permanent Paper Standard issued by the National
Information Standards Organization (Z39.48–1984).

10 9 8 7 6 5 4 3 2 1

This Book is Dedicated in Loving Memory to
Mordechai Nessyahu "Z'al"
Dr. Haim (Haimi) Nessyahu "Z'al"
Yehudit Nessyahu "Z'al"

Contents

Foreword by Gad Yaacobi   ix

Preface   xi

Acknowledgments   xiii

Introduction: The Task of the Jewish Futurist   xv

Chapter 1   The World We Live In   1

Chapter 2   The Triumph of Zionism   13

Chapter 3   Zionism in the Twenty-First Century   27

Chapter 4   The Special Case of American Jewry   43

Chapter 5   Israeli Grand Strategy: A Historical Critique   53

Chapter 6   Reinventing Israeli Grand Strategy   69

Chapter 7   Reinventing Israel-Diaspora Relations   89

Chapter 8   The Future of Arab-Jewish Relations   103

Chapter 9   The Future of Ethnic Relations and Israeli Culture   115

Chapter 10   The Future of Jewish-Christian Relations   135

Chapter 11   The Future of Jewish Identity   155

Chapter 12   The Cyber World We Live In   169

Chapter 13   The Future of Jewish Spirituality   179

Chapter 14   The Future of Jewish Learning   199

Chapter 15   The Jewish Community in Cyberspace   215

Appendix: A Brief Introduction to the Cosmotheistic Hypothesis
of Mordechai Nessyahu   231

Glossary   235

Bibliography   245

Index   251

Foreword

This ambitious book, *Futurizing the Jews*, presents a comprehensive critique of where the Jewish People are at the beginning of the twenty-first century, how they got there, and where they should be going if they want to survive.

The book is original, iconoclastic, and in some ways revolutionary. Its analysis treats the Jews as an integral part of what the authors call "the global *human* ecology." This approach represents a timely and forthright rejection of what they call the "Nation that Dwells Alone Syndrome" based upon a populist misinterpretation of the biblical injunction to be "a nation dwelling alone...not reckoning itself among the nations" (Numbers 23:9). Timely because it runs counter to present trends of Israeli isolationism that find ideological justification in this biblical passage.

It would be absurd to deny that the Jews and especially Israelis live in hostile environments and that many international organizations and countries "judge" Israel by a double standard unparalleled in modern times. This is a given, but Israel and its supporters amongst world Jewry must not give in to the temptation to respond with an emotional indignation that assumes that "the entire world is against us."

Indeed, the emotional anxiety with which we respond to our enemies might be a greater danger to us than the hostility of our enemies. Clarity of mind based upon clarity of analysis has to be the Jewish People's greatest asset. This book offers us a large portion of clear, realistic analysis in the sense that it deals with the global and Jewish reality as we find them and not with ideological wishful thinking. But it is also an idealistic book that presents a positive, even heroic, vision of what the Jewish future could be if we choose to apply our rational faculties to the new global reality and not give in to defensiveness.

The book is so wide-ranging in its scope that I would not attempt to inventory here the many original ideas it contains. My short list of its most salient contributions would include:

A stress on the Jewish future replacing our preoccupation with the Jewish past

A neo-Zionist ideological analysis of modern Jewish life that serves as an alternative to both post-Zionism and classical Zionism. This is particularly important because post-Zionism is essentially nihilistic and classical Zionism is increasingly irrelevant for growing numbers of Jews in Israel and the Diaspora.

The conceptualization of Jewish Grand Strategy and a clear delineation between ideology, policy, grand strategy, strategy, and tactics. The confusion of these various frames of reference has caused much mischief in Israeli politics and decision making since the Six-Day War.

Clear and compelling proposals for what an all-Jewish Grand Strategy might consist of.

An entirely new concept of Israel-Diaspora relations based upon the principles of an all-Jewish Grand Strategy and the potential of the information technology revolution. What I have called a "New Partnership."

A description of a Jewish spiritual renewal that could be as appealing to the secular Jew as to the religious Jew.

The book is rich with additional ideas, analyses, and proposals. It challenges inherited assumptions and calls for positive action. I believe we have before us a book that must become a reference point for Jewish policymakers as quickly as possible.

Gad Yaacobi, former Israeli ambassador to the
United Nations and cabinet minister

Preface

Some words about the style and methodology of this book are in order. For the sake of grace of language we have decided to use the first person "I" throughout much of the book instead of the collective "we." In those places where we have reverted to the collective "we," we have no scientific explanation, we simply went by what seemed most comfortable and appropriate.

The first-person emphasis is fitting both because this book is interlaced with objective analyses and individual experience and anecdote and because this is really two books in one. Chapters 1 through 10 were written by Tsvi Bisk and deal mostly with social and political analyses of the Jewish situation with suggestions for future trends. The methodology for this part of the book is critical and historical. It is a critical analysis of where we are, how we got here, the inadequacies/faults of the present situation and approach and some alternative policies we should be following in light of present world trends and Jewish challenges. Tsvi Bisk also wrote chapter 11 with substantial contributions by Dr. Moshe Dror.

Chapters 12, 13, 14, and 15 were written primarily by Dr. Dror with substantial contributions by Tsvi Bisk. They deal mostly with the spiritual and practical potentialities of cyber-reality vis-à-vis the future spiritual and communal development of the Jewish People.

It may seem strange at times that a book on the future should dwell so much on historical critique, but it is our firm belief that unless we anchor our presentation in both historical and current reality we run the risk of Jewish "futuristics" degenerating into Jewish "fantastics." Indeed this has been the fate of much futurist speculation.

Similarly, because we want this book to be accessible to the widest possible audience, we have dispensed with all references. Both of us are writing this book after long careers of writing for publication and for our own pedagogical use. Some of our writings were research papers, which included all the academically appropriate references. Including these references would have been cumbersome for the reader and would have destroyed the flow of the narrative. The strategy of writing is telescopic: in other words, a theme or idea touched upon in an early chapter is repeated and or expanded upon in later chapters. This will explain the repetition of certain themes or ideas throughout the book.

One last word on style and narrative flow: we use a great many terms that most Gentiles and many Jews find unfamiliar. Instead of explaining these terms in the body of the book, a procedure that might distract the reader, we have decided to define them in a glossary. This way, the Jewishly informed reader can read right through, while the less-informed reader can refer to the glossary when need be.

Acknowledgments

Tsvi Bisk must, first and foremost, acknowledge his unpayable debt to the late Mordechai Nessyahu, a man of deep spirit and discernment whose intellectual life work and loving friendship have framed and stimulated Tsvi's intellectual and human development in their entirety throughout his adult life. Little if any of Tsvi's contribution to this book would have been possible if not for his long partnership and friendship with Mordechai Nessyahu.

Tsvi must also pay tribute to the memory of his adopted "little brother" Dr. Haim Nessyahu, a mathematics prodigy whose premature death and only partially realized life work has reminded him of the fragility of human life and has driven him to finish this book. Tsvi regrets the lost opportunity to argue over the contents of this book with both Mordechai and Haimi.

Both Dr. Moshe Dror and Tsvi Bisk are indebted and must pay tribute to the memory of Mrs. Yehudit Nessyahu who, in addition to serving as a surrogate mother to Tsvi over the years, managed to transcend the double tragedy of losing her husband and only son to, amongst her many other activities, dedicate herself to the typing and formatting of this book. We are both deeply saddened that Yehudit passed on before being able to see this book published. Yehudit's life was the essence of the modern Jewish experience. Most of her extended family was exterminated in the Holocaust and as a young adult she was the only female member of the Mossad team that captured Adolf Eichmann and brought him to justice in the Jewish State.

Both authors are also greatly indebted to Ms. Micaela Ziv for her dedicated editing and editorial comments in general, as well as for playing the part of intelligent but critical lay person for whom this book is targeted. We are additionally obliged to Mr. William (Zeev) Cohen for his detailed stylistic comments, which have made the book readable for the lay person. A special thanks goes to Professor Joseph Levinson for his critical commentary on several important chapters in the book.

Lastly, we would like to thank Mr. Gad Yaacobi, former minister in various Israeli governments as well as Israel's ambassador to the United Nations, for writing his generous foreword.

At the personal level, both authors are grateful and thankful for the tolerance both their families have shown for that consuming preoccupation without which no serious book can be written.

Dr. Moshe Dror wishes to pay tribute to his wife Simcha for her love and support, without which this project would not have come to fruition. He would also like to acknowledge those individuals who have influenced his thinking in a significant and powerful way: Menachem Alexenberg, Reb Zalman Shlomi-Schecter, Florence Ross, Phillis and Harvey Sandler, as well as his son Amos Davidowitz. He takes this opportunity to express profound appreciation to the Reverend Dr. Richard Kirby for years of collaborative and challenging thinking. Also a debt of gratitude to the staff of the Bet-Yatziv Study Center of the Israel Ministry of Education in Beersheva, especially its director, Dr. Oded Avissar for untold hours of discussions and programs that have contributed to his thinking. A special thanks is in order to the hundreds of participants in Bet-Yatziv workshops and seminars who have enriched his thinking.

Tsvi Bisk wishes to pay tribute to his wife Ziona for her long-suffering forbearance in putting up with a husband who lives his life in a most unorthodox way. He also wants to express his most profound love and appreciation for his children—Yonit, Drorit, Natanel, and Mor—without whose love and very being he would not have summoned up the strength to prevail.

It also goes without saying that both authors wish to show appreciation to those many thinkers and writers whose ideas have anticipated, paralleled, and informed their own work.

Introduction: The Task of the Jewish Futurist

I believe the twenty-first century can be the Jewish century. The century in which one's Jewishness will no longer be a burden or barrier, or constitute a sacrifice. The century in which Jewish individuals can realize their human potential without sacrificing Jewish ambitions and realize their Jewish potential without sacrificing human ambitions. I believe that no other people on earth is better prepared by virtue of education, temperament, and proven historical adaptability to face the challenges of the space age. Two thousand years of travail have prepared the Jews for these challenges.

In what Alvin Toffler calls "Third Wave" civilization, the Jewish People are favorites, not underdogs. But, while not forgetting, we must stop making a fetish of past suffering and begin to create a new Jewish civilization based on our relative advantages. Classical Zionism sought to use the past as an inspiration to build a better future. Yet in recent years much of Jewish life has been characterized by the desire to sacrifice the future in order to rebuild the past.

Neither Israel nor Diaspora Jewish organizations have created frameworks capable of researching current world trends and their possible influence on the future of the Jews. There seems to be a collective refusal to recognize that present technological and political developments will affect the Jewish People's struggle for meaningful survival in the twenty-first century; this despite the fact that futurism and futurology have become a multibillion dollar business and that some of the most prominent futurists are themselves Jewish.

Many of the problems that agitate Israel and world Jewry derive from our inability to reevaluate our circumstances in conjunction with world developments. Israel, especially, appears to be out of sync with the political and moral evolution of the democratic developed world it so wishes to be a part of.

The task of the futurist is not to predict, but to try to envision achievable desirable futures and to formulate strategies by which we might achieve such futures. We are not speaking about deterministic or inevitable futures but rather about desirable futures determined by us. A futurist is, therefore, a long-term social strategist, trying to construct a future-oriented social science based on a rigorous critique of the history that has created our present as well as idealized visions of human capabilities. It is a value-laden science. It does not deal with what *will be*, it deals with what *should be* or *could be*.

The task of the Jewish futurist is to state the self-evident truths that (1) the Jews are part of world developments whether they like it or not and that (2) the future is more important than the past. We cannot live in the past, but we will either live or die in the future. We cannot change the past, but we can create a better future.

David Ben-Gurion once remarked that the past 1,000 years of Jewish history were important but that the next 1,000 years are more important. What was his meaning? Simply this: that the past—its glories and its sufferings—can never be anything but an inspiration for our future. If we make it anything else, if we make it an idol to be worshipped, we threaten our very survival and by doing that betray those past generations we claim to celebrate and respect.

This obligates us to ask the relevant questions. For example, how is technology likely to affect the social, economic, political, spiritual, and Zionist development of Israel and the Jewish People? How are social developments likely to affect technological developments and what opportunities and hazards does this present to Israel and the Jewish People? What are the *likely* ramifications of the new global economy in general and for the Jewish People in particular? How are global political developments likely to affect the long-term planning and policy making of Israeli and Jewish organizations? And how are internal developments within the Jewish world likely to affect the character of world Jewry? I stress the word *likely* since we need room in our thinking for what futurist Arthur Shostak has called "wildcard events": dramatically unexpected and unanticipated events such as the attack on the Twin Towers and the subsequent war on terror.

Some developments that must guide Jewish thinking in the next several decades are telecommunications, the creation of a world market and a world cultural market, ecological concerns, and the creation of a unified European Community from the Atlantic to the Urals by the end of the second decade of this century. More specific issues include Israel becoming the largest Jewish community in the world by the end of the first decade of this century and the continuing growth of hostile Moslem populations in Europe and North America. This book will deal with these subjects.

Progressive countries and companies around the world have made futurism and anticipatory thinking a systematic part of their planning. Ongoing educational projects within organizations are dedicated to developing futurist habits of thought. Researching the future implications of current developments and intuiting possible future developments engage thousands of the best minds around the world. Creating scenarios of possible alternative futures and conducting simulations of how to behave as we engage the future are part and parcel of the long-term planning of any organization worthy of its name.

In light of all this, it is remarkable that the organized Jewish world has not actively adopted the mechanisms and methodologies of these developments. It is doubly remarkable because so many Jewish individuals are prominent futurists, because Zionism is the quintessential futurist ideology, and because some historians attribute the very invention of the concept of the future to the Jewish religion—a religion that describes a God who is the maker of the entire universe, acting within history to create a better human and cosmic future—a view that makes the prophets protofuturists.

IDENTIFYING THE PROBLEM

The problem is general to the human condition and specific to the Jews. We are limited by what we know and because all that we know, we know from the past. Yet every problem exists by definition in the future. Problems do not exist in the past. If they are past, they are solved and are therefore no longer problems. The present is but a theoretical point, analogous to a point in mathematics. The minute we say the word *present* it is past. Life is a constant carrying the past into the future—a future that cannot be predicted or forecast because it does not yet exist. As futurist Edward Cornish has noted, the nonexistence of the future is the basic assumption of futurist thought.

Futurism teaches us how to ask the right questions about current developments, how to develop futurist habits of thought and the ability to envisage desirable and possible alternative futures. It also cultivates the ability to recognize the opportunities in unexpected events when they occur.

Futurist thinking differs from long-term planning. The planner discerns demographic trends and suggests building more old-age homes or creating more gerontological services for an aging Jewish community. The futurist asks what are the implications of the Jews being the oldest ethnic group in the United States: how will this affect Jewish political power over the next decade? How will it affect support for Israel? What will it mean culturally, psychologically, and spiritually when Israel becomes the largest Jewish community in the world? What will be the political status of world Jewry when the Moslem population of the United States surpasses the Jewish population and becomes increasingly organized and wealthier?

Our knowledge acts as a filter that prevents us from envisaging alternative futures that differ qualitatively from the past. Ironically, the greater the success of past methods of problem solving and habits of thought, the greater the difficulty in envisaging alternative futures. We educate our children for twelve years about the past expecting them to be good citizens in the future and wonder why it does not work. We educate them about the past but give them no tools with which to envisage themselves in a hopeful and optimistic future. Consequently young people today are often filled with foreboding and despair and rates of suicide increase all over the world. Teaching our children how to develop anticipatory thinking and futurist habits of thought are necessary for creating high standards of citizenship in the future. They are also necessary survival tools for our civilization.

People who address the future through a spiritual filter of despair, pessimism, and hopelessness will almost certainly create a future of despair, pessimism, and hopelessness. People who acquire the tools and the habits of thought that enable them to envisage alternative futures of hope and fulfillment will become optimists possessing creative energy and belief in the value of their efforts. They will thus have a better chance to create a better future. It is a simple rule: pessimists create negative environments and optimists create positive environments. In popular terminology it is called "the power of positive thinking," and, although denigrated by haughty intellectuals, we all know it is true.

The human race had no need of anticipatory thinking until the Industrial Revolution. Before that, what we learnt from our grandparents we could teach to our great-grandchildren and know it would have relevance for their lives. Indeed, the very aim of education was to pass the values and culture of past generations onto future generations, a kind of benevolent dictatorship of the past over every aspect of our lives. But after the Industrial Revolution the rate of change increased exponentially, and since World War II it has been increasing at an even more explosive rate. Changes no longer occur over several lifetimes, unfelt by the people experiencing them; radical changes occur constantly, every day of our lives. Individuals living today experience more change in one year than entire generations experienced only several hundred years ago. Hence, what I thought I knew several years ago I am not so sure I know today. How can I educate my children when I have to constantly reeducate myself, when facts *and* "morality" seem to be in a constant state of flux—and when the word *morality* must be placed in inverted commas to indicate both its temporal and cultural relativity?

For despite popular belief, moral perspectives also change, not only facts. Consider the moral and ethical implications of medical technology. Ten years ago I *knew* that the taking of a human life was a contemptible thing in every possible event: murder, manslaughter, wars, and even traffic accidents (resulting as they usually do from human negligence). Yet how do I judge people who pull the plug on terminally ill loved ones because they have begged them to do so? What right do I have to sustain the inquisition-like torture of people who are prevented liberation from their pain by modern medical technology but given no hope?

THE NATION THAT DWELLS ALONE

This world we live in serves as a general frame of reference for the Jews as it does for other peoples. But this leads us to a specifically Jewish problem. I call it the "Nation that Dwells Alone" syndrome. The populist and ignorant misuse of this biblical phrase has caused the Jews no end of mischief. Its application in Israel's present political and economic situation could be a recipe for disaster.

The Jews have an ancient tradition of dividing the universe into two parts. There are four hundred billion stars in our galaxy alone and hundreds of billions of galaxies in the universe, and all this is divided into the Jews and the "Goyim." In Israel we have carried this tradition two steps further. First of all, we have created a new geography. The planet earth is divided into two: the Land of Israel and outside the Land of Israel *(Ha'aretz* and *Hotz l'Aretz)*. Some years ago my six-year-old son asked me if Brazil was in *Ha'aretz* or *Hotz l'Aretz*. This would be amusing if not for the fact that these geographical concepts seem to be held by senior Israeli policy makers who talk about the world and Israel as if they were two separate places and Israel was not part of the world. In recent years we have created a new division: Israel and the Jewish World. On the one hand is Israel and on the other hand is the Jewish World.

As dismayingly déclassé as it may seem to many, we must recognize that the Jews are part of the universe. If a star supernovas within one thousand light-years from our solar system the Jews will die also, not only the Goyim. Israel is part of the planet Earth. If the hole in the ozone continues to widen, we will have solved the Israeli-Palestinian conflict forever. And if wind patterns had been different when Chernobyl exploded, Israel would not have had an agricultural sector for the next 50 years.

Israelis are also part of the Jewish People. The aspirations, ambitions, and dreams of the young modern Jew from Tel Aviv, Degania, or Dimona are not substantively different from the aspirations, ambitions, and dreams of the young modern Jew from New York, Los Angeles, Montreal, London, or Paris. Even the younger generation of Israel's non-Jewish minorities have begun to develop the same aspirations and ambitions as their Jewish counterparts. If we do not recognize and understand the essential similarity between young Israelis and Diaspora Jews we cannot build a social, economic, and Zionist policy that rationally addresses the problems, challenges, and opportunities of modern Jewry, whether in Israel or in the Diaspora.

We must recognize and acknowledge that the individual Jewish human being is the center and focus of our concerns, that the individual is a finite, one-time entity compelled to fill his or her life with meaning within an infinite universe. If we do not recognize this we will continue to alienate growing numbers of young Jews, who will not perceive spiritual added-value in being Jewish. Young Jews will see no reason to cultivate Jewish ambitions, and history will see this period as the last sad chapter of the Jewish historical drama.

THE CRITERIA

The following describes the appropriate perspective for viewing the relationship between the individual and his or her human environment. I will discuss this from an Israeli point of view, which is most natural for me. But I also believe it is relevant for most self-identified Diaspora Jews.

The Individual. Classical Zionist ideology always placed the human being in the center. Zionism saw the human being as the aim of its endeavors, the uplifting of the Jewish human being as its raison d'être, and the fulfillment of the individual (*Hagshama Atzmit*) as the only real means by which this could be accomplished. Unfortunately, like many other utopian ideologies of the past several hundred years, it was usually referring to the Platonic ideal of the human being—not the concrete, real human being. For years much of Western culture has sacrificed the concrete human being in favor of the abstract idea of the human being. The experience of Communism has demonstrated that this approach is a recipe for disaster. Communism sacrificed millions of real human beings in the service of an unsubstantiated, abstract concept of an ideal humanity. This must be a cautionary for the future of Zionist thinking.

The Community. No human being is an island. No one can live alone, and certainly no one can fulfill their individual capacities and give meaning to their lives in isolation. We live in communities. What kind of communal frameworks and communities do we need to realize our capacities and give fulfillment to our lives? The kibbutz was to have been the proper answer to this question. But its own Platonic problem has been its undoing, as it pursued an unsubstantiated kibbutz *ideal* instead of asking what *real* live individual kibbutzniks required in order to realize their human potential.

The Economy. No community dwells alone. It survives within an economic framework. What kind of economy can sustain the kind of community we need to realize our capacities? It would be a dynamic, innovative, productive, profitable economy with ever-increasing options that reflect the striking opportunities of human potential within the new global reality. A sluggish, undynamic, unprofitable, unproductive economy hostile to the new global reality and limiting our options will not suffice. True, an economy can be super efficient and because of its social ideology still tolerate immoral social situations such as: inequality before the law, racial discrimination, and grinding poverty. An inefficient economy, however, can never over the long term sustain a moral society, no matter what the abstracted, idealized, "moral" level of its social ideology. In such a situation the declared social values become objects of contempt and cynicism and produce a social reality opposite to what was intended.

The Society. No economy survives in isolation; it is subsumed within a more general social reality. What kind of society do we require to sustain the kind of economy we need without selling ourselves to economic considerations only? For me, society takes precedence over the economy. In this I am still a social democrat. I have never agreed with the basic assumption of classic capitalism and Marxism that the human being is primarily economic and motivated primarily by economic values. The human being is *also* economic and motivated greatly by economic values, and any social ideology that ignores this and does not enable and encourage a dynamic economy is guaranteed to fail. For the individual will strive to realize himself or herself no matter what, and this requires a dynamic modern economy. In this I oppose the new antimodernists as represented by the fundamentalist Greens, who express the wish to return humanity to a pretechnological reality.

The Culture. Man is primarily cultural and symbolic; a psychological animal motivated by the abstract as much if not more than by the material. Unless we understand this we cannot understand the political history of the past several decades. How was it, for example, that Reagan won 60 percent of the vote when close to 60 percent of the voters, in poll after poll, supported social policies that reflected the Democratic national platform? How was the Thatcher phenomenon possible when 70 percent of the English public still identified themselves as working class at the height of the Thatcher era? The answer is that both Reagan and Thatcher conquered the national symbols, the prisms through which each people saw its own identity. Reagan co-opted patriotism and religiosity and projected a friendly, humane humor, the quintessential American. Mrs. Thatcher, the iron lady, projected an image of a world role and values for which apparently many postimperial English were nostalgic. In addition she played the petit bourgeois character of the English working class for all it was worth when she all but gave away council flats to their tenants, thereby satisfying the popular English creed of "my home is my castle." Unless we understand man's cultural and symbolic nature we cannot understand "solidarity," all but destroying the Polish economy and lowering living standards, in order to make Poland ungovernable by the communists, the army, or anyone else that did not reflect the will of the Polish people to achieve national independence and freedom. The first Palestinian *Intifada* lowered living standards by 50 percent for abstractions such as national independence and sovereignty. And Israeli politics have reflected the American reality for the past two decades; a majority vote for *Likud*-led governments, whereas a majority support Labor Party policies. The reason? The Likud has conquered the national symbols. If culture forms the basis of both society and economy, what cultural values and symbols are required to sustain an economy and society in which we can fulfill ourselves as human beings?

The Country. What kind of country do we need? We need a Jewish country: demographically, socially, culturally, politically, and even economically. A country in which the modern Jewish individual can realize his or her ambitions as part of the new global reality and not sacrifice these ambitions in stubborn opposition to the new world reality now being created. We need a country that creates both Jewish and human added value within the context of the global reality of the twenty-first century.

The World. What kind of world do we need and what will be our relationships to it, of our community, our economy, our society, our culture and our country? For no country or nation dwells alone, it never has, it does not now, and given the new global reality, it certainly never will. Yet no myth has had such a pernicious effect on how the Jews interrelate with the world than the misinterpretation and misrepresentation of a "Nation that Dwells Alone." No myth has caused the Jews to misinterpret their recent history more. For the universal developments of the past 200 years have influenced the course of Jewish history as much if not more than any other national history on the face of the earth.

HISTORICAL ANALOGY

Let us ask the questions that the Jewish futurist must ask in regard to historical events before we ask them in anticipation of future developments. For a futurist must first of all be an historian. A futurist must understand historical context and historical method and must be a student of the history of ideas. One description of futurism could be the application of the history of ideas to the future. There are various methodologies of futurism, including extrapolation, analogy, scenario writing, simulations, and Delphi polls.

A serious futurologist must use a combination of all these methods if he or she wishes to be responsible. Yet for me, the most valuable and creative method is analogy to historical developments in other periods and developments in other societies. Comparing the impact of revolutionary changes in the past gives one a good idea as to what impact present revolutionary changes might have on the future, leaving room, of course, for Arthur Shostak's probable wildcards. For in periods of great upheaval and rapid change we must expect wildcard events, even though we cannot anticipate or predict the specific event. We must learn, therefore, to live with ambiguity. This does not release us, however, from the responsibility of trying to create better futures.

Paradoxically, the historical method of analogy releases one from the bondage of history. History becomes a living thing to be used in a creative way—not a museum of mythologized, heroic past events to be worshipped. Worshipping the past is a human disease that also infects the Jews. Applying futurist methodology to the past allows us to use it creatively by enabling us to understand it in different ways. We must ask how technology and social and political developments have influenced the Jewish People in the past 200 years before we go on to a futurist analysis.

THE INDUSTRIAL REVOLUTION AND THE JEWS

The Industrial Revolution affected the Jews more than any other event in Jewish history and arguably had a greater effect on the Jews than on any other people on the planet. The three most important events of the past 200 years of Jewish history, the creation of North American Jewry, the Holocaust, and the creation of the state of Israel would have been inconceivable without the means of production and transportation provided by the Industrial Revolution.

The first Zionist Congress, which took place in 1897 in Basle, could not have taken place 100 years earlier on anywhere near the same scale or format. Hundreds of Jews from every corner of the earth came to Basle at a specified time and took part in a discussion pertinent to the future of the Jewish people. They came by railroad and steamship, they slept in hotels, they were informed about it through the mass media of the times (newspapers and periodicals), they coordinated and planned the proceedings by way of relatively reliable international mail and telegraph systems, which also enabled them to plan and keep to a timetable. Up until the nineteenth century and the Industrial Revolution such a mass convocation would have been impossible.

In 1797 no railroads and steamships existed and hence no mass movement of people and no large hotels; we had no mass-distributed newspapers (lacking both the technical means to produce them and the literate market to consume them); we had no reliable mass international mail and no telegraph system. In other words, the very organizational existence of the Zionist movement depended on the means of production of the Industrial Revolution. So, too, was the very physical existence of the Zionist enterprise in the Land of Israel.

Opponents of Zionism often used the argument that Zionism was an unrealistic pretense because a wasteland could not absorb millions of Jews and become a Jewish homeland. Zionists replied, by implication if not by articulated word, that this may have been true in the past but the technical and engineering skills and the scientific knowledge of the Industrial Revolution would enable them to turn the wasteland into a flourishing garden productive enough to absorb as many Jews who wished to come. The greening of the desert became both a polemical tool and a practical reality enabling the implementation of the Zionist Revolution. It was possible because of the Industrial Revolution.

During the Civil War the population of the entire United States (North and South) was 31 million. This represented a tenfold increase over the period from the Revolutionary War. Yet by this time only about 50,000 Americans were Jewish—a puny community compared to Russia, Poland, North Africa, and Germany. This changed radically during the economic expansion following the Civil War.

An estimated 30 million people immigrated to the United States between 1870 and 1914. This great human tide was necessary to operate the huge new industrial plant being built in the United States and became possible with the new transportation technologies of steamships and railroads. The railroad companies encouraged immigration to settlements alongside railway tracks in order to rationalize them and make them more profitable.

Western and northern Europe could no longer supply the requisite human resources, so immigration was encouraged from southern, middle, and eastern Europe, areas with large concentrations of Jews. As a result, out of the 30 million immigrants, 1 to 2 million were Jews. From being a minor Jewish community during the Civil War, American Jewry had become, by World War I, one of the largest and certainly the most powerful and influential community in the Jewish World.

Industrialization, and the Enlightenment values that had made it possible, created new concepts of human civilization and human interaction that stimulated German Jewry to create the Reform, Conservative, and neo-Orthodox versions of Judaism—the modern Judaism we are so familiar with.

The rise of Nazism and the industrial methods of murder employed by the Holocaust made North American Jewry the largest Jewish community in the world by the end of World War II. Democratic capitalism, the quintessential product of the Industrial Revolution, as well as its precondition, made American Jewry the richest, freest, most powerful and self-confident Jewish community in history. American Jewry's power mobilized wisely was one of the primary preconditions for the creation of the state of Israel, an event that altered the course of Jewish history and increased the self-confidence of the Jews as American citizens even further.

All of the above was a direct consequence of or was enabled by the advent of industrial civilization. It was truly the most revolutionary period in Jewish history since the Exodus from Egypt. We would do well to keep this in mind when considering the revolutionary implications for the Jews of the postindustrial communications revolution. Using analogy we can conceive of even more far-reaching changes, challenges, and dangers awaiting the Jews in the twenty-first century.

THE FUTURE

This is a book about the survival of the Jewish People in the twenty-first century. It attempts to answer two questions: (1) what means and habits of thought must the Jewish People cultivate in order to guarantee their survival? and (2) why should a young, non-Orthodox, university-trained Jew even be concerned about remaining Jewish?

These two questions are intertwined and constitute the two major components of a strategy of Jewish survival. Survival depends on power: physical, intellectual, and spiritual power. For human beings in general and Jews in particular, physical and spiritual survival cannot be separated. If the physical body of the Jewish People fails to survive, it goes without saying that the spirit of the Jewish People cannot survive. Alternatively, if the spiritual energy of the Jewish People cannot be developed in a manner conducive to the needs and interests of the young, non-Orthodox, university-trained Jew, then the Jewish body will not create and sustain the energy it requires to survive.

The Jews have never accepted the Platonic/Cartesian dualism of body and spirit that has characterized Christianity. The Jews do not deny the body or separate spirit from body, or place the spirit on a higher plane than the body. For the Jew, spirit and body are not two distinct entities. They are, rather, two aspects of one being—the human being. The Jew says, "If there is no bread, there is no Torah." In other words, if there is no body, there is no spirit.

If rationality separates the human from the animal and constitutes the primary tool of human survival, it cannot be contrasted to spirituality. Spirituality is not by its nature irrational, as much of New Age mysticism would have us believe. For the Jew it can never be antirational. For if there is no Torah without bread and if we can only obtain bread by the rational application of our minds, then there can never be Torah (spirituality) without rationality as the primary principle of our society and of the individuals that compose it. The analytical method employed in Talmudic study is rational at its base.

The very term *spirituality* may be problematic. As we shall see, in subsequent chapters, Jews have been forced to use Greek/Christian terminology, which may not be suitable to the Jewish worldview; as a consequence of being a minority culture subsumed in a Greek-based Christian culture.

For the Jews to survive as human beings they must conform to the rules of survival of all human beings within the context of the particular historical socioeconomic reality in which they exist. For the Jews to survive, as Jews, requires a serious physical/intellectual/spiritual added value for the modern Jewish individual, in return for the added effort it takes to remain Jewish. In other words, the physical and spiritual options of the individual Jewish human being must be increased as a result of his or her Jewish identification.

But neither Jewish added value nor Jewish survival can be achieved in contravention of the rules of human behavior as these manifest themselves in the twenty-first century. On the contrary, the Jews must conduct their struggle within strict conformity to the economic, technological, social, and political norms of the modern democratic postindustrial reality. But conformity is not enough, else why be Jewish at all? Jewish identity must add new dimensions to one's humanity if it is to promote Jewish ambitions amongst our young, non-Orthodox, university-trained Jews. A Judaism that requires one to subtract dimensions of one's humanity in order to remain Jewish will not encourage these Jewish ambitions; it will encourage assimilation.

Consequently, a space age Jewish civilization must be based, first and foremost, on the optimal self-fulfillment and self-realization of the individual. It cannot be based on the self-sacrifice of the individual. In the space age no society can long survive, let alone flourish, if it bases itself on the self-immolation of the individuals that comprise it. Every society is but a reflection of the collective self-fulfillment of the individuals that comprise it.

Not only are individual human rights an inherent value in themselves, pertaining to the very nature of the human being as a human being, they are now a utilitarian necessity for the collective survival of society as a whole. The tremendous real time changes and human skill requirements of the global space age society require the optimal empowerment of the individual and the optimal encouragement of the individual's rationality in order to enable him or her to make their optimal contribution to society. In the space age, individual egoism is a societal virtue and individual self-sacrifice is a societal sin. That is why above, in the criteria, I began with the individual and built everything else on the bedrock of what the individual rational human being needs. When we speak about *Futurizing the Jews* we must first begin with the Jewish individual.

The first part of this book includes the following chapters. Chapter 1, "The World We Live In," describes the significance of the technological and cultural developments that serve as the backdrop for any rational discussion about the future of the Jewish People. "The Triumph of Zionism," chapter 2, explains how the Zionist Project has come to dominate any debate about the future of the Jewish People. Chapter 3, "Zionism in the Twenty-First Century," describes how a reevaluation of classical Zionism is a fundamental necessity for the rejuvenation of Jewish life and culture in Israel and in the Diaspora. "The Special Case of American Jewry," chapter 4, describes why American Jewry stands outside the classic Zionist analysis and why American Jewry must take upon itself a special role in regards to the future of the Jewish People as a whole. Chapter 5, "Israeli Grand Strategy: A Historical Critique," consists of precise definitions of the various levels of Israeli policy making, concrete critiques of past successes that have turned into current failures, and the lessons to be drawn. Chapter 6, "Reinventing Israeli Grand Strategy," is a detailed description of the environment in which Israeli policy making will take place and how this should direct future planning. "Reinventing Israel-Diaspora Relations," chapter 7, demonstrates the special physical and the spiritual roles the Diaspora must play in order to guarantee Jewish survival. It delegates a special role to the Israeli Diaspora. Chapter 8, "The Future of Arab-Jewish Relations," severely critiques the attitudes and policies of the Israeli right and the Israeli left, and it suggests a new nonsentimental and nonchauvinistic approach to the subject.

Chapter 9, "The Future of Ethnic Relations and Israeli Culture," is both a historical critique and an attempt to define the parameters of a pan-Jewish culture in the twenty-first century. "The Future of Jewish-Christian Relations," chapter 10, formulates a radical redefinition of the ground rules of Jewry's relationship with the Christian world in the twenty-first century, and chapter 11, "The Future of Jewish Identity," outlines the parameters or imperatives of Jewish identity in a culturally pluralistic world.

The second part of this book includes the following chapters. Chapter 12, "The Cyber World We Live In," explores the revolutionary potential that information technology offers the human race. Chapter 13, "The Future of Jewish Spirituality," describes how much of the Jewish tradition anticipated the spiritual possibilities of the communications revolution and envisions the spiritual possibilities of a renewed Judaism joining its historical traditions to the cybertechnical possibilities of the twenty-first century. "The Future of Jewish Learning," chapter 14, redefines the methods of Jewish education and draws attention to the correlation between traditional Jewish educational methods and the general postmodern educational reality. It deals primarily with education in the Diaspora but with ramifications for Israel also. Chapter 15, "The Jewish Community in Cyberspace," describes the new information revolution's possible effect on how world Jewry will "Jew it," based on discussions in chapters 12–14. The Appendix, "Cosmotheism: A Worldview for the Space Age," is a brief summation of the life work of the late Israeli thinker Mordechai Nessyahu. We believe that Nessyahu's thinking offers a spiritual and intellectual anticipation of the human potentiality of twenty-first-century civilization.

CHAPTER 1

The World We Live In

Any rational discussion about the future of the Jewish People must be framed within a discussion about the future of the human race. For, self-evidently, Jews are part of the human race. This may be shocking news to some Jews and anti-Semites but it is nonetheless true. There is no need to demonstrate the shock of the anti-Semites, but a word about the shock of the Jews might be in order. This includes the aforementioned misuse of the concept of a "Nation that Dwells Alone" by political and spiritual populists in order to indicate that the Jews can and even must ignore historical trends that affect the entire human race. This is of course a recipe for self-destruction. Just ask the Serbs.

The Jews are not alone in dividing the world into them and us. This is a universal tendency across time and geography. The ancient Greeks divided the world into Greeks and barbarians. So did, and sometimes still do the Chinese and Japanese. The famous headline in the London *Times*—"Fog in Channel—Continent Isolated"—shows that imperial England was no less insular.

The Jewish penchant for giving special status to the Land of Israel is also not unique. The Japanese, Chinese, and others have done the same. Indeed, even calling the Land of Israel *the* Land is not unique. The Irish call Ireland "Ye Sod," *the* Land.

But this book is not about the survival capabilities of other peoples in a rapidly changing world. It is about the survival capabilities of the Jewish People and as such must deal with those aspects of Jewish culture that enhance the chances of Jewish survival as well as those that are inimical to Jewish survival.

A discussion about the future of the human race will indicate the planetary framework the Jews must relate to in order to survive and prosper in the future. This requires a preliminary overview of where we *as human beings* are at present, and how we arrived here. It requires a broad outline of the technological, economic, cultural, and political trends now affecting the human race as a whole and therefore affecting every Jew in the world.

THE TURNING POINT

The entire Earth, as represented by its highest life form, the human race, is in the midst of what scientist/philosopher Fritjof Capra has called the "Turning Point." This is a historical crease wherein inherited assumptions, values, and understanding are being upset by a combination of some of the most radical changes in the history of the human race.

Capra's working assumption is that we are trapped in our inherited paradigms. This causes us to fear the future rather than to perceive the opportunities within current developments. A paradigm is a social and cultural totality that reflects the state of science and technology at a particular historical moment, the modes of production that reflect that state, and the social and political frameworks that reflect the inherent requirements of those modes of production. A good historical example would be the transformation of human consciousness as a consequence of the transformation of agricultural society into industrial society. Cultural and spiritual life systems always influence and are influenced by the dominant paradigm. A turning point is when a paradigm we have become acculturated to is in the process of being rapidly replaced by a different paradigm.

OUR INHERITED PARADIGM

Our inherited paradigm is extremely compelling, and this may explain why it is so difficult for us to escape its limitations. It is a conjoining of the Enlightenment and the Industrial Revolution, both of which have their roots in the Renaissance and the Scientific Revolution. All our values, perspectives and prejudices are filtered through these historical developments. This includes our perspectives on Israel, Zionism, and Diaspora institutional life. This filter hinders us in the necessary task of envisioning alternative futures, a universal human problem that becomes especially acute in the case of the Jews.

The Renaissance-Scientific-Enlightenment-Industrial paradigm has two fundamental characteristics: quantitative measuring tools and secular humanism. These two are inextricably tied to one another.

Mathematical language gave us the quantitative measuring tools that made the Commercial and Scientific Revolutions possible. The Scientific Revolution enabled us to manipulate our environment for our own benefit and thus even conceive of the idea of human progress. The Commercial Revolution provided the material means for human progress to become a reality. Science and commerce were the basis of the modern humanist Revolution. They were also prerequisites for eventual Jewish emancipation. Both science and commerce are ethnically neutral; they reward competency and imagination and are indifferent to the religious or cultural affiliation of the individual demonstrating that competence and imagination. Together, they formed the basis of a major paradigm shift. Countries that took part in this paradigm shift prospered, those that turned their backs to it became backward.

It is no accident that Holland, the first commercial republic, possessed a built-in resistance to ethnic discrimination and it is therefore no accident that Spanish and Portuguese Jews found refuge there from the Inquisition. Renaissance humanism, the Scientific and Commercial Revolutions it fathered, and the European Enlightenment that was coeval with them are therefore the prerequisites to Jewish emancipation and the birth of modern Judaism and the modern Jew. I refer the reader back to the Introduction and the role of the Industrial Revolution in the development of modern Jewish life.

If human beings had the power to manipulate their environment and to exploit their productive abilities for their own benefit and improvement, they no longer completely depended on God but could control their own destiny. Human beings were at the center of social interest and activity (hence the term *humanism*), and not God. God was still a creator who wound up the universe (like a cosmic clock) but afterwards took no active part in his creation. This view of God was fundamental to natural theology, a theology based upon living one's life according to the laws of nature and not according to the real-time dictates of a supernatural being who took personal interest in every human being. Deism, the theological outlook that characterized most Enlightenment thinkers, developed out of natural theology.

THE AMERICAN ENLIGHTENMENT

This was especially the case in regards to America's founding fathers. Jefferson, Madison, Franklin, Payne, Adams, and so on, were all Deists. God for them was an indifferent "First Mover." They believed that human beings must depend therefore on their own reason and not on supernatural miraculous interventions. The American Declaration of Independence begins with those immortal quintessentially Deist words:

When in the course of human events, it becomes necessary for one people to dissolve the political bands which have connected them with another, and to assume among the Powers of the earth, the separate and equal station to which *the Laws of Nature and of Nature's God entitle them* ...We hold these truths to be self-evident, that all men are created equal, that they are endowed by their Creator [that is, Nature's God and the Laws of Nature created by Nature's God] with certain *unalienable Rights, that among these are Life, Liberty and the pursuit of Happiness.* (Italics mine)

America is the ultimate Enlightenment project. There is no American Jewry without this, as it was America's Enlightenment outlook that eventually granted Jews the same unalienable rights as others. There is no modern Israel without American Jewry; there is in short no modern Jewish life, as we know it (and perhaps no Jewish life at all).

The American and Enlightenment worldview was the consequence of a useful philosophical tautology. Reason had been enthroned. God being God was by definition the ultimate rational force in nature. It was, therefore, inconceivable that God did not create nature according to rational laws. Natural law was therefore, *by definition*, rational law. God subsequently gave human beings reason (by creating us in his "image"). He did this in order to enable human beings to discover the rational laws by which he created nature. Since God did everything for a reason (that is, according to reason), this was the only purpose to give humankind reason. Since rational law and natural law were one and the same and both flowed from the mind of God, the scientific project that gave birth to the Enlightenment was often called "knowing the mind of God."

When human beings saw they could influence their lives and make them better on this earth and not only in heaven, they began to concentrate on the things of this world and not the world to come. Hence, society became more concerned with *this* world.

Secular humanism means that human beings (not God) are at the center of their own lives dealing with things of this world (not of the world to come). Political organization, economic system, and commerce were all things of this earth and thus were by definition secular humanist activities. Democracy and capitalism are secular humanist systems that are concerned with *human* activity in *this* world. The Jews have thrived in this secular humanist world of democracy and capitalism and consequently have been more influenced by secularist trends than most other ethnic groups.

SECULAR HUMANISM

Secular humanism is one of the foundation stones of modernism and hence of Jewish emancipation. Its growing spiritual inadequacies based, in part, upon some of the self-doubt of its physical scientific basis has led to the radical moral relativism of postmodernism on the one hand, and a return to the bedrock "certainties" of religious fundamentalism on the other hand. Both extremes feed off one another and both, together and separately, are dangerous for the future of human society in general and for the Jews in particular.

To reiterate, science, the language of science (mathematics) and the technology and commerce they spawned enabled human beings to both conceive of and implement the possibility of the humanist project. Science was the first humanity since it made modern humanism possible by empowering human beings to control their fate. This of course contradicts the modern educational practice of separating the sciences from the humanities, a practice with dreadful social and cultural consequences.

No longer were human beings dependent only on the compassion of a God influenced by human prayers. Now they could improve their own welfare based on their own rational efforts. Rationalism (an "-ism") as opposed to rationality, became the new dominant ideology replacing religion. Religion was now forced to make its peace with the rational scientific worldview. This led to the natural theology and Deism discussed above. These general developments served as the cultural foundation and intellectual backdrop that helped contribute to the development of Reform, Conservative, and neo-Orthodox Judaism as well as to the development of Zionism, Bundism, and Yiddishism. Once again, modern Jewish society is inconceivable, except as an integral part of general human developments.

The fact that humanity could now exploit nature for its own benefit was rationalized into an axiom of western civilization that nature existed for human beings to exploit. God was rational; therefore, he created creation according to rational laws. He then created man and gave him rational capability. It was thus self-evident in this new Enlightenment worldview that man's proper task on this earth was to exploit his rational capabilities to unlock the rational laws of God's rational creation. This would enable man to create rational economic and social organizations of benefit to human beings rather than to create theological structures to celebrate God. Men such as Newton wanted to "know the mind of God," which meant to understand the laws of nature. Societies and cultures that lacked this ideological base were considered inferior. It became the task of modern imperialism to enlighten the benighted non-Western masses (the so-called white man's burden).

Zionism imbibed many of these modernist Enlightenment assumptions, and they have been responsible for some of the greatest achievements in Jewish history. They have also been responsible for some of the graver mistakes of the Zionist Project. The paternalistic, condescending attitudes toward Arabs and Jews from African and Asian countries that derive from this worldview have been responsible for many of our political and social problems. Our recent attempts to correct these attitudes have led to a politically correct multiculturalism that is just as uncritically one dimensional and destructive as the cultural chauvinism it was designed to alleviate.

NATURAL RIGHTS, SCIENCE, AND IDEOLOGY

The Enlightenment belief was that the tools of rational/empirical inquiry with which human beings unlocked nature's laws would also enable humans to discover economic and social laws by which to create a rational (that is, natural and therefore just) society. Rational and just were seen as equivalent—anything rational by definition could not be unjust. God, consequently, was by definition rational and just, and anything created by God would be rational and just. Accordingly, if we built a society based upon rational natural law it would also be just. God created a rational universe and gave human beings reason so that they could prosper in that universe. If human beings created a rational society, all rational beings could prosper in it and this would be just.

The secularization of these concepts lies at the foundation of all modern liberal and socialist political theory, including Zionism.

Economic and political theorizing became less moralistic and more rational, or scientific, that is, less concerned with ethics and more preoccupied by sociology and history. The systematic inquiry into the nature of economic and political life had paralleled the Scientific Revolution and was central to the Enlightenment gestalt. "Scientists" delved into economic philosophy and "economists" delved into moral social issues and the mutual cross influences were almost impossible to discern. In fact, the terms *scientist* and *economist* were invented much later, well into the nineteenth century. Isaac Newton held the chair of natural philosophy and Adam Smith held the chair of moral philosophy at their respective universities. If you had addressed Newton as a scientist and Smith as an economist, neither would have known what you were talking about.

This was the basis of modern political ideologies, and the economic and historical theories that were their midwives, and the Scientific Revolution that was their mother. Adam Smith, along with many other Enlightenment philosophers, wished to become the Newton of human society. Newton discovered the rational mathematically mechanical laws that made nature run and thus enabled us to improve the material human condition. Adam Smith, and the proto-economists who went before him, wanted to discover the rational, mathematically measurable laws that made human economic life function, thus enabling us to create a more rational, hence more productive and consequently a more just and moral society (hence the term moral philosopher).

The assumption that material progress and the rational organization of society would make better human beings, that this unity automatically connects material progress to moral progress became that ideology we now call modernism. The realization that material progress does not automatically lead to moral progress, that rational and fair social institutions do not solve the problem of human evil, has resulted in the anti-ideology we call postmodernism.

Karl Marx, a late Enlightenment figure, shared all of Adam Smith's rationalist and scientific assumptions and wanted to become the Darwin of society. Darwin wanted to uncover the internal laws of development of organic history, and Marx wanted to uncover the internal laws of development of human history. Marx wanted to be a *scientific* socialist as opposed to the naive, idealistic, and moralistic early socialists. He assumed that once we perceived these inevitable deterministic historical laws (the iron laws of history), we could begin to conform to them in a conscious way, thus hastening the advent of a more rational, therefore more just and moral society. In hindsight, it is clear that Smith (the godfather of capitalism) and Marx (the prophet of communism) were part of the same Enlightenment project. They were both looking for a more rational, scientific way to organize and run human society and they both believed that this was a job for human beings and not for God. Capitalism, democracy, idealistic socialism and "scientific" (Marxian) socialism are all secular endeavors. They aim to improve human life on this earth and not in the world to come.

Zionism was a much later product of this same gestalt. Inherent parallels appear between Bacon's axiom that it was humanity's task to penetrate Nature and tear her secrets from her and the Zionist axiom to conquer the wasteland. Smith's and Marx's hope that their enterprise would result in a new man (more rational, just, and moral) are reflected in the Zionist aim to create a new type of Jew (more independent, less obsequious, and more heroic). Without the Enlightenment concept of the "New Man," it would have been impossible to develop the Zionist concept of the "New Jew."

Indeed the entire reality of modern Jewish life would have been inconceivable without the development of science and capitalism. As mentioned previously, both science and commerce are ethnically neutral; therefore, the cultural dominance of both within the framework of a constitutional democracy has created a civilization most amenable to the Jews on both a practical and a moral level.

FROM SCIENCE TO SCIENTISM

The transition from philosophy to science as the fundamental intellectual superstructure of human inquiry occurred in the nineteenth century. This is when science also became "Scientism." Scientism implies that what cannot be described in precise scientific terms (preferably by way of mathematical language) is not worth discussing and probably does not even exist.

Scientism achieved its grotesque extreme in the philosophy of behavioral psychology of Watson and Skinner. They denied the very existence of volitional human consciousness because it could not be seen, felt, smelt, or measured. *Mind* was a meaningless word because it could not be scientifically described. Behavior could be observed, described, and statistically measured. Human beings ceased to be human beings and became human behaviors. Science, the first humanity, was now transformed into scientism, which denied the very humanity of humanity (that is, if we accept that the volitional reasoning mind is what separates the human from the animal).

This became grist for the mill of postmodernists who denied reason as the universal objective characteristic of all humanity and deemed it rather an ideological construct of Western culture. These postmodernists denied that reason had any intrinsic objective value and affirmed that nonrational, irrational, and even antirational ways of relating to reality should be treated with equal respect. Postmodernism retreated into premodernism and put the metaphysical on the same plain as the physical.

Multiculturalism was born. Medicine men became equal to medical men. Pretensions to any hierarchy of values became politically incorrect if these corresponded to cultural origin. Objective rational discourse based upon a universally accepted language of meaning became totally impossible in the social sciences and the humanities. New Age affirmations went unchallenged because no one could challenge them other than by applying critical reasoning, an effort a priori preempted by the prejudices of postmodernism. One who dared to apply the standards of critical reason was accused of cultural jingoism. Anything went. Analytical and critical questioning became a sign of poor taste and cultural intolerance. The human mind was turned into uncritical mush, which was ideal for advertisers and politicians but disastrous for our civilization. Reason created science, science created scientism, and scientism created antireason.

Consequently, we are now in the midst of one of the greatest turning points in human history. Every area of our lives seems to exhibit a breakdown of inherited assumptions and ways of functioning. We have entered the twenty-first century armed with the outmoded conceptual weapons of the seventeenth, eighteenth, and nineteenth centuries. The twentieth century was a conceptual Waste Land, a kind of new Dark Ages of conceptual thought. We only barely muddled through, and humanity (especially the Jews) paid a terrible price. We only survived at all because of the positive inertia of the paradigm of the previous centuries. But inertia is no substitute for a conceptualization of new visions and new institutions more in keeping with the realities of the new global economy and a rising consciousness of planetary citizenship. Postmodernism might be an accurate critique of the twentieth-century wasteland, but it is not a positive program around which human beings can construct their lives. Neomodernism will strive to create a positive program for "Third Wave" society.

THE UNPRECEDENTED REVOLUTION

We find ourselves in the midst of a historically unprecedented revolution. Computers, genetic engineering, the conquest of space, nuclear energy, robotics, and telecommunications are having a greater impact on human destiny than the Agricultural and Industrial Revolutions combined.

The joining of human imagination and creativity to the speed and memory of the computer has resulted in an evolutionary development. We have become in effect a new species, as different from our forebears in our potentiality as the Cro-Magnon man was from the Neanderthal.

The conquest of space is as significant in the history of evolution as when the first amphibian left water and came on land. The "natural" environment of life on this planet, as represented by its highest manifestation (conscious life) is no longer only its crust, but potentially the entire cosmos. The advent of genetic engineering has given the human race ultimate responsibility for the evolutionary process itself. The development of fusion power has placed the most basic motive force of the entire universe (the transformation of hydrogen into helium, the fundamental process of every star in the universe) into the hands of the human race.

All these developments joined to robotics and telecommunications are creating new means of production and information interchange that are radically altering concepts of society, economy, and culture beyond recognition.

A single world market and communications system is now in place. The concept of sovereign nation-states interrelating with one another is evolving into a transnational reality first in the economic and then in the political realm. The concept of the correspondence of political and economic sovereignty with cultural autonomy is being replaced by concepts of cultural integrity within a transnational economic reality.

The Jews, as usual, are disproportionately represented in every one of these developments. Jewish individuals have been at the cutting edge of this new Scientific Revolution as well as the development of the new information transfer and financial instruments required and made possible by that revolution. What does classical Zionism or any of the extant Jewish organizations have to do with any of this?

THE CURRENT CRISIS OF CIVILIZATION

The following developments have led every aspect of our lives to convey a general sense of breakdown:

Existential. The *who* and *why* of what we are as human beings and the meaning of our world and of our existence in it has never been more confused and amorphous. Medieval, Renaissance, Enlightenment, and Victorian human beings knew who they were and what society and God expected of them. Since World War I, with the collapse of nineteenth-century optimism and the advent of the theory of relativity and the new physics, with its uncertainty principle, we have been living in an age of anxiety without spiritual or intellectual anchor. One of the aims of the postmodernist project was to attack human certitude (moral, scientific, or political) as insufferable hubris. Although this project has performed a valuable service in critiquing modernist ideology, it is essentially nihilistic. It offers no coherent substitute for modernism. Indeed, it would view the very search for coherence as a modernist pretension. But if humanity is to survive, the intellectual project of the twenty-first century must be to move from postmodernism to neomodernism. We must reinstate the Enlightenment human project at the center of our concerns, sans hubris.

Economic. No serious question remains that only the market economy can and does work in an environment characterized by rapid change. Even so, its social and cultural consequences and the fact that we have not yet harnessed it for the benefit of all humanity disquiet us. Economic theory and practice have reduced the human being (and here I use the term *human being* in its most literal sense) into production and consumption. We are not considered unique individuals, we are either consumers or producers. In order to increase sales, modern advertising has atomized the family into its constituent parts. Advertising 30 years ago featured the family car and pictures of the family sitting around the television set. Incipient consumer capitalism celebrated the family. Today every family has a car and a television, so advertising promotes the idea that every *member* of the family should have the car of his or her choice, and of course every room in the house should have its own television. Advanced consumer capitalism celebrates the atomized individual. We are no longer human beings, we are consumer beings. Several years ago, in America, in the middle of a heated debate on child-targeted advertising in general and Saturday morning television in particular; a television reporter challenged an advertising executive as to the ethics of child-targeted advertising. The executive's response was one of genuine surprise. "But you don't understand," she said; "you have a misperception; you should not look at them as children, but as little consumers." Isn't it ironic that in the United States some of the most radical free marketers are often those most publicly vociferous about family values? Is there anything in today's culture more corrosive to the traditional nuclear family than the inherent dynamic of advanced consumer capitalism? Consider the following headline, which appeared in the *International Herald Tribune* on June 3, 2000: "Rise in Joblessness Delights U.S. Markets." This monstrous headline reflects the classical economic fear that an imbalance between the supply of labor (labor, not human beings) and the rate of growth will cause inflation. Its reductionist approach to economics totally divorces the economy's functioning from the human aims of human economic activity. It is a totally dehumanized economics; dehumanized in the most literal sense in that it ignores the humanity of the human beings it is designed to serve.

Political. All over the world, traditional political systems and institutions are becoming ever less adequate to the needs of the new paradigm. Our social/political life in modern times has also become organized around quantitatively measurable social units. If it had not, the disciplines of sociology, political science, and statistics would have been impossible. We are trying to cope with a Third Wave economic, social, and cultural reality by means of Second Wave ideologies, methodologies, and political institutions. Modern politics reduces human beings to voters and representatives and human community to voting districts, voting blocs, and such. Political theory speaks of the balance of power while economic theory refers to the balance of trade. Both phrases have their genetic roots in the classical mechanical physics of the Enlightenment. Both appeal to mathematically reducible abstractions rather than to real human beings. Both are inadequate to the challenges of the twenty-first century, which are qualitative in their essence.

Social. The increased speed of change has produced a general feeling that our social values and the institutions that reflect them are under siege. Our entire educational system is based on the industrial factory model, even today. We take raw material (children), put them into a factory (school), and move them along an assembly line with various stations (grades). Workers (teachers) add subject matter to the children and mold them into useful parts (citizens) to be placed into society (the giant machine). The great video clip of Pink Floyd singing *The Wall* is an outstanding critical visual dramatization of the essence of the modern educational system.

Cultural. Since World War I and the simplistic, often ideologically driven popularizations of scientific developments such as relativity, indeterminacy, and chaos theory, humanity has witnessed the almost universal demise of objective standards of cultural product and the worship of the subjective. This has characterized almost all of modern art, which has degenerated, in recent years, to a point wherein the pretension to make a value judgment about a cultural product is judged as antidemocratic philistinism. We are supposed to tolerate and even pay tax dollars for any kind of pretension as long as someone with a knowing tone of voice declares it "art." The fact that so-called intellectuals defend this state of affairs is one of the reasons anti-intellectualism, even amongst university graduates, has become so widespread. Our reasoning intellect is our primary survival tool, which makes this anti-intellectualism dangerous. The very concept of culture has been industrialized. In culture and recreation we speak of the entertainment industry and the leisure industry. The use of the word *industry* is not just a semantic affectation. It reflects a general attitude of our relationship to human needs. It reflects how we have made commodities out of our responses to these needs and how we have used industrial techniques to produce and deliver the "products" geared to satisfying these needs. Mass spectator sports and mass popular culture are direct responses to the leisure needs of mass human populations after the Industrial Revolution. Mass urban concentrations, mass transportation, mass communications are all prerequisites for the very existence of mass sports and mass popular culture.

Scientific. Many are deeply troubled by ethical implications of advanced lines of scientific inquiry such as human cloning. The advance of medical technology has helped turn medicine from healing to torturing the terminally ill. In earlier times, people sickened, suffered for a short while, and died. Today, some people sicken and then suffer and suffer and suffer until they beg loved ones to help end their misery. Ethical questions surrounding euthanasia are staggeringly numerous and complex.

Jewish and Israeli. Jews, being perhaps the greatest benefactors from modernism, are now the most influenced by this breakdown of the Enlightenment secular humanist paradigm. The effects are apparent for all to see. Only the most benumbed Jew would fail to be disturbed by the present status of Israel-Diaspora relations, Orthodox–non-Orthodox relations, the moral level of Israeli society and the weaknesses of Diaspora Jewry. One reason for the current crisis in Jewish life is that we have no public agenda to address the previous points in a particularly Jewish way. Therefore, Jewish identity per se provides no real added human value, especially to the modern non-Orthodox Jew. For the first time in Jewish history, the best Jewish minds of our era do not take substantive part in specifically Jewish discourse.

CONCLUSION

Nothing was inherently wrong in the Enlightenment/Industrial Revolution paradigm or is especially tragic in its current breakdown. Quite the opposite, it has been responsible for the greatest material progress in human history. Its very technological possibilities have prompted a quantum leap in our moral, ethical, and even spiritual expectations.

The next time you feel nostalgic for some mythical, pristine, preindustrial age, consider how life was in those eras. Would you be willing to go back to a period when 70 percent of children died before the age of five (as was the case in Europe as late as 1750)? Would you be willing to live without electricity? Would you be willing to live without modern dentistry? If you go to a dentist when your teeth ache you give indirect sanction and affirmation to the entire Industrial Revolution: the metallurgical industry, the chemical industry, the pharmaceutical industry, the electronics industry, and so forth.

Or consider the case of Professor Steven Hawking. Consider the horror of that magnificent mind trapped in that crippled body and the blessing of modern technology that enables him to function as a true human being. Whatever the idyllic dreams of the radical greens, we should not be seduced by them. The Industrial Revolution was the greatest *spiritual* event in the history of the human race.

But as management guru Peter Drucker says: "nothing fails like success." The limitations of the Enlightenment/Industrial Revolution paradigm have become increasingly self-evident as a consequence of its very success.

A new paradigm of society is being born, based on radical new developments in science and in the organizational possibilities of industrial, scientific, and technological civilization. We call this paradigm, which reflects the success but growing inadequacy of the Enlightenment/Industrial Revolution paradigm, neomodernism.

This is the framework that the Jewish People must relate to if Jewish culture is to impart spiritual and practical added value to the young, university-trained, non-Orthodox Jew striving to find meaning. We are speaking about real value, not the warm feeling of nostalgia. What can we take from the cultural resources of the Jewish tradition that will enable us to confront this reality in a creative way that would provide that added value to the modern Jew in the twenty-first century?

Like it or not, this is the world we all live in. These are the practical, spiritual, and moral challenges we must all deal with. If the Jewish People cannot develop a cultural paradigm that relates to this world in constructive ways particular to itself, then the 4,000-year historical odyssey of the Jewish People will probably end by the end of the twenty-first century.

CHAPTER 2

The Triumph of Zionism

This chapter evaluates the success of classical Zionism and the consequent ideological crisis that this success has engendered. The intellectual attitude called post-Zionism is one manifestation of this ideological crisis. The fundamental Zionist ideological analysis and the political program that derived from that analysis are in the final stages of realizing themselves. Despite its myriad detractors over the years—within and without the Jewish community—Zionism remains the only nineteenth-century ideology that continues to demonstrate its relevance in this early part of the twenty-first century.

The question is not whether Zionism is the right direction for the Jewish People to take (the classic dispute) but whether its self-evident triumph is good for the Jewish People. Will its past and present relevance remain pertinent further into the twenty-first century, or will it become the same kind of obscurantist block to Jewish evolution and the Jews' ability to survive in a meaningful way, as some streams of Orthodoxy had become in the nineteenth century? Zionism has been a triumphant success, but this very success might be one major cause of its current crises. The aims of classical Zionism were to (1) create a Jewish state, (2) concentrate a majority of the Jewish People within that state, (3) integrate peacefully into the Middle East, (4) achieve relative economic independence, and (5) build a model society.

NORMALITY AND ABNORMALITY

The question of normality and authentic collective and individual existence has been a preoccupation of Zionism since its inception. Zionism's basic assumption was that Jewish existence without Jewish sovereignty in a Jewish homeland was abnormal and dangerous. Since the Holocaust, this has been an almost universally accepted norm of world Jewry, with only a few anecdotal exceptions. The only debate has been whether Zionism requires the entire Jewish People to settle in Israel or only a sizable segment—but even this debate has declined in light of objective developments.

According to classical Zionist analysis, the dispersion was not only a physical exile from the Land of Israel, it was also a spiritual exile from the Jewish individual's own authentic self. Zionists viewed exile as the primary cause of the distorted economic structure of Jewish society, what they termed the "inverted pyramid." Exile was also responsible for creating a peculiar kind of Jewish personality and mode of behavior: insecure, fearful, self-conscious, hyperenergetic, and over compensating. Exilic Jews were characterized by a unique combination of self-loathing and self-love that exiled them from their genuine selves. Indeed, some Zionists went so far as to claim that this collective socioeconomic abnormality combined with the behavioral abnormality of so many Jewish individuals discomfited the Gentiles and that this contributed to anti-Semitism. Zionism, therefore, would not only cure the Jews of their abnormality, it would also cure the Gentiles of their anti-Semitism.

Exile and cure are recurring themes in Zionist literature. Exile was the disease; return to the homeland was the cure. The various social and psychological abnormalities were the symptoms. To this day, the Israeli use of the word *gola* (exile) angers American and European Jewish leaders, as it implies abnormality. They prefer *Tfuzot* or Diaspora. Most sophisticated Israelis with ongoing contacts with Diaspora Jewry would probably agree that Jews in the West are not living an abnormal existence in exile. Notwithstanding that the classic Zionist analysis might leave a lot to be desired in its particulars, in its broad terms, Zionism's basic ideological assumptions seem to have stood the test of time.

NATIONALISM AND UNIVERSALISM

Classical Zionist ideology claimed that Europe and European civilization could not sustain vibrant Jewish communities in modern times. Anti-Semitism and the appeals of assimilation would eventually erode and destroy the possibility of Jewish existence in Europe. Naive faith in modern universalistic solutions to Jewish survival such as liberalism or socialism was a delusion. The success of these ideologies would lead to increased assimilation, their failure, to profound mass disappointment and social frustration, which would result in virulent anti-Semitism. This two-pronged prophecy has been fulfilled. Ideology alone could not extract the culturally rooted anti-Semitism of the European individual and its eventual expression in concrete social behavior and political polemic. One could be a liberal anti-Semite and one could be a socialist anti-Semite even as one spoke of universal brotherhood. Cultural and intellectual inference can also be anti-Semitic, such as the pejorative "Talmudic Argument," which so many liberal intellectuals use. This will be discussed in chapter 10, "The Future of Jewish-Christian Relations."

The apparent contradiction was resolved in the mind of the "progressive" European by predicating the Jew's social and political liberation on his ceasing to be a Jew and becoming a member of the general human community. Many Jews, anxious to please this "enlightened" opinion, flocked to the banner of the mythological cosmopolitan human being. That weird cultural mutation, the cosmopolitan Jew, with a pathological desire to be free of his Jewishness, was born. "Jew, Jew, Jew," cried Portnoy in Phillip Roth's *Portnoy's Complaint*. "Why can't I just be a human being?"

Zionism posits that no unique general human community exists, but rather, myriad national, ethnic, and religious communities interacting with one another to their mutual benefit. The true progressive aim should not be to homogenize our differences but to create frameworks within which these interactions between different human communities can be positive and creative. In this particular context we must replace the mechanical either/or analogy of classical Aristotelian logic (either universal or national) with an ecological analogy of inclusion and noncontradiction between the two concepts. Environmentalism now recognizes that " monoculturalism" (that is, the extensive cultivation of single crop or species over extensive areas) endangers the health of the entire ecological system.

An ecological system that has an ever-growing variety of species, variations of species, and ever-growing interactions between these species is healthy, vigorous, and robust. An ecological system that has an ever-diminishing variety of species, and therefore an ever-diminishing interaction between these species, is sick and susceptible to collapse. Each species preserves its own identity and integrity and by doing so, in dynamic interaction with other species, enhances the essential robustness of the entire ecological system.

What is true of natural culture is also true of human culture. A vigorous human society would be characterized by an ever-increasing number of human subcultures contributing their particular outlook and creativity to society. In other words, a people that strives to preserve its integrity and identity in civilized interaction with the rest of humanity enhances the essential robustness of all human civilization. It is by now generally agreed that a complete homogenization of human culture into a cosmopolitan "monoculture" would impoverish the human spirit to the point of endangering the very prospects of human survival.

Moses Hess's *Rome and Jerusalem* anticipated this ecological analogy by predicting the universal contributions a renascent Italian state and a renascent Jewish state would make to universal human civilization *not as their primary purpose but as a natural consequence of performing the tasks necessary to reconstituting themselves*. Here, he was following the lead of Mazzini, the liberal Italian nationalist.

How has Hess's thesis stood the test of reality? How have the necessary tasks of the Zionist enterprise to reconstitute the Jewish commonwealth contributed to universal human civilization? On a recent trip to the United States I happened to be sitting next to a gentleman from Wales on an internal flight. In the course of our conversation he began bragging about the resurgence of Welsh national identity and the fact that "ulpans" all over Wales are generating a rebirth of the spoken Welsh language. When I asked him if *ulpan* is a Welsh word, he admitted that he did not know. When I informed him that *ulpan* was a Hebrew word and that the entire Welsh language teaching system was a result of a visit of Welsh nationalists to Israel in the early 1970s, he was genuinely surprised. The Irish, too, use *ulpan* to describe their framework for the resurrection of the Irish language. Similarly, the Basques have copied the Israeli ulpan system, and their basic Basque grammar text is titled the *Ulpan*. The Dutch use the Israeli ulpan system to teach Dutch to new immigrants to Holland.

The Zionist necessity of regenerating the Hebrew language (one of the greatest achievements of Zionism) has become a light unto many Gentiles. Through the Zionist necessity of creating a modern human society in an arid ecology, Israeli foresters have been asked to oversee and advise massive arid zone reforestation projects in countries as diverse as Mexico and China. Israeli water engineers and agronomists have also been asked to advise developing peoples all over the world. In the early 1980s the Navaho Indian tribe observed that their "Painted Desert" was similar to the Negev and asked Israel to send an adviser to help them to adapt the technology of drip irrigation to their particular situation. Many leaders of Third World countries (even those who consistently vote against Israel in the United Nations) cite Israel as an example of what they believe they can accomplish themselves.

These universal contributions were a natural consequence of Israel fulfilling its national needs and not of a desire to be politically correct universalists dedicated to uplifting downtrodden Third World masses. If one were to compare the universal contribution of Israel in its more than 50 years to that of France or England (both 10 times the size of Israel) during the same time, Israel would come out most favorably.

Enlightened nationalists (I prefer this term to *nationalist*) believe that human beings cannot "just be human beings" in the abstract, they are always human beings within concrete and particular cultural and historical contexts. There exists no Platonic idealized human being, only real human beings living in historical and cultural context. The Enlightenment call to the Jews to join the general human community meant predicating Jewish liberation on assimilation and the end of the Jews as a people. Particular collective Jewish existence was thus delegitimized by the ideologies of modernism (see Hertzberg's *The French Enlightenment and the Jews*). This was but a short step from delegitimizing the very physical existence of the Jews.

ANTI-SEMITISM AND JEWISH SELF-HATE

The pathology of Jewish self-hate (*not* Jewish self-criticism, which reflects authentic Zionism), whereby the Jews themselves legitimized their own dele-gitimization, was born out of this modernist Enlightenment view. No one could be more contemptuous, sarcastic, and venomous against any expression of Jewish particularity (religious or Zionist) than the cosmopolitan Jew striving to be part of Gentile society. This, as we now know, did not solve the problem.

Cosmopolitan Jews were also attacked by anti-Semites *because* they were cosmopolitan and therefore without authentic cultural roots. *Rootless cosmopolitan* became a synonym for Jew in Stalinist literature and almost always was a prelude to some anti-Semitic activity. The cosmopolitan Jews, in paroxysms of self-justification did not blame their "progressive" attackers, they embraced universalistic ideologies of brotherhood—how could they be anti-Semitic? Instead they blamed the Jews. They blamed the *OstJuden*, the Jews of Eastern Europe who refused to give up their particular Jewish behavior and mannerism. "How can the Gentiles be expected to accept us as part of their community if we remain separate?" They blamed the Zionists who raised questions of dual loyalty while embracing the reactionary and anachronistic positions of nationalism (which, of course, all "enlightened " people were try-ing to do away with). "How can we expect the Gentiles to accept us as loyal and patriotic citizens of our respective countries if we keep talking about this nonsense of a Jewish State?" "How can we expect progressives to accept us if we become reactionary nationalists?"

As Zionists never tired of pointing out, the Jews were attacked (1) because they wanted to remain separate communities, (2) because they presumed to national sovereignty, and (3) because they dared to assume that they could ever assimilate and be true Germans or true Frenchmen. The *OstJuden* were resented because they spoke poor German and French with a terrible accent, and the cosmopolitan Jews were resented because they spoke perfect German and French, often better than "authentic" Germans and French. I once asked an expert in the German language in what part of Germany the best German was spoken. His answer, given with a wry smile, was "the Jews of Prague."

Today, Jews are attacked in Russia because they presume to be true Rus-sians. Whether separated from or integrated into Russia, Jews are hated and attacked. Germany could not tolerate the Jews, nor could Poland, Rumania, Hungary, or the Ukraine. Vast areas of Europe have or soon will become *Judenrein*. The Zionist prediction vis-à-vis most of Europe has come true.

SELF-EMANCIPATION

European cultures, unlike American culture, are aesthetically normative, with centers and peripheries. They include a national language, national cus-toms, and national music and literature. In the view of Romantic nationalism, these are natural organic products of the internal developments of the peoples. Outsiders can imitate and pretend to be a part of these cultures, but they can never truly be so. In the view of modern anti-Semitism, which is largely a mutated outgrowth of modern Romantic nationalism, the very attempts at imitation infect both the national culture and the spiritual health of the nation, and such a disease must be expunged. Indeed, the extreme expression of this sentiment led to the Nazis. Cosmopolitan Jews were hated and despised because of their cultural pretensions and their success in assimilation and in contributing to the national cultures of their adopted lands. The Jews were in a no-win situation.

All of this was quite clear to early Zionist thinkers. In 1882 Leon Pinsker, a Russian Jewish supporter of the Enlightenment and assimilation, rethought his position after a pogrom at Kishinov and wrote his profound tract *Auto-Emancipation*. Analyzing current events and anticipating some of the above dilemmas, he concluded that the only solution to the Jewish problem was to be found within the Jewish will to self-emancipation, that is, the Jews taking ultimate responsibility for their own future. Putting one's faith in universalistic ideologies to solve the Jewish problem would result in even greater suffering. It is a self-deception, he said.

Instead, the Jews must take responsibility for their own fate and cease to base their future on the modernist fiction of human progress and the eventual perfection of humankind. Human progress is no guarantee for producing better human beings; it is only a guarantee for increasing human power. In this particular context, Zionism could be viewed as a proto-postmodernist movement!

Zionism said: do not depend on the liberals to emancipate you; do not depend on the socialists to liberate you. Arise and emancipate and liberate yourselves. If the Jews wish to earn the goodwill of the Gentiles they must do so in the old-fashioned way—through power. Jews must become political and gain power. In the era of nationalism and the nation-state, this means Jewish nationalism as a means to Jewish self-emancipation.

Later, Theodore Herzl, an assimilated Jew who had no knowledge of Pinsker or his *Auto-Emancipation*, came to the same conclusion as a result of the famous Dreyfus affair (1894). Dreyfus was a French Jewish officer framed for treason by Gentile colleagues. Vicious anti-Semitism accompanied the trial and what followed. Herzl was shocked to hear cries of "death to the Jews" in Paris, the cultural and spiritual capital of enlightened Europe, and concluded that the Jews had no future in Europe. He wrote the *Jewish State* (1896) in response. Less intellectually profound by far than Pinsker's *Auto-Emancipation*, it was written in a much more compelling and popular scenario form (Herzl was a playwright) and was more straightforward about what the Jews required: in his view, they required nothing less than their own nation state, the Jewish State.

The Zionist analysis was eurocentric but assumed its relevance for Jews in the Islamic world. Zionists believed that the inevitable rise of nationalism in the Moslem world, in response to European nationalism, would also exacerbate the inherent precariousness of Diaspora Jewish existence, until viable Jewish communities could no longer be sustained.

America, on the other hand, was recognized as different from the outset. Leaders such as Ben Gurion and Jabotinsky (living in the United States during Turkish and English rule of Palestine) realized that a different kind of Jewish community was being created. Yet most Zionists believed that sooner or later viable Jewish communities would also be difficult to sustain in America. The reasons might differ from those in Europe and the Islamic world, but in the end Jewish viability would also erode in America.

The conclusion was that Jewish survival in the modern era (the era of industrialism, liberalism, nationalism, socialism, and individualism) depended on creating and sustaining a modern, democratic Jewish State in the ancient Jewish homeland where, because of objective and subjective developments, the majority of Jews would eventually find themselves living.

THE SUCCESS OF THE ZIONIST ANALYSIS

What is the historical record of this Zionist analysis? In the Islamic world, millennia-old Jewish communities have all but disappeared. The only viable Jewish community in the Middle East is Israel. Progressive opinion blames Zionism and Israel for this development. Progressives claim that the Jews always lived well under Moslem rule; that Islam only *appeared* to become anti-Jewish because of the unjustified provocations of Zionism (unjustified because Jewish nationalism itself is unjustified). In truth, the so-called Golden Age of Moslem Spain ended several hundred years before the Inquisition when fanatic Moslems exiled many Jews (Maimonides amongst them) from Moslem Spain.

The remainder of the Golden Age was under Christian rule until the Inquisition. The Jews always lived under the sufferance of the Moslems. Jews were always a protected "People of the Book" as long as they agreed to their inferior position and, like the Blacks in the American South, kept their place.

In reality, the Islamic rejection of Zionism sprang from Jewish pretension to equality. It was intolerable that an inferior people presumed to assert their national and hence their human rights alongside of Islam and in the process create a sovereign state within which even Moslems were bound by laws passed by a Jewish majority. The theological problem that Islam has with Zionism and Israel is similar to that of the Vatican. Jews can be tolerated, but Judaism and Jewish aspirations cannot be treated as being of equal value. The Zionist hypothesis of the *gola*'s abnormality was, therefore, no less relevant for Jews in Moslem countries, even though Zionism rarely, if at all, analyzed the concrete situation of the Jews in the Moslem world. Blaming Zionists for anti-Jewish violence in the Middle East and elsewhere is akin to blaming American Blacks for anti-Black violence because they dared to assert their rights and refused to accept the role designated for them by others.

Unfortunately, the Zionist prediction about what would happen to the Jews of Europe as a result of persecution and assimilation has also been vindicated in the twentieth century. The Nazis all but physically exterminated European Jewry. The Communists all but spiritually exterminated Soviet Jewry. European Jewry numbers dropped from about nine million before the war to about three million after the war, and to about two million at the fall of Communism. Hundreds of thousands have disappeared because of assimilation in the Soviet Union. English Jewry has declined from a community numbering well over 400,000 in the 1960s to a community numbering well under 300,000 today, mostly due to assimilation and emigration. The 600,000-strong French community is racked by mass intermarriage (estimated by some to be around 70 percent). In less than eight years since the fall of Communism, well over a million Jews have emigrated from the Soviet Union, mostly to Israel, the United States, and Germany. Fewer than 1 million Jews remain in the former Soviet Union, and with only 1 birth for every 8 deaths and approximately 80,000 leaving every year, the future appears bleak.

We have witnessed the radical numerical decline of European Jewry in this century, a decline that apparently will continue for the foreseeable future. More and more Jewish communities will shrink below the critical mass necessary for sustaining viable communal life. What will remain will be aging remnants visited by American Jewish missions "seeking their roots." As Zionism predicted, physical and spiritual persecution has combined with tolerance-induced assimilation to spell the end of European Jewry. Within the next several decades—little more than a century since Herzl and Pinsker—less than one million Jews will live in Europe and less than one hundred thousand in the Moslem world, less than one-tenth the population of a century ago.

The Zionist claim that the *galut* cannot sustain viable Jewish communities in modern times appears vindicated. There is, however, a powerful argument for one major exception to the Zionist case: American Jewry, which will be discussed in chapter 4.

THE ZIONIZATION OF JEWISH CULTURAL AND COMMUNAL LIFE

In the meantime, Zionism has already triumphed indirectly from within the Diaspora communities themselves. Jewish People the world over have become Zionized through their personal involvement with the ongoing drama of Israel. Many Jews are still more emotionally troubled by what goes on in Israel than what goes on in their own communities. However, in recent years, a growing fatigue with Israel and its problems is becoming increasingly apparent in many parts of the Diaspora.

Israel is the preeminent Jewish fact of the past 50 years. Since World War II, the larger part of Diaspora Jewish communal life has, for better or worse, revolved directly or indirectly, around Israel. One cannot possibly divorce the fact of Israel from an understanding of the internal sociological and organizational developments, modes of behavior, and cultural expressions of American, European, former Soviet, Australian, South African, and Ethiopian Jewry.

How many Jewish organizations are based in some way upon Israel-focused activity? What is their relative weight within the community? Can a Jewish organization with no Israel-centered activity whatsoever even survive? Over the past 50 years, anti-Zionist Jewish organizations have all but ceased to exist, and anti-Israeli Jews have by definition become marginalized.

Look at the year's program of activities of any synagogue. Look at what programs attract people. Consider revisions in liturgy to include mention of Israel and the Israeli army and the almost universal use of Sephardic pronunciation in Ashkenazi synagogues, which is a Zionist innovation. Look at the way holidays are now celebrated and investigate the educational content of day and afternoon Hebrew schools. In modern Orthodox, Conservative, and Reform synagogues, Israel the reality and Israel the symbol play central roles in the way the community identifies itself and interrelates with its Jewish and non-Jewish surroundings.

THE ZIONIZATION OF HAREDI JEWRY

The one exception often cited to demonstrate the possibility of an authentic Jewish existence without the State of Israel is the ultra-Orthodox Haredi community.

But even this historically anti-Zionist community has become "Zionized" by the living fact of Israel and the central place Israel plays in modern Jewish life. Only a fringe minority of the ultra-Orthodox would today call themselves anti-Zionists. The vast majority today would call themselves non-Zionist, while a growing number would call themselves national Haredim, in both Israel and the Diaspora. Indeed the national Haredim might now outnumber the anti-Zionist Haredim. Two profound internal changes within the ultra-Orthodox community directly and indirectly affected by Israel have brought this about:

The vast majority of ultra-Orthodox Jews now living have been born and reared in Israel and the United States and have acculturated many of these countries' values and habits of thought. In Israel, young Haredi men and women are becoming increasingly Israeli in language and modes of social and economic intercourse with the non-Haredi community. Haredi educational facilities are becoming increasingly dependent upon the Zionist state. In the United States, while still keeping separate, the Haredim have been greatly affected by general American attitudes (one notable area being education for women). It is also difficult to be anti-Zionist in a country in which the Gentiles are so Zionist. Religious reasons have prompted a growing number of American Haredim to move to Israel. They may not call it *aliya*, and they may say that it is not Zionist, but their *aliya* is made possible by the very existence of the

Zionist entity and the assistance of the Zionist state of Israel. Ironically, the rate of western *aliya* amongst the so-called anti- or non-Zionist Haredim is higher than amongst other Jewish groups. This cannot but have long-term effects on modes of behavior and habits of thought.

In Israel, the Haredim have built an impressive institutional and communal infrastructure that takes an increasingly active role in the political, economic, social, and cultural life of the country. In their daily lives, they speak Hebrew with the Sephardic accent, conveniently ignoring the Zionist origins of this cultural fact. Their Israeli infrastructure is a focus of American Haredi life. American Haredim raise money for it, lobby politically for it, are emotionally involved in its fate, and are galvanized when its vital interests seem challenged. In a word, an almost exact copy of how the general Jewish community relates to Israel.

The greatest irony is that the so-called anti-Zionist Haredim have used the fact of Israel to put forward their own program better than any other Jewish group. The many rootless young Jews who pass through Israel in the hope that they may "find something" makes the *baalei tshuva* industry possible. It is also made possible by the fact that Israel has become the yeshiva center of the Jewish People. Zionism in turn made this possible.

In Israel, Sephardic Haredim will soon constitute the numerical majority of the Haredi community. The Sephardim have never been anti-Zionist, and it would be difficult even to call them non-Zionist. They form a major component of the national Haredim and might even in some cases be called Zionist Haredim.

Other profound internal developments are causing the Haredi community to integrate into general Israeli society and in this sense to become Zionized, and thus, indirectly, Zionizing their American (and European) counterparts. These developments are not as yet apparent to the general or even to the Haredi community. But by simple quantitative and qualitative extrapolation one could build a future scenario, based on objective developments and characterized by solid internal logic in which within several decades the status of women and Haredi attitudes to secular education will have undergone a radical change.

Numerous academic *baalei tshuva* concerned about the lack of secular education on the part of their children are already changing the norms of Haredi society. This is reinforced by American Haredim greatly influenced by American attitudes to education and to education for women in particular. In addition more Haredi businessmen desire professional education for their sons and, in some cases, daughters.

The changing job market also requires educated and professional Haredi women in order to compete. Here, the "traditional" role of the Haredi woman as primary breadwinner plays a subversive role vis-à-vis traditional Haredi society. Demand is growing for family, education, child, and other counseling services within the Haredi community, too. Traditionally, women filled these roles, and the competitive need to be educated and professional means more Haredi women must develop analytical and critical thinking skills. Such skills have, historically, resulted in radical change, and this will most likely repeat itself in the Haredi community. Signs of a Haredi feminist phenomenon have already begun to appear as more Haredi women pursue higher secular education. All of this is reinforced by the problems of an over-built, nonproductive Haredi infrastructure that has generated a financial cri-sis within Haredi institutions. Because of these developments, the first decades of the twenty-first century will see increasing numbers of young Haredi men and women compelled to integrate within Israeli economic life.

More Haredim will therefore become integrated into mainstream Israeli life and will become more Israeli. They will feel more social and psychologi-cal pressure to assume the full burdens of Israeli citizenship (including some kind of army or other national service) and in this way will de facto become Zionized (whether they call themselves Zionists or not). Zionizing Israeli Haredim will lead to the Zionization of American Haredim.

THE SUCCESS OF THE ZIONIST POLITICAL PROGRAM

Zionism has almost fulfilled its entire political program. Indeed, it might do so within the first decade of the twenty-first century. It has created a state, and has become part of the world community despite Arab hostility. It has created a vital and highly developed economy despite what some researchers estimate as 44 billion dollars' worth of damage caused by the Arab boycott since the establishment of Israel. It has been slowly integrating into the region over the past two and a half decades.

Sadat's visit to Jerusalem and the subsequent peace agreement with Egypt, the Madrid conference, the Oslo agreements with the Palestinians, and the peace agreement with Jordan represent the greatest triumph of Zionism since the creation of the State of Israel. Zionist grand strategy strove for Israel's peaceful integration into the region; Arab grand strategy was to drive the Jews out of the region. The peace process is an unstated Arab admission that their grand strategy has failed and that Zionism's has succeeded. This remains true no matter what the fate of the peace process following the second *Intifada* of 2000–2003 or any other future crisis. What has been done cannot be undone, no matter how hard radical Islamists and Arab nationalists try.

The West does not, has not, and never will accept Israeli views on the occu-pied territories. Conversely, however, most Western countries accept the Israeli view as to the essence of peace. An Israeli prime minister could have made President George Bush senior's speech at Madrid about the type of peace he envisioned, wherein he chided the Egyptians for their cold peace attitude toward Israel.

The West wants stability. This means Israel accepting the Arab position on the territories and Arabs accepting Israel's position on the essence of peace. Peace is impossible without territorial compromise, hence no stabil-ity. Without Israel's conception of peace and full normalization threat of war will continue, hence no stability. The question of justice and the relative merits of the Arab or the Jewish position matter little. Most Israelis have accepted the Arab view on the territories, but most Arabs, especially the Palestinians, have yet to accept the Jewish view on peace. They make their agreement to peace contingent on Israel accepting principles that, if accepted, would mean the destruction of Israel. An example would be United Nations Resolution 194 giving Palestinian refugees the right to return to their homes in Israel proper.

In regard to world Jewry, Israel has long since ceased to be dependent on Jewish philanthropy. Funds raised for Israel by all Jewish organizations represent the equivalent of about 1 percent of Israel's GNP and less than 2 percent of Israel's budget. Diaspora Jewry, on the other hand, derives 100 percent of its budgets from their share of the fundraising. If Israel's problems are still a major marketing device in the fundraising process and if fundraising still plays a central role in the identity of Diaspora Jewry, then raising funds for Israel is more important for the Diaspora than it is for Israel. A decline in dependence is a major indication of success.

Imagine the effect on Jewish life in Israel and the Diaspora if full-page ads sponsored by the State of Israel appeared one day in major newspapers in the United States thanking American Jewry for their past support and informing them that their financial contributions were no longer necessary. Israel would have to tighten its belt one notch. American Jewry's entire organizational, social, cultural, and even financial life would be traumatized. What would American Jewry do without work for Israel as the central fact of Jewish life? This is not a theoretical question. The likely gradual removal of direct American government aid over the next several decades will even detract from the value of American Jewry as a political lobby for Israel—the second major Jewish activity after fundraising.

The declining impact of the financial costs of the Arab boycott, the opening of formerly closed world markets and the subsequent legitimization of Israel as an object of international investment will more than make up for the end of Jewish and American aid. At that point, Zionist voices in Israel will be raised to cut the umbilical cord of Jewish aid. The argument will be "how can we present ourselves as the vehicle of meaningful Jewish existence while continuing to beg for money from rich Jews in the Diaspora?" Israel cannot on the one hand present itself as a welfare case to Diaspora Jewry and on the other hand as a place to which one makes *aliya*. This is not an illogical argument; it has been made in the past; and it will certainly be made with more conviction over the coming years.

SO WHAT?

The question is, so what? Does the apparent triumph of Zionism prove its value? Does it guarantee Jewish survival in the twenty-first century? Historical conditions change. Who can say that what has been relevant will continue to be relevant?

Let us assume that the State of Israel will guarantee the physical survival of the Jews. Who is to say that Jewish culture will continue to make meaningful contributions to world civilization or will provide meaningful frameworks for the self-realization of the individual Jew? There is a branch of Zionism I call the Zionism of mediocrity. It is a position advocated by Jacob Klatzkin, of whom Arthur Herzberg said in his book *The Zionist Idea:* "he is the most important Zionist thinker to affirm that a third-rate, normal, national state and culture would be enough" (p. 315). It is a position also held by Klatzkin's latter-day spokesman Hillel Halkin in his book *Letters to an American Jewish Friend.* This branch of Zionism finds comments about meaningful contributions to world civilization at best amusing irrelevancies. The Jews have the right to survive, the Diaspora does not have the right to survive, and therefore the only place the Jews can and should survive is in Israel. If the price means trading Jewish quality for Jewish mediocrity, so be it.

Most Zionist thinkers, however, seem to have concluded that the Zionist enterprise must have cultural and social pretensions above and beyond the national program. This was both an ideal and a necessity.

They ask, is the conclusion of 4,000 years of Jewish history to be a third-rate Levantine country? Is this what the Jewish historical travail has been all about? What right have we to be satisfied with such an outcome? Are we not morally obligated to justify Jewish history by creating a moral society? This view would say if contemporary Israel is the final stage of Jewish evolution, the result is singularly inadequate to the prodigious process of Jewish history. Redemption cannot be third-rate politicians and fifth-rate rabbis arguing over nonefficacious ideological nonsense. After the historical travail of the Jews, this would be too cruel a joke.

For many the question of a first- or third-rate Jewish State goes beyond moral responsibility to past generations and a sense of embarrassment about Jewish mediocrity. This view holds that creating a model society, and the social, economic, and cultural policy required to do so, is an absolute necessity for the very survival of the national program. The Jews are not like other nations and the Jewish State cannot be like other nation states. Moral self-justification is not the rationale for a model Jewish State, but rather an existential necessity

The Jewish State must be—*for its own sake*—a light unto the Gentiles. If Israel is not a light unto the Gentiles, it will not be a light unto the Jews; if it is not a light unto the Jews it will not be able to survive.

No less a personage than David Ben Gurion held this position, which has deep roots in Zionist thought. From Moses Hess's *Rome and Jerusalem* to Herzl's *Old Newland,* which portrayed the Jewish State as an entrepôt of human culture and a model for independent Arab and African states, it saw a capacity in renascent Israel to "serve as a model" for other peoples. To some extent this is already the case, as pointed out above in the references to Israel's impact on the rebirth of other languages and on arid zone forestation, agriculture and water engineering and management.

The question remains—so what? Zionism is triumphant and Israel will soon have within its borders a majority of the world's Jews. Is this a cause for Zionists to celebrate and congratulate themselves? Or is it rather a time to quake with trepidation over the awesome responsibility that now rests *solely* on our shoulders, the responsibility for the continued physical and meaningful survival of the Jewish People?

For despite the pose of Zionists that Zionism represents the Jewish future, in practice Zionists have functioned as if alternatives existed (America, for instance) and that ultimate responsibility for the Jewish future was not really theirs. Over the next several decades, Zionism will be called upon to put up or shut up. The outcome will determine whether Zionism was indeed a redemptive movement or a terrible historical mistake.

CHAPTER 3

Zionism in the Twenty-First Century

If Zionism is to remain relevant, we must engage in a critical reexamination of its assumptions, arguments, and symbols. We must attempt to reformulate it or, in the language of modern management theory, to reinvent it. Zionism must reflect the needs of the Jewish People in the twenty-first century. This is a prerequisite to any comprehensive discussion of the Jewish situation in general, because the past 100 years of Jewish history have involved supporting Zionism, opposing it, or coming to terms with it and the product of its labors, Israel.

Zionism is the elephant in the Jewish bed, something that cannot be ignored. You may like it, you may resent it, you may be amused or bemused by it, but you cannot ignore it. It occupies the landscape of modern Jewish culture like a great mountain. It is always before your eyes, and whenever you want to act Jewishly you must go through, over, or around it. Ignoring it or dismissing it coincides with Jewish irrelevancy. This makes the current crisis of Zionism so central to any discussion of the Jewish future, especially in the Diaspora.

One need not witness the frenetic behavior of recent Zionist Congresses, the ongoing decline of the World Zionist Organization, or Israel's loss of direction, or dwell on the fiction of meaningful Zionist activity in the Diaspora to conclude that Zionism is in crisis. It is enough for the modern Jew, Diaspora *or* Israeli, to ask, "Does classical Zionism resonate with meaning for my own life, for the experiences I undergo, and for the challenges I must face?"

Zionist apologists dismiss this kind of question as the sort of self-indulgent radical individualism that reflects decadence, a loss of values, and a decline of commitment to Jewish survival. But does decadence cause the question to be asked or is decadence a result of the question not being answered? I believe the latter, for no ideology can truly address the problems of the collective unless it is meaningful for the living individuals who constitute the collective. The lack of a positive answer constitutes the emotional foundation of post-Zionism.

No ideology can remain moral, let alone relevant, if it sacrifices the tangible individual on the altar of the abstract collective. The collective acquires true meaning only when it is a harmonious reflection of the combined aspirations of individuals. Whenever ideologists abstract or mythologize the collective and set it above the aspirations of individuals, judging them by fantastic standards of an imagined "organic community" or "objective scientific analysis of historical developments," they provide rich soil for the growth of gulags and other totalitarian manifestations. As Professor Nathan Rotenstreich has pointed out, "The existence of the State of Israel is by definition a structure of the activities of individuals taking place within the framework of a collective existence" (*Midstream*, May 1990).

In other words, a collective is only real when it provides historical place and time in which *individual* human beings can fulfill themselves. Zionism's purpose was to solve the problems of living Jewish human beings; to allow them to enjoy and realize their human being without sacrificing their Jewish being; to enable them to enjoy and realize their Jewish being without sacrificing their human being. This can be the only justification for the existence of Israel and Zionism. Yet it seems that Zionism and Israel have grown distant from the aspirations of many young Diaspora and Israeli Jews over the past several years.

The reason is that Zionism is a nineteenth-century ideology trying to come to terms with a twenty-first-century reality. To borrow Alvin Toffler's metaphor of the three waves, it is a Second Wave instrument trying to address and answer the problems of a people who as individuals are at the very forefront of creating a Third Wave civilization. Therefore, Zionism finds it difficult to provide solutions for a growing list of modern Jewish problems. The persistence of an outmoded expression of Zionism has tended to exacerbate these problems, especially in Israel.

Survey all that is wrong with modern Israel, and in almost every case you will find a Zionist position or polemic that ceased to be pertinent decades ago. Preoccupation with the leftover questions of classical Zionism is depriving increasing numbers of Israelis and Diaspora Jews of the historical space they require to actualize themselves as individuals. This is true for the Left, the Right, and the religious wing of Zionism.

WHAT IS ZIONISM?

In its broadest terms, Zionism is the growing concentration of ever-larger numbers of Jews in the State of Israel in order that they may optimally actualize both their human being and their Jewish being. It strives to create particular expressions of Jewish life suitable for modern times. Or, to be more precise, it strives

To facilitate the *collective* integration of the Jewish People into modern life in order to enable the individual Jew to fully realize himself or herself as a modern human being without having to sacrifice Jewish identity.

To conduct this collective integration in such a way as to create specifically Jewish frameworks that give Jewish identity an *added value* to the Jewish individual's ambitions to actualize his or her capacities. Jewish identity must change from something an individual must *sacrifice for* to something an individual will *benefit from*.

From Herzl to Ben Gurion, Zionism has been preoccupied with the future and not with the past. Ben Gurion's desire that Israel be a "light unto the nations" for both moral and practical reasons sprang from his concern for the future of Jewish existence. The moral and the practical are inextricably interlocked within this interpretation of Zionism. Zionists who moralize in the abstract instead of finding practical solutions are part of the problem. Israel's citizens and world Jewry are judged by these self-appointed guardians of the faith and found inadequate.

I would rather treat Zionism as part of the social and political history of the Jews, demonstrate its relevance in a certain time and place for many Jews, and show how it has become increasingly irrelevant over time as it has succeeded in changing the social and political reality of the Jewish People. So, again, what is Zionism? Let us define our terms.

Zionism is an ideology and not a theology. It is not a religious dogma, which one believes in, but rather an intellectual tool for analyzing the situation of the Jewish People as well as a program, based upon the conclusions of the ideological analysis, for improving that situation. *Policy* is the means by which we hope to implement the ideological program. *Grand Strategy* is the efficient mobilization of economic, social, military, cultural, and moral power in order to implement policy aims. *Strategy* represents the ways and means by which one implements any one of the components of Grand Strategy. *Tactics*, in comparison, is but a component of strategy and can be further divided into concrete and verbal tactics.

One of the errors of post-state Zionism has been to confuse ideological conclusions with policy aims, policy aims with grand strategic instruments, and grand strategic instruments with strategic maneuver and strategy with tactics. Consequently the *tactic* of talking tough has taken on the mantle of *ideological* value.

Another error has been the failure to note that the character of every one of these categories constantly changes. The ideological conclusions pertaining to a given situation at a certain point in history do not necessarily pertain to a different situation at a different point in history. If this is true, policy aims must of necessity also change as new grand strategic instruments are created and old ones are reformed or even eliminated. Strategies and tactics must also adapt to changing realities of political, military, and economic power. Nothing is more foolish than to endorse a certain way of doing things because it was done and worked in the past. A course of behavior that worked in a past radically different from the present is almost guaranteed to fail in the future.

All of these categories have been confused with values and ideals. Thus, the army and Jewish settlement and certain Histadrut (Israel Labor Federation) institutions were transformed from grand strategic instruments into values; and fervently held idealism became a substitute for creative ideological thinking. These and other issues will be dealt with in detail in the chapters having to do with Grand Strategy.

IDEOLOGY AND IDEALS

We must differentiate between ideology and idealism. All ideologies are based on ideals, but ideology and idealism are not synonymous. Some examples of positive ideals would be brotherhood, equality, justice, freedom, and liberty. One may be a liberal, a socialist, a conservative, or religious and embrace various interpretations of these ideals. People advocate ideologies that combine analytical conclusion and programmatic device into the most efficient means of realizing their ideals. Honest people embracing radically different ideologies can sustain civilized cooperation with great mutual respect when their basic ideals are the same. This attitude is the very foundation of democratic society.

We must never forget, however, that ideals and idealism can be negative, and that ideologies based on negative ideals are, by commonly agreed opinion, immoral. Adolph Hitler was an idealist. The Ayatollah Khomeini was an idealist. The Kamikazes and the Red Guards were idealists. Their ideals and the ideologies based on their ideals were and are immoral according, I would assume, to most readers of this book. This is why when, in the context of the current Israeli political debate, we hear the phrase "at least they are idealists," we should want to know what ideals we are talking about before we generate enthusiasm. If the ideals in question reflect explicit or implicit racism, or contempt for judicial due process or democratic procedure or equality before the law, we should not be impressed.

When this kind of idealism is framed by a fanatic belief system that absolutely knows the will of God vis-à-vis current political questions and is capable of morally justifying every kind of behavior no matter how outrageous, it is time to draw a line and say,: "Over this line we are no longer one." The ultimate product of such idealism was Yigal Amir—the murderer of Yitzhak Rabin.

If ideology is in part a tool for analyzing a situation and drawing conclusions geared to change or improvement, then when the situation does change we must search for new ideological expressions that will provide us with new analytical tools. With these we can draw new conclusions about our new situation and thus create new programs, new policies, and new grand strategic instruments to change or better serve that new situation. New means of analyzing a new situation will almost certainly result in new conclusions and indicate ways and means of creating new grand strategic instruments and efficiently reforming old ones. It should be noted that our situation has changed not only because of objective historical developments but also because of the programs and policies of previous successful ideological analysis.

Dogmatic loyalty to old ideas, organizations, and ways of doing things is no proof of the purity of one's Zionist credentials; it is a proof of stupidity and is guaranteed to bring failure. Nothing fails like success because success breeds loyalty to the instruments that made it possible. This loyalty creates a hidebound conservatism, which balks every attempt at constructive change. It is our generation's task to reinterpret Zionism. To do this, we must first examine how our period differs from that which gave birth to classical Zionism.

HISTORICAL BACKGROUND

Zionism developed on the background of nineteenth-century European civilization in response to the unique conditions of nineteenth-century European Jewry, especially East European Jewry. It drew inspiration from the 2,000-year-old Jewish desire to return to Zion but was not synonymous with that desire. It was and still is a nineteenth-century political development.

That Zionism developed in Europe in the nineteenth century has special significance, considering that more than half of Israel's Jewish population and close to 60 percent of her soldiers and students are of non-European origin. More than two-thirds of the Diaspora lives outside Europe. Twenty percent of Israel's total population is not Jewish (and not European). We no longer live in the nineteenth century but have entered the twenty-first century. These compelling facts demand a reinterpretation of Zionist ideology.

The Industrial Revolution most characterized nineteenth-century Europe. The rise of capitalism, liberalism, nationalism, socialism, and cultural nationalism were concomitant with the Industrial Revolution. These developments released forces that made the situation of the Jews increasingly intolerable but also supplied the means by which they could liberate themselves. In this, they were no different from other colonized peoples. Zionism reflected and incorporated all of these developments and could not have arisen in any other historical context.

The opponents of Zionism asserted that a wasteland could not possibly absorb millions of Jews. The Zionists responded that using new industrial means of production, the Jews would redeem the land, converting it from a waste into a garden. This, in fact, became the historical case. The industrial reality of the nineteenth and twentieth centuries was more than a concrete instrument of the Zionist enterprise, it was a propaganda tool.

Historical context also applies to the cultural renewal that Zionism hoped to effect. The father of modern Hebrew, Eliezer Ben-Yehuda, did not decide in a cultural vacuum to try to revivify the Hebrew language. His initiative, along with the progenitors of modern Hebrew literature, was part of a universal historical phenomenon that may be termed cultural nationalism. When Ben-Yehuda and his Hebrew language associates appeared on the historical scene, many peoples of Central, Eastern, and southern Europe were already modernizing their language and their literature, transforming them into useful tools for their modern national aspirations. The Poles, Russians, Hungarians, Czechs, and Italians were already well advanced in this direction. The Jews may have had a longer road to tread, considering that Hebrew of any sort was not their daily spoken language, but the project itself was embedded within the cultural developments of nineteenth-century Europe.

In addition, every political party and movement within the World Zionist Movement and since 1948, also within the State of Israel, has its ideological and organizational roots deep within the nineteenth-century European reality. The various -isms of nineteenth-century Europe, such as liberalism and socialism, provided Zionism (another nineteenth-century European -ism) with the raw material to construct its political culture. This dependence on nineteenth-century -isms is also the case for other nations, but the Jews feel its negative consequences more because of their particular character and their greater survival need to adapt to the environment of the twenty-first century.

Nineteenth-century Jews were characterized by their lack of a state, their abysmal poverty, and their lack of basic human rights. More than 80 percent of world jewry lived under tyrannical or authoritarian regimes, and thousands of Jews died of malnutrition every year. Jewish life was characterized by what socialist Zionism called an abnormal socioeconomic structure, the so-called inverted pyramid. This concept posited that "normal" nations possess a pyramidal social and economic structure, with most of the population in industrial and agricultural production, a minority in services, and an even smaller minority in intellectual and spiritual endeavors. The word *normal* derives from *norm*, that which is standard. The Jews were the mirror image of this universal norm, common to every other nation at the time. A tiny minority of Jews were in agriculture; a small minority were in industry while the majority were in the services and intellectual and spiritual pursuits.

The consequences of this abnormality, according to classical Labor Zionists such as Borochov, Syrkin, and Gordon were unhealthy social, cultural, and psychological characteristics that contributed substantially to anti-Semitism. After all, why shouldn't presumably normal peoples be troubled by the presence of an abnormal people living in their midst?

One of the main tenets of Labor Zionism was that the Jews had to cure themselves of their abnormality through the catharsis of physical work. The creation of Jewish working and peasant classes became not only a political, economic, and social necessity but increasingly became of spiritual, almost religious, value in and of itself. Out of this was born the myth of the *halutz* or the pioneer. The early pioneers of what is known as the Second and Third *Aliyot* (immigrant waves) saw themselves as national, social, cultural, and spiritual pioneers. This tiny band produced all the great leaders of the pre-state Jewish entity and the early and middle years of the state. These included David Ben-Gurion, Levi Eshkol, Berl Katzenelson, Pinhas Sapir, and Golda Meir.

During this historical phase, the Zionist project was self-evident: to create a Jewish State that, by guaranteeing the civil rights of the Jews, would release their productive energies, allowing the natural creation of a Jewish working and peasant class thereby solving the problems of abject poverty and the supposedly abnormal socioeconomic and psychological-cultural structure of the Jewish People. Zionism had tremendous impact on the great masses of East European Jewry because both its analysis and its program resonated with meaning for their lives as individual Jewish human beings living in a particular historical context. Zionism's very relevance provoked the Communists to invest so much energy in disputing it. If its message had not been so compelling, Zionism would not have enjoyed so much attention from the Communists.

This Zionist project made the Labor Zionist program attractive. The self-evident rightness of the Labor policy and strategy as well as the social and economic instruments they created (kibbutz, moshav, Histadrut, Hagana, and such) and the practical and dynamic leadership this policy produced made them attractive even to the non-Labor voter. Many saw the kibbutz especially as at the forefront of the Zionist enterprise: settling the land, defending it, creating a Jewish agriculture, and absorbing immigration. It represented the essence of Zionism and enjoyed universal respect. But what is the situation today?

THE PARADOX OF SUCCESS

The very triumph of Zionism has created a paradox. Classical Zionism's primary purpose was to substitute normality for the abnormality of a totally exilic existence. It succeeded. We now have a Jewish State that has been in existence for more than 50 years. This fact alone completely changes the character of Jewish existence, not only for the Jews who reside in the state but also for Jews the world over. It is impossible to understand the psychology, the organizational structure, and the behavior of Diaspora Jewry today other than in the light of Israel's existence. Statehood, not statelessness, is the major Jewish fact. The major operating principle behind any analysis of American, former Soviet, Western European, or Latin American Jewry is the fact of Israel's existence.

But Israel's political life is still dominated by pre-state Zionist polemics. All of this is completely meaningless for the everyday concerns of the modern Jew *including the modern Israeli Jew*. The fact that the educational content and the organizational structure of much of Zionist life still rely on this outmoded paradigm holds the key to much of what is wrong with current Jewish life: in Israel, in the Diaspora, and in regard to Israel-Diaspora relations.

Classical Zionism claimed that the creation of the state would radically alter the character of Diaspora Jewry. They would be prouder, more independent, more autonomous, and more self-confident. This prediction came true, yet its consequences are uncomfortable for Zionist functionaries and state representatives. They have not even begun to come to terms with it as it implies the normalization of Diaspora Jews. This contravenes a bedrock assumption of classical Zionism regarding the inherent abnormality of Diaspora life.

Many Diaspora Jews—uncomfortable with the implications of Jewish statehood—are almost thankful for this failure of Zionist functionaries and state representatives to redefine Zionism. This failure, in effect, turns Zionism into a kind of cultural fast food that requires no real effort to consume and satisfies a spiritual hunger that might have been filled by something more profound. The spiritual space filled by a kitsch version of Zionism, which no one takes seriously, is one cause of shallowness in Jewish life today. Zionism's biggest problem is that it has realized all its aims and its so-called representatives have failed to construct on its success an up-to-date message that resonates with meaning for modern Jews, in Israel as well as in the Diaspora. Zionism has become a quintessential example of the principle that nothing fails like success. The state exists; Jews are normal; now what? This situation has given birth to post-Zionism.

Classical Zionism claimed that the Jews required a state of their own to guarantee their civil rights. The paradox is that the vast majority of Jews live in the Free World and possesses more civil rights as individuals than the citizens of Israel. Most Diaspora Jews have more religious freedom than Israeli Jews. They are free of the surveillance and control of an Orthodox rabbinate in regards to marital affairs, and they have the freedom to choose or not choose any trend of Judaism without fear of discrimination within the general or the Jewish community. No censor limits their freedom of speech. They are unhampered by the need to perform reserve duty and need no permit from the army before they travel overseas, as was the case until recently. I am not decrying these last two points: Israel's objective situation requires their perpetuation, within reasonable limits. But it *is* the objective reality and obviates, in practice, if not in principle, the classical Zionist claims regarding Jewish civil rights. A more sophisticated Zionist argument would demonstrate that the status of Jews in the West reflects, in no small measure, the very success of Israel and Zionism.

A third paradox relates to the Zionist claim that the Jewish State was a prerequisite to ending Jewish poverty. At the outset of the twenty-first century we note that the vast majority of Diaspora Jews are not poor. There are Jewish poor, but poverty is no longer a sociological characteristic of Diaspora Jewry, quite the opposite. Diaspora Jews usually have higher per capita incomes than other ethnic groups in their various communities. This is not only true for American and Canadian Jews but also for English, French, and Australian Jewry.

It was also the case for most Soviet Jews before the collapse of the Soviet Union. By the social and economic standards of the Soviet Union, the Jews were firmly ensconced within the middle and upper middle classes. Their problem was not material, it was spiritual and cultural: if a Soviet Jew gave no public expression to Jewish ambitions and stoically bore official and unofficial anti-Semitism, he or she got along in society not much worse than other Diaspora Jews. Now, with the collapse of the Soviet Union and the ongoing mass emigration of the Jews from the Commonwealth of Republics, the least materially established organized Jewish community in the world will soon be the State of Israel. The most materially dependent Jewish community in the world is the State of Israel. Israel is *not* an independent state; it is a state whose very survival depends on continued support of the American people and the American government.

The fourth paradox relates to the so-called abnormal social and economic structure of the Jewish People—the inverted pyramid. The paradox is that this inverted pyramid has become the norm for the entire developed world. Since World War II, developed societies the world over have been in an accelerated process of inverting the pyramid. In the United States, for example, less than 2 percent of the work force is employed in agriculture, less than 15 percent in manufacture, and the rest in services or the creation, processing, and exchange of information of one form or another. What was once considered abnormal has become the norm or standard by which modern societies judge themselves. The social and economic structure of much of the developed world has become Judaized. In the light of historical hindsight, the inverted pyramid was not an abnormality but a forerunner of Third Wave civilization.

A NEW ZIONIST VISION

Zionism for the twenty-first century must mobilize and direct the energies of the Jewish People into practical and creative activity as intense as the pre- and early-state eras. It must strive to transform Israel into a society with the highest possible economic, scientific, cultural, and social standards. This must be an integral part of the search for new ways of living in and thinking about the civilization we are creating. Israel must become a social and economic leader enlisting the ability of the entire Jewish People in order to create new frameworks and services geared to answering world needs in the twenty-first century.

Our national vision must evolve into a national-universal vision with national-universal obligations for a national-universal people. This is not a return to the utopian Romanticism of those nineteenth-century cosmopolitan Jews who denied the very legitimacy of Jewish particularity and advocated assimilation. On the contrary, it is predicated on the assumption that unless we develop a new national-universal paradigm of Jewish existence we will fail to develop the instruments necessary for particular Jewish existence in the twenty-first century. In short, this is more a universal vision for the Jews than for the non-Jews. It recognizes that Israel cannot truly become a Jewish center unless it becomes a world center and conversely that it cannot become a world center unless it becomes a Jewish center. This is a practical requirement of Jewish existence and not a *moral* imperative.

This would be an updated version of Hillel's famous dictum: "If I am not for myself who will be for me" and the Jewish concept of *tzdekah*, which is usually wrongly translated as charity. Charity derives from the Latin word *caritas* or caring, *tzdekah* derives from the Hebrew word *tzedek* or justice and recognizes that according to Hillel, justice begins with the egoistic *I*. Christianity has given indirect affirmation of this Jewish view in the phrase charity begins at home.

In other words, this is not a call to Jews to become international do-gooders but to guarantee that they use Israel to become an indispensable contributor to the solution of world problems. To do this, we might consider making it a national goal to turn Israel into a bridge between the developed and the developing worlds.

The small nation-state is rapidly becoming an *economically* irrelevant concept, even as ethnic and cultural nationalism increases throughout the world. Economically, Israel is not even a country—it is a medium-sized city. What must supplant and supercede the concept of the sovereign nation-state is not the uniformity of cosmopolitanism but a growing profusion of transnational nation-states interacting with one another in a growing complexity of human activity. The analogy of species diversification in ecological systems makes the case that the devastation of cultural and ethnic diversity endangers the ability of the emerging world system to succeed and perhaps even the human race itself to survive. Lush variety provides ecological systems with their resilience. Species uniformity in an ecological system leaves it susceptible to disease and sudden collapse: as with ecological systems, so with human society.

Transnational nation-states would be entities capable of preserving the cultural integrity of ethnic groups or nations while facilitating their economic and political integration into the new transnational reality. Paradoxically, integration into the new transnational reality is becoming basic to the preservation of the national and cultural sovereignty of small peoples.

THE NEW PARADOX OF NATIONAL SOVEREIGNTY

In order to preserve sovereignty, we must give up sovereignty. This is the new paradox: to guarantee national strength—if not survival—we must attach ourselves to new transnational frameworks such as the European Union. This means giving up a great deal of our economic and political freedom of action.

If we want to successfully absorb another 1.5 million Jews (immigrants and native born) by the year 2010, we must strive to become a member of the European Union, further strengthen our ties with the United States, and reach out to the new powers in Asia. The European Union has become an important key. As Dr. Dore Gold, a former Israeli Ambassador to the United Nations, has pointed out, the end of the Cold War has created a new multi-lateral concept of collective engagement that seriously endangers America's traditional relationship with Israel (*Jerusalem Post*, February 28, 1992). Collective engagement, according to Gold, means the sharing of responsibility. This is why the peace process itself is of Zionist value, notwithstanding the second *Intifada* and other crises that will almost certainly arise.

Unless Israel eventually becomes an integral part of the new European Union (and, let us hope, a new Middle Eastern security arrangement) even her special relationship with the United States will be in danger. Israel cannot become part of Europe without a Middle East peace arrangement (*arrangement*, not peace in the Western sense of that word). On the other hand, Israel might use the peace process to become a member of the European Union, thus becoming an integral part of a major international bloc and preserving her special relationship with the United States.

However, the very fact of membership in the European Union entails significant compromising of historical concepts of national sovereignty. Israeli passports will have *Europe* written in them in uppercase letters and *Israel* in parentheses in lowercase letters. The European unification agreement, more than just an economic treaty, has profound political and cultural implications.

Both Israeli citizens and non-Israeli European residents of Israel will be able to defend their human and civil rights *as defined by the European Community* in European Union courts. For example, an Israeli woman will be able to sue the State of Israel in Europe if she feels Israeli laws do not give her equality before the law. She will almost certainly win, and Israeli courts will honor this decision because the primacy of European courts in civil rights issues is an integral part of European Union membership and will have been sanctioned by the Knesset, Israel's parliament. A Reform Jew will sue the state (or any one of the municipalities) for permission to build a Reform synagogue and will most probably win.

The point is that this new reality represents a significant change in the concepts of national political sovereignty. Combined with the economic limitations placed on members of the European Union, the autonomy of the nation-state is seriously compromised.

THIRD WAVE ZIONISM: ISRAEL AS A WORLD METROPOLIS

Even within the classical conceptions of the nation-state, Israel is not really economically a country. In terms of population, Israel is smaller than greater

Boston, greater San Francisco, or greater Philadelphia. Greater New York and Los Angeles are empires compared to Israel. An entity smaller than medium-sized cities and isolated from its immediate geographic surroundings cannot pretend to copy Japan or the United States or even Korea and Taiwan.

Israel's model must be cities like Boston and San Francisco, for we are in competition with them for the hearts of the modern Jew. They, not Baghdad, Damascus, Tripoli, or Teheran represent Zionism's greatest survival challenge. This being so, we must transform our self-perception from pioneering outpost to cosmopolitan metropolis providing services to the entire world, thus reflecting the aspirations and utilizing the skills of a world people (*Am Olam*).

Boston's largest economic activity is education. An estimated quarter million university students reside in greater Boston and generate billions of dollars of economic activity. Other major economic activities include health services and science-based industries and services related to these education and health resources. Boston serves not only Massachusetts or even New England, but the entire continental United States, and indeed the world. It is not a regional city but a world city, a metropolitan node within the planetary communications and services delivery system.

Israel too can become such a metropolitan node, rather than a nation-state economy producing goods and services for six million residents and another two or three million export customers. Israel, with its multicultural, multilingual composition, can surpass other metropolitan nodes in many areas. Boston's model should be a light unto the Jews. Using it, Israel's disadvantages turn into advantages and she becomes a more suitable instrument for serving the needs and aspirations of the modern Jew.

When Israel properly understands and exploits modern telecommunications, she can become a world-class supplier of educational, engineering, health, legal, financial, and various other types of consulting services. These services will provide rich soil for the growth of numerous new kinds of science-based industries. We will absorb growing numbers of communications and medical personnel, scientists, lawyers, engineers, and educators. These are professions Israel has difficulty absorbing and in which Jews, *including Israelis*, world over are so disproportionately represented.

How can such an approach help us solve many of the most pressing problems of Israel and world Jewry? Let us engage in a mind experiment and apply this hypothesis to some concrete problems and dilemmas.

Population Increase and Immigrant Absorption

Israel has had trouble absorbing its own native sons and daughters, let alone the massive skilled *aliya* from the former Soviet Union, in the rewarding and interesting occupations they desire. By constructing a society, culture, and most of all economy on the inadequate paradigm of the Second

Wave nation-state, we have created frameworks and policies actually dys-functional to our national interests. Transforming Israel into a world metropolis serving the needs of the world economy in the space age will cre-ate a chronic shortage of academically trained personnel as well as raise the standard of living. Both of these developments will radically improve Israel's absorption potential. The advent of Israel as "Silicon Wadi" is one sign that Israel has already begun this process. And notwithstanding the periodic crises of the so-called New Economy, it is manifestly self-evident that Israel's future lies in just this direction.

Jewish Work and Foreign Workers

Moralizing about Jewish unwillingness to work has assumed the dimen-sions of a national sport. Yet, upon examination, this judgment clearly is drawn from that image of work left over from the classical Zionist myth of the inverted pyramid and the need to create a new Jewish class of peasants and proletarians. The truth is that Jews have traditionally been allergic to nonre-munerative and boring work and are not impressed by the various Tolstoyan ideologies singing the praises of physical work, which supposedly raises the spiritual level of the individual engaging in it. They know that boring, by any other name, is still boring.

On the other hand, anyone connected with Israeli high-tech industry and services knows that well-paid, interesting employment often produces a work ethic higher than that of the Japanese or the Americans. So, have we built an Israeli economy suitable to the temperament, aspirations, and skills of the Jewish People? No, the inverted pyramid work myth has led us to copy West-ern industrial development and build in essence a Second Wave economic base that is excellent at absorbing peoples who are in the process of moving from the first to the second wave. Tens of thousands of non-Israeli Arabs, Turks, Portuguese, Africans, Rumanians, and Thais are currently working in Israel. This economy is poor at absorbing Jews, who are either at the forefront of creating Third Wave civilization or have the aspirations and temperament of Third Wave civilization.

Economic development depends more on cultural values than on the vari-ous economic theories. The Japanese succeeded because they built a Japanese economy, an economy that reflected the relative strengths and the mentality of the Japanese people. It is incumbent upon us to build a Jewish economy, an economy that reflects the relative strengths and mentality of the Jewish Peo-ple, a Third Wave economy.

Israel-Diaspora Relations

Israel-Diaspora relations have been based on self-righteous Israelis preach-ing about immigration or Diaspora Jews giving money to or lobbying on behalf of Israel. Since Western *aliya* has all but dried up, the entire relation-ship has become based upon Diaspora philanthropy and political activity on behalf of Israel. The effectiveness of Diaspora Jewish political activity on Israel's behalf reflects the political clout of raising large sums of money for favored political candidates. This model has never succeeded in involving more than 25 percent of the Jewish community. In recent years both the per-centage and the absolute number of people contributing to Israeli causes have dropped. More contributors are looking for different kinds of Jewish causes to support, and the *real* value of the Diaspora's yearly contribution to Israel has declined by about 50 percent since 1973. Although investment in Israel is a proposed alternative model, realistically this can involve only 1 or 2 percent of the community in any significant way.

Both models effectively shut out huge segments of the Jewish community, educators, scientists, engineers, artists, media personnel, and even managers. In addition to fundraising and investments, we should be developing a United Jewish Appeal of Jewish human resources where people could contribute their skills and not only their money. But this can be done only if we cultivate the concepts of world metropolis and global tribe. The same conditions under which we can absorb limitless immigrants and Israelis will also enable us to absorb (partially or temporarily) many professional Diaspora Jews in mean-ingful activity centered on national-universal projects.

Individuals could spend their sabbaticals or several weeks or months in Israel working in these projects. A growing class of people—managers, scien-tists, consultants, and such—spend tens of thousands of miles a year in the air, and a disproportionately high number of them are Jews. Jews could also remain at home and with the aid of a computer, modem, and fax, as well as other telecommunications and information exchange technologies, make sig-nificant contributions to Israel- or Jewish-oriented projects, a kind of elec-tronic *aliya*. The revolution in transportation and telecommunication and information exchange must radically alter all previous concepts of both Zion-ism and Israel-Diaspora relations. Air travel times New York to Los Angeles and New York to Tel Aviv differ by four hours. By telephone, computer, or fax, travel to either is instantaneous.

This model of Israel-Diaspora relations can assist in the fight against assim-ilation by investing our practical and educational endeavors with new future-oriented content. We can stimulate our Jewish young people's ambitions by both exciting their idealism and satisfying their self-interest within Jewish contexts. An Israel that becomes a "Light Unto the Nations" in many areas is capable of doing just that.

The Social-Ethnic Gap

Only a Third Wave society is capable of erasing both the disgrace and the danger of Israel's social gap. Social solidarity is not only an ideal, it is a practical necessity for survival. Israel's social gap constitutes a greater danger to the survival of the Zionist enterprise than the Arab armies.

We cannot cut the educational budget several years running and hope to close the social gap. We require tremendous resources in order to expand the educational system. We cannot generate such resources from a Second Wave economic base; just as we cannot hope to close the income gap on the basis of what industries in competition with India, Pakistan, and the Philippines can possibly pay.

Those who still might boast about Israel's past success in creating a "real" Jewish working class should note that most of those workers were Oriental Jews who did not want to be workers. They certainly did not want their children to be workers and resented the Ashkenazi ideologues who sang the praises of physical work that they themselves would not think of doing or educating their children to do. Not only is the existence of a Jewish working class in Israel not part of the solution to the Jewish problem, as the early Zionist pioneers posited, it is a major part of Israel's social problem. Conventional industry in competition with cheap-labor countries creates a strong vested interest in keeping educational and social levels low to create cheap pools of labor. This perpetuates the gap.

The facts speak for themselves. More than one million Israeli workers earn less than $750 a month. The Zionist myth of creating a Jewish working class has created a Jewish serf class. Knowledge-based enterprises, on the other hand, have a strong vested interest in raising educational and social levels to create a talented labor pool. It is time that Zionism undertook a conscious rejection of the inverted pyramid myth.

Jewish-Arab Relations

The Grand Strategy of enlightened Zionism was, is, and must continue to be to integrate peacefully into the region. Our relations with the Arab countries, the Palestinians, and Israeli Arabs cannot, however, rely on such empty concepts as trust, goodwill, or the brotherhood of all men—our relations must reflect our own long-term interest deeply rooted in a foundation of power. Power and enlightened self-interest, not holding hands and singing "we shall overcome," must underlie our relationship with the Arab world and indeed the wider world at large.

Only a Third Wave Zionism, based upon the concept of Israel as a world metropolis, can provide us with the requisite power to serve our interests vis-à-vis the Arabs in the twenty-first century.

CONCLUSION

We are living in a time of great upheaval and change. The Jewish People must either take a leadership role or perish. They are favorites and not underdogs, however, in facing the challenges of Third Wave civilization. No other people on Earth is better prepared by virtue of education, temperament, and proven historical adaptability to succeed in the twenty-first century. A Zionism that presumes to be the survival ideology of the Jewish People must take the lead. With the instrument of the State of Israel as the concrete manifestation of the Zionist dream placed in their hands, the Jewish People will be prepared to confront their future. The task of Diaspora Jewry is to help Israel create an environment conducive to this transformation.

CHAPTER 4

The Special Case of American Jewry

Unlike most Zionists, I accept as indisputable the claim that America is different vis-à-vis the "Jewish Problem" and hence that American Jewry is different. Moreover, I claim that little if anything in the classical Zionist analysis is relevant to the American Jewish experience. This is probably why American Jews, despite being the most important and vital supporters of the Zionist enterprise, are often indifferent to the fundamental Zionist argument and contemptuous of Israeli politicians preaching the classical Zionist message. Unlike European Jewry in the nineteenth century, the Zionist argument has had little resonance for the American Jewish experience as it is lived by the individuals that make up the community. American Jewry *is* a special case.

But the questions remain: is American Jewish life normal, and can America in the long run sustain a viable Jewish community? Given extrapolations of present quantitative and qualitative trends, what will American Jewry look like in 2048—the State of Israel's centennial year?

WHY THE UNITED STATES IS DIFFERENT

The United States is different because its cultural origins and its foundational mythologies are radically different from every other Western country. The United States is the only Western country whose mythologies are not pagan but Old Testament. And although it may be unarticulated or unconscious, this fact must surely have had a profound effect on American attitudes toward Jews and Jewish causes and on the feeling of being at home that appears to come so naturally to American Jews.

The Bible and biblical metaphor form the foundation of American culture, not the Greco/Roman, Teutonic, or Druidic myths. When Europe looks to its cultural roots, it invariably ends up in paganism. This is certainly true for continental Europe and for England. For even though the Bible has been called the national saga of England and even though this aspect of English culture has parented the Old Testament characteristics of American culture, England's cultural roots are pagan—whether Druid or Greco/Roman.

The claim for the uniqueness of the United States is true even on the American continent. Canada is more European than American. Its culture has none of the moralistic overtones so characteristic of the United States and so easily traced to the Old Testament foundations of Puritan culture.

Latin American culture is a mix of Catholic, Indian, and African cultures. There is little Old Testament influence. Indeed, much of Latin America's popular culture has pagan roots—especially in Brazil.

Exodus and the search for the Promised Land is the preeminent metaphor of the United States. America has transmuted the concept of the Promised Land into an amorphous concept called "The American Dream." The Exodus metaphor appears in various degrees in all five of the foundational cultures of the United States: the Pilgrim Forefathers, the Blacks, the West, the mass immigration, and suburbia.

THE PILGRIM FOREFATHERS

The entire metaphor of the Pilgrim experience was Hebrew. England was Egypt, which they left to do God's work. James I was the pharaoh, the Atlantic Ocean their Red Sea, America New Canaan, and, later, Jefferson, Madison, and Washington became Moses and Joshua.

Some historians even trace Thanksgiving to the Jewish holiday of Succoth, or as the Christians call it the Festival of Booths. Both are harvest holidays commemorating redemption in the wilderness. Both commemorate a God-inspired and God-guided deliverance. As the Pilgrims constitute the primary foundation culture of the United States, we begin to see the influence of Jewish metaphor on American culture. America's Puritan heritage, as well as other fundamental Protestant influences, has engraved the American character with the Hebrew imprint. While Europe entertains visions of her barbaric past in her mythology, America's mythology is Old Testament. Neither Thor nor Jupiter lie at the bottom of the American character, but Moses, the Chosen People, the Promised Land, and redemption.

Evidence supporting this thesis is plentiful and is provided largely by the founding fathers themselves. In 1788, a former president of Harvard, Samuel Langdon, called for the establishment of an American republic based on ancient Israel, and saw in the republican form the means to attain universal morality and justice. John Adams said, "Hebrew mortar cemented the foundations of American Democracy."

Many Puritans studied Hebrew and were called by Hebrew names. Hebrew, not Latin, was their holy tongue. The president of Yale proposed that Hebrew be the official language of the new young republic.

The Puritans saw their religion as the covenant of Israel in continuum, although under a different administration. To the Pilgrims, the outstanding lesson of the Old Testament was that a nation as well as an individual could be in covenant with God. And they intended to establish such a nation, doing God's work, on the shores of the New Canaan of America. Many of these early Americans found full justification for their distaste for absolutism and divine right in the Old Testament. They believed that democracy is moral before it is political, as it presupposes a moral basis and background. The equal protection clause of the Constitution has its genetic roots in the belief that all men are equal in the eyes of God.

The infatuation of the Jews with America repays in equal measure the infatuation of Protestant Americans with the Hebrew heritage. Early Sephardi Jews believed that the American Indians were descendants of the Ten Lost Tribes in an attempt to identify America with the Promised Land. Ashkenazi Jews called America "Die Goldene Medine"—the golden country (that is, land of milk and honey). The word *America* has quickened the hearts of Jews for years, in ways that may be surpassed only by the word *Israel.*

Revolutionary America and modern Israel are also strikingly similar. They are the only countries in the world to be established en toto as a country, a society, and a culture, by a group of founding fathers inspired by clear visions of a universal role. It is the messianic prophetic message that informs both experiences, for better or for worse.

THE BLACKS

The second foundational culture is that of Black America, which is also based on the Exodus metaphor, although in both negative and positive ways. It is both an escape from the Egypt of America and a journey to the promised land of America. The Black spirituals, rooted as they are in the slave experience, sing of deliverance from slavery, going into the Promised Land ("Go Down Moses"), and crossing the river Jordan (the Mississippi serving as a substitute—how we Israelis wish it were so!). Examine the speeches of Martin Luther King and other Black civil rights leaders and see how often the Exodus metaphor and the redemption metaphor repeat themselves. In King's last speech before he was murdered, he likened himself to Moses: "I may not enter the Promised Land with you; I may only stand on the mountain top and look in, but you will enter." While the Blacks are a minority in the United States, constituting perhaps 15 percent of the population, it is indisputable that Black culture has made a *disproportionate* contribution to American culture in general. What, after all, is American music? Jazz, rock and roll, blues. The roots of this music trace back to Black church music, founded upon biblical mythology and metaphor.

THE CONQUEST OF THE WEST

America's third foundational culture is the conquest of the American West. The great migration to and conquest of the West is another great Exodus, and the West with all that it represents (cowboys, individualism, freedom) is still one of the most profound myths of American culture. It parallels the importance of the Samurai myth for Japan. The pioneers were looking for their own promised land. They wanted to leave the injustices of the East for freedom, dignity, and happiness. The Great Plains was the Sinai desert. Read the correspondence and the diaries of these pioneers and discover redemptive biblical language in its full force. James Mitchener's popular novel *Centennial* transmits the sense of destiny of these pioneers. Prayers of guidance and of thanksgiving were their daily lot.

The phrase *Manifest Destiny*, when speaking about the conquest of the West, connotes a God-given right and task, similar to the God-given right and duty of the Hebrews to conquer the Promised Land. American politicians spoke about the God-given rights of the God-fearing nation to these lands. In this context, the American Indians were sometimes seen as hostile Canaanites who had to be eliminated to make room for God's people. To justify the elimination of Native Americans, the white settlers often called them Amalek (biblical enemy of the Israelites).

The Mormon saga was the quintessential expression of this western Exodus metaphor. Their founder, Joseph Smith, received holy tablets from God. In order to escape persecution, his followers made their way west, enduring hardship and purifying their faith and themselves. This wilderness sojourn became in Mormon tradition analogous to the Israelite's wandering 40 years in the desert, until they were delivered unto their Promised Land. Like Moses, Joseph Smith never saw the Promised Land. It was left to his Joshua, Brigham Young, to conquer the land and forge a commonwealth. The Mormons built a theocratic republic ruled by elders similar to the Sanhedrin and constructed their Mormon Tabernacle Temple. As coincidence would have it, the very geology of Utah is similar to the Land of Israel—complete with its own great Salt Sea, fed by its own "Jordan" river.

THE IMMIGRANT SAGA

The immigrant saga is the fourth foundation of United States culture. America was the promised land of a mixed multitude of downtrodden peoples looking to escape the persecutions of modern day pharaohs and find freedom and dignity. Their Exodus was in steerage, not on camel or donkey, and the ocean, as with the Pilgrims, was their Sinai wilderness. Their sightings of the Statue of Liberty at the gateway to the promised land after their travails and suffering remind one of the Israelites looking over the Jordan from Mount Nebo into their Promised Land after 40 years in the desert.

Is it a coincidence that the American Jew, Emma Lazarus, wrote the poem inscribed on the pedestal of the statue, a poem that celebrated the immigrant saga and America as the Promised Land? Is not the very language of the poem reminiscent of the language of the prophets? "Give me your tired, your poor, your huddled masses yearning to breathe free, the wretched refuse of your teeming shore, send these, the homeless, tempest-tost to me: I lift my lamp beside the golden door!"

SUBURBIA

The foundation cultures of the Puritans, the Blacks, the West, and the immigrant saga are all variations of the Exodus metaphor. In addition, we have the materialistic redemption dream of suburbia, a kind of kitsch perversion of the Exodus metaphor, but no less powerful for that in molding the American persona. Fleeing the imperfect city—looking for the American Dream of perfect happiness and harmony in the promised land of new perfectly designed communities.

The promised-land American Dream of suburbia has resulted in a peculiarly idiosyncratic American-style literary form called "suburban angst," based upon the failure to find perfection and harmony, something that only Americans would even seek. One may claim that the elusive "facticity" of this American Dream has had primary formative impact on the American psyche, culture, and polity. How un-French, how un-German, how un-Italian, how Jewish! Is this one reason that so many Europeans feel foreign in American culture and so many Israelis feel right at home?

AMERICAN CULTURE AND PATRIOTISM

Europeans often deride the United States for having no culture. This is both true and untrue. The United States certainly has culture and profound cultural creativity but, unlike Europe, America has no generally agreed upon *normative* culture. It is a *mosaic* of these foundation cultures in addition to myriad other subcultures. Neither Jews nor anyone else can be accused of not assimilating, like the *OstJuden* in Germany, or assimilating too much, like Stalin's rootless cosmopolitans in the Soviet Union. American cultural life has no center and no periphery. Given the benefit of historical perspective, we now see that the United States has always been a proto-postmodernist country. Can anything be more amenable for Jews than this? Indeed, the United States, as a mosaic, is the prototype of a transnational nation-state in its very essence.

Even patriotism in the United States is different. It is not measured by swearing loyalty to Volk, Fatherland, or hereditary sovereign; it is measured by swearing to uphold and defend the Constitution. Civil rules of behavior, not race, blood, or mythical appeals to the land and historical legend determine what is a true American. Americanism is a confessional identity, not a tribal identity. One does not pledge allegiance to the tribe; one pledges allegiance to the flag and the republic for which it stands: that is, to the Constitution, which *is* the republic.

A true American is one who adheres to Americanism, to the American way of life, not to particular bloodlines. This is why Chinese, Blacks, and Jews can talk about "our Pilgrim forefathers" with no sense of absurdity. And even though Jewish identity is tribal and relates strongly to a particular land, the very style of American constitutional law has strong parallels to *Halachic* law. It is basically an ongoing contextual commentary about a fundamental legal document intended to govern the behavior of a polity. Is it only coincidence that the Bill of Rights is composed of 10 amendments and these 10 amendments constitute the 10 commandments of American civilization? American culture is redolent with Jewish symbols.

AMERICAN JEWRY AND THE AMERICAN DREAM

So is it any wonder that few other ethnic groups in the United States have surpassed the Jews in believing in or taking advantage of and fulfilling the American Dream? Judged by the practical standards of Americanism, the Jews are the most American of all the American ethnic groups.

In addition, the Jews are the wealthiest, best educated, most professional, most organized ethnic group in the United States. They have a higher percentage of political representatives in proportion to their size than other minorities—even representing areas that have no sizable Jewish vote. In recent decades, they have become more traditional and more publicly ethnic. Jews wearing yarmulkes have been White House and Pentagon advisers. Jewish food and Yiddish slang have become an integral part of Americana.

So why, with all this, is Jewish existence in the United States still a matter of doubt over the next 50 or 60 years? The question is not idle. It has to do with demographic trends and the residual abnormality of an exilic existence, even in the United States. In other words, it has to do with both quantitative and qualitative questions.

OBJECTIVE CHALLENGES

The organized American Jewish community has significant pretensions in regards to Jewish history. It has developed the two-center theory of modern Jewish existence in opposition to the one-center theory of Zionism. By this, American Jews would agree that Zionism is right in regard to the rest of the Jewish world but wrong in regard to the United States. The rest of the Jewish world may be in *galut* (exile) but American Jews are not: "We are obviously not in our ancient homeland, but we are still at home," would be their claim. They would claim that the American Jewish relationship to Israel is similar to that of Babylonian Jewry during the Talmudic period and the formation of Rabbinic Jewry. They would claim that modern Jewish life can, does, and will survive in at least two more or less equal centers: Israel and North America.

Certainly, all cited above would confirm this proposition. Under close examination, however, this proposition must be challenged. The many positive developments within American Jewry of the past 20 years are often cited by the proponents of the two-center theory as proof of the vigor of the American Jewish community. But these great developments must be examined in light of more basic negative trends; trends documented and commented upon in great detail by the American Jewish community itself.

First among these developments are demographics. Although the Jews have always been a small people, and although size itself is not a prerequisite to cultural greatness (the Jewish community of greater Los Angeles is larger than both Spanish and German Jewries at the height of their cultural efflorescence), survival is first of all biological and numerical. Below a certain critical mass, even small peoples have difficulty sustaining communal identity and cultural creativity. In this regard, the long-term statistical trends are no more promising than in England or in France.

The American Jewish Committee's Yearbook (the bible of American Jewish communal life) has reported that American Jewry is shrinking by about .5 percent a year (in contrast to Israel's Jewish community, which is growing by around 1.5 percent a year *before aliya*). Other indicators show that this rate of shrinkage is likely to increase. By the end of the first decade of the twenty-first century, 50 percent of all marriages involving Jews may be intermarriages. And even though some of these intermarriages result in the couple rearing their children as Jews, most do not. In addition, the Jews are already the most elderly ethnic group in the United States. Some reports claiming that the median age of the Jewish community is already over 45 (as compared to about 35 for the general American community and 25 for Black and Hispanic Americans). The median age of American Jewry is, therefore, already beyond the age of reproduction.

Moreover, various social factors lead Jews of reproductive age to marry later than other ethnic groups, including proportionally higher feminist consciousness. The biological future of the American Jewish community, therefore, is not bright. One reason why this has not been more dramatically felt is the large influx of Israeli, Russian, and Latin American Jews into the United States over the last three decades of the twentieth century. It is significant that even with this influx, demographic erosion continues, as documented by American Jewish organizations themselves.

SUBJECTIVE DILEMMAS

But even more important than the quantitative argument is the qualitative one. Is American Jewish life normal? Unlike the quantitative science of demographics, one cannot objectively prove or disprove the essentially subjective claim of abnormality. Normality or abnormality is a totally subjective feeling. Trying to argue this through so-called objective historical analysis is absurd. Zionists say the American dispersion is abnormal; the American Jews say it is normal. End of argument.

The question of normality is specific and concrete. Specific individuals feel normal or abnormal in concrete historical contexts. I, for example, felt my life as a Jew in the United States was abnormal. I could not articulate this feeling at the time and indeed was barely conscious of it. In retrospect, I now know that this is what led me to come to Israel. I will give some personal examples of why I felt this way, and use these personal examples to challenge the American Jewish reader to confront the normality or abnormality of his or her own situation. Again, I readily confess that I came to see what I am about to relate as abnormal only with the wisdom of hindsight—after I had been in Israel more than 20 years and began to meditate on what had, after all, brought me there.

First, I have faint childhood memories of the Rosenberg trial and my father and other Jewish neighbors calling for the death penalty. The innate sensitivity of the child perceived disquiet and worry behind patriotic protestations. The Kennedy assassination, however, gave me my first conscious inklings of how unnatural American Jewish life really was. The first reaction of my parents was "I only hope a Jew was not involved." When I commented that I didn't see what difference that made, I was told not to be stupid. When it was reported that Jack Ruby (Rubenstein) had assassinated Oswald my parents and many other Jews were visibly upset.

Two years later, I was drafted into the American army. The two-week induction period included a rousing sermon by a Black Baptist army chaplain before approximately 3,000 inductees. He called on all present to remain true to their particular religious traditions while in the army. At the end of the sermon, he asked for a show of hands. "How many Protestants are here?" (Two thousand hands went up.) I knew immediately what was about to happen and had about two seconds to make one of the most difficult decisions in my life. "How many Catholics are here?" (One thousand hands went up.) "How many Jews are here?" (Mine and two or three other hands went up.) I felt as if 3,000 pairs of eyes were boring into the back of my head. Later, several other Jews in my unit came up to me and asked me how I had the guts to put my hand up. Now, if anyone asks me what Zionism is, I answer it is the ability to put your hand up without self-consciousness when someone asks how many Jews are present; all the rest is commentary.

The Pollard incident is perhaps the most recent example of American Jewish abnormality. I was stationed in the United States during this period as an emissary for a Zionist organization. The reaction in the Jewish community was astounding. I am not talking about the justified criticism of Israel's stupidity in using an American Jewish citizen for espionage, thus breaking one of Ben Gurion's ironclad rules. I am talking about the visceral fear, demonstrated by so many Jews, of possible accusations of double loyalty—their basic insecurity and fear for *their own positions* as a consequence of the incident. One might legitimately ask if a WASP would become hysterical if another WASP were discovered spying for England, an Italian American if an Italian American was discovered spying for Italy, or an African American if an African American were discovered spying for Nigeria? For me, fears such as these point to an unnatural or abnormal situation.

If a Jew can truly say to himself or herself that these reactions are normal, or that he or she would not have reacted thus, then their Jewish life in the United States is normal. If he or she cannot truly say one of these two things then his or her Jewish life in the United Sates is abnormal. Is a normal and authentic communal Jewish life possible in the United States? In my opinion, yes. I also believe that the vast majority of individual Jews are still fraught with feelings of marginality and insecurity that make this question academic.

THE FUTURE OF AMERICAN JEWRY

This may, however, be a generational dilemma. Baby-boomer Jews may strongly feel the schizophrenia described above, while Generation-Xers feel it less, and *their* children not at all. The irony being that those most motivated to creating a Jewish/American synthesis are the most psychologically inhibited from doing so, and those most psychologically capable of creating the synthesis feel no real reason to do so.

Historical development is, however, indifferent to opinion. According to current demographic trends, Israel will become the world's largest Jewish community within the first decade of the twenty-first century (depending on relative rates of immigration to and emigration from Israel). What cultural, psychological, and spiritual repercussions will arise for both communities when Israel passes American Jewry in size? This profound question has not even entered the discussions of any Jewish organization; this is a question for Jewish Futurology. Within the first two to three decades of the twenty-first century, more Jews will be living in Israel than in *all* Diaspora communities combined. This is about the same amount of time that has passed between the 1973 Yom Kippur War and the beginning of the twenty-first century

As the largest, wealthiest, most powerful Diaspora Jewish community in the world, American Jewry must redefine itself and play a special role in the creation of a new Judaism and a new Zionism. Its special character, unique intrinsic potentials, and vital position within the American republic—the one partner the Jewish People must have to prevail—make its contribution to the Jewish future indispensable.

America's democratic principles, scientific knowledge, and technological power make it the natural spiritual and practical partner of the Jewish People. America's heritage seems to have predestined her to become the primary supporter and partner of a renascent people and the State of Israel.

American Jewry must, however, create a coherent "ideology" of what defines American Jewishness. It must be an American, not an inherited European or Asian ideology. This is to say, it must be an updated reexpression of America's Hebraic roots. It must offer a coherent framework to enable American Jews to correlate being world, American, *and* Jewish citizens.

American Jewish educators might conclude that teaching about America's Jewish roots in Hebrew school outweighs running bar mitzvah "factories." Teaching children to declaim prayers they do not understand has not proven effective in preserving Jewish identity.

Schizophrenia is the natural condition of today's thinking American Jews. Fascinated with and enthusiastic about America, American Jews have always struggled to relate to America and their Jewishness at the same time and with integrity. They are uneasy Americans and uneasy Jews. The 2000 Democratic vice presidential candidacy of Joseph Lieberman, while of great historical importance, failed to ease this angst in a meaningful way.

American Jewry's emotional and material involvement with Israel can no longer be written off as having no bearing on their American Jewish character. It is too deep, too involved with the very survival of Israel to be shrugged off in a dispassionate way. Non-Orthodox American Jewish identity seems to involve little more than material support for the State of Israel, emotional reaction when Israel is in danger, Holocaust remembrance, and kitsch nostalgia. The average non-Orthodox American Jew is at once alienated from his Jewish heritage and identity—he no longer responds to religious appeals—and from true American belonging.

American Jewry is compelled to confront what it means to be Jewish in modern, secular twenty-first century, pluralistic America. Nostalgic *Yiddishkeit* can no longer suffice—as more and more Jews move further from the East European tradition that still speaks to the hidden recesses of their parents' hearts.

A *real* American Jewry must be created—with its own values and agenda that *must* stand in dialectical tension with Israel—not only for the sake of Jewish survival in general but for the sake of Israel.

CHAPTER 5

Israeli Grand Strategy: A Historical Critique

This chapter identifies and critiques past Jewish Grand Strategy. No Grand Strategy can be coherent and logical unless it conforms to the ideological assumptions and policy goals it is designed to serve. We have defined our ideological assumptions and policy goals in previous chapters, and what follows is a logical consequence.

Jewish Grand Strategy refers to an integrated use of Jewish resources to assure meaningful Jewish survival in the twenty-first century. It deals with the military, economic, professional, intellectual, social, cultural, scientific, and moral resources of the Jewish People.

The analytical principles of this chapter derive from the ideas of B. H. Liddell Hart, the renowned British military philosopher who, in his classic book *Strategy*, endowed the "policy of limited aims," the "strategy of the indirect approach," and the predominance of "grand strategic resources" with overriding policymaking status. Some of his disciples included German generals Rommel and Guderian, the American general George Patton, and General Yigal Yadin, the Israeli army's chief of staff during the War of Independence.

Liddell Hart believed that responsible leaders should adapt their aim to circumstances or develop new means to make the aim more possible. In other words, one's aims should reflect one's grand strategic resources or one must devote one's energies to increasing those resources. Wasting resources on unachievable ideological aims is a recipe for political disaster.

It is interesting to note that Liddell Hart's philosophy of conflict management molded the Israeli army's operational principles in its early days but has had little if any policymaking influence on Israel's political leaders. This may explain why Israel's early military operations were usually more successful

than its political policies and why later military operations dedicated to absolutist aims (such as the Lebanese War and the so-called "War on Terror")
have been markedly unsuccessful.

DEFINING OUR TERMS

In chapter 3, "Zionism in the Twenty-First Century," we defined the terms
ideology, policy, grand strategy, strategy, and *tactics.* In this chapter, we present
more extensive and precise definitions. Each term is defined according to the
Random House Dictionary (College Edition) and may include my own particular
construal based upon the particular interpretations of Liddell Hart. All italics
in these definitions are mine.

Ideology. (1) The body of *doctrine,* myth, symbol, etc., of a social movement, institution,
class, or group; (2) such a body of *doctrine*... with reference to some political or cultural plan.

Policy. (1) A definite course of action adopted for the sake of *expediency and facility;* (2)
actions or procedures conforming to or considered with reference to *prudence or
expediency.* This means the conversion of ideological doctrine into concrete, under-
standable, and *achievable* goals. Achievable is the critical word, because, as Liddell
Hart points out, available resources and general political and economic context
always constrain plans. Hence his advocacy for policies of limited aims. Policy
might be prescribed by ideology but grand strategic limitations must define policy
aims. Therefore, an ideology of a "Greater Israel" on the part of the Jews or a
"Greater Palestine" on the part of the Palestinians can never succeed given the present historical context. The attempt to achieve such a goal entails a waste of
resources and energy so as to endanger the entire national projects of both nations.

Grand Strategy. Interestingly enough, the dictionary has no definition for Grand Strategy. This reflects Liddell Hart's contention that Grand Strategy is the most
neglected aspect of policy planning. My interpretation of Hart's description of
Grand Strategy would be a rational analysis of the economic, political, military,
social, and moral resources of a people and how best to optimally mobilize them in
order to minimize weaknesses and achieve *vital* goals. Grand Strategy defines the criteria and priorities by which we determine policy goals; it is the filter through which
we pass our policy goals to see if they are appropriate. In a sane and rational entity,
Grand Strategy determines policy *more than does ideology.* Ideology might strive for
an ideal, but in real life we must construct policies based upon reality, even as we
strive to alter that reality. Grand Strategy is the keystone of any policy.

Strategy. (1) A plan, method, or series of maneuvers or stratagems for obtaining a specific goal or event; (2) the *applied* planning and mobilization of grand strategic
resources vis-à-vis one's policy aims. Strategy mobilizes resources, forms alliances,
and makes specific plans for implementation.

Tactics. (1) Adroit maneuvering, technique, or procedure for gaining advantage or success; (2) tactics are the means by which strategic aims are pursued in specific situations or in regards to specific aspects of the overall strategy.

All of the above rubrics are both aims and resources. One has tactical aims and resources, strategic aims and resources, grand strategic aims and resources, policy aims and resources, and ideological aims and resources. Thus *aim* and *resource* will be used interchangeably throughout this and subsequent chapters.

GRAND STRATEGY AND THE QUESTION OF VALUES

Formulating a coherent Grand Strategy requires clear distinctions between primary values, secondary values, and periodic values. Primary values are universal in time and place. Secondary values serve primary values, optimizing their chance of fulfillment. Periodic values are vital for assuring primary and secondary values within a particular historical environment and context.

Examples of primary values would be freedom, dignity, justice, and equality before the law, values of *inherent* value. Examples of secondary values would be equal access to education and diminished income inequalities as major instruments for guaranteeing optimal legal justice and equality. This recognizes that in a free society poverty restricts freedom of choice in practice, while discrepancies in education and standards of living almost guarantee inequality before the law.

Equality is *not* a primary value; it is not inherently valuable in and of itself *unless* it serves freedom, justice, and legal equality. If equality was inherently valuable, Pol Pot's Cambodia and the Taliban's Afghanistan would have been moral entities, characterized by radical equality in standards of living—that is, *everyone* at the same abysmal level of poverty and deprivation of fundamental human rights. Equality is without moral standing unless it serves primary values.

Periodic values might refer to specific programs, practices, or rules established in a certain historical period in support of secondary and primary values that might over time become dysfunctional to the very secondary and primary values they originally served. In a general context, this might refer to certain aspects and particular programs of a welfare state. In a particular period they might have reinforced equality and sustained human freedom and dignity, but in another period they might perpetuate poverty, creating dependent and manipulatively obsequious welfare recipients.

In our particular Zionist context, the collective and cooperative settlement projects (kibbutz and *moshav*) that characterized so much of the Zionist enterprise's heroic period might be termed periodic values. These entities were of value because they were a vital component in the fight for the primary values of Jewish independence and freedom. They functioned in a highly egalitarian way thus guaranteeing high morale. In other words, during a particular historical period these settlements manifested important secondary values vital for sustaining primary values. If, however, these settlements have become just another place where people live, making no special contribution to either national independence or individual freedom, and their most talented members leave, of what special value are they in this historic period?

Jewish Grand Strategy must be founded on futuristic thinking and clarity of values. The price we pay for nonfuturistic thinking, for being rooted in and infatuated by past successes, is the loss of garand strategic focus. The consequence is the pursuit of self-defeating and dysfunctional policies, which reflect confusion between primary values, secondary values, and periodic values. Examples of this lack of grand strategic focus abound in Israel's recent history and help explain the gap between our present security, social, economic, political, democratic, and ecological circumstances and the expectations and desires of most of Israel's citizens. A critical historical review of some of these examples would be a useful prologue to reinventing Israeli Grand Strategy.

SETTLEMENT POLICY: 1948–1967

The most outstanding example of loss of grand strategic focus, deriving from confusion between primary and periodic values and resulting in a huge gap between reality and expectation, has been settlement policy following the creation of the Jewish State. Our expectation had been to create a democratic state, in which even its non-Jewish citizens would feel at home, much as non-Danes feel at home in Denmark. A state based upon social justice, characterized by diminishing inequalities of education, opportunity, and income, as well as equality before the law and state institutions.

Present reality does not reflect these expectations. This is a consequence of loss of grand strategic focus deriving from confusion about values. It is not a consequence of the inherent immorality of the Zionist project as Arab Nationalists and Jewish post- and anti-Zionists would have us believe.

During the pre-state era, kibbutz and *moshav* settlements epitomized Zionist grand strategic value and activity. Their contribution was crucial in the struggle to create the Jewish State, and they were a primary force sustaining effective Jewish possession over land purchased by the Jewish National Fund and other Jewish organizations.

Their very existence had security value in the communal struggles with local Arab populations as well as against hostile Arab incursions from outside the Mandate area. They played a vital role in the absorption of Jewish immigrants and were the backbone of creating Israel's agricultural economy. This was of both economic and spiritual value in the context of a worldview that saw a Jewish return to the land as vital to curing the Jews of their exilic disabilities.

Their heroic attempts to sustain equality of means as well as equality of opportunity invested the entire Zionist enterprise with a moral self-confidence that not only energized the Zionist pioneers but also inspired world Jewry and earned the admiration of progressive non-Jews. This resulted in significant political benefits. Many liberal, socialist, and labor organizations around the world were predisposed toward the Zionist enterprise and the nascent Jewish State because of the kibbutz experiment (as well as the Histadrut economy). Israel's standing in the Liberal and Socialist Internationals as well as with the AFL-CIO and other labor organizations was a valuable political asset second only to organized Jewry. Before 1967, these progressive forces were a greater political asset than an ambivalent United States. The so-called special relationship between Israel and the United States developed after the Six-Day War, thanks in large measure to the political power of American Jewry.

During the War of Independence and throughout the 1950s and early 1960s, the kibbutz and *moshav* settlements played a vital security role in establishing and sustaining the nascent Jewish State. This role is illustrated by the heroic stories of the Syrian tank stopped at Degania, or Kfar Darom and Yad Mordechai holding out against the Egyptian army.

If you wanted to be a dynamic Zionist during the pre-state and early state periods, you would become a member of a kibbutz or a *moshav*. By doing so, you would be contributing territorial, security, economic, moral, political, spiritual, and immigrant absorption value to the Zionist enterprise and young Jewish State.

But the weaknesses of this pre-state settlement policy began to manifest themselves soon after its creation. The classic Zionist approach of filling up empty spaces with as many Jewish settlements as possible continued to be the backbone of immigrant absorption policy during the Jewish State's first two decades. This policy reflected the pre-state Zionist view that occupying empty spaces would guarantee Jewish possession, contribute to security, and determine state borders.

As a consequence, hundreds of thousands of new Jewish immigrants, mostly from Africa and Asia, were directed to development towns in under-populated peripheral areas called development areas. They were also directed to cooperative farming villages called immigrant *moshavim*. Cultural reasons ruled out the kibbutz format as unsuitable for this mass immigration.

This project also had a domestic political dimension. The various modes of settlement were the backbone of the practical activity of Labor Zionism. Since the Labor Party, in its various guises, ruled the country until 1977, these settlement policies also reflected the self-perceived long-term interests of Labor Party political power. Yet even in the early 1950s, several young Labor Movement activists and youth leaders active in the absorption process cautioned against this policy. They warned that it was an outmoded leftover from the pre-state era, unsuited to the needs and abilities of the newborn Jewish State.

They noted that most of these immigrants came from technically backward societies and possessed few of the skills required to prosper in a modern technological society. They further noted that it would be impossible to supply hundreds of small villages and dozens of small towns with the full menu of social, educational, and employment services and opportunities this particular population needed most in order to catch up to their Western brethren. They predicted correctly that this settlement policy would perpetuate and deepen the social gap. It also alienated large segments of Israel's population from the basic values of the Israeli Labor Party with profound long-term political consequences for Israel's domestic and foreign policies.

These critics claimed that the advent of the Jewish State, including an organized police force, border guard, army, and other requisite institutions, as well as recognized international borders, represented a radical transition from the pre-state Zionist project. The entire policy of filling up the country with a Jewish population to prevent Arab squatting and the development of an Arab majority in certain regions such as the Galilee and the Negev was in their view anachronistic.

One activist, Zvi Kesse, proposed a different settlement concept. Instead of hundreds of tiny villages and dozens of small development towns, he suggested creating three or four major metropolitan areas capable of absorbing masses of immigrants. This would allow for less per capita investment in infrastructure, increasing the effectiveness of these investments. It would also enable Israel to supply more efficient public services and employment opportunities to those people who needed it most.

Kesse recommended developing Beersheba into a major city of one million inhabitants and Afula, Safed, and Tiberias into cities of a quarter million each. Such a policy would guarantee Jewish majorities in both the Negev and the Galilee as well as better enable us to confront the inherited social gap.

Veteran Labor Party leaders, such as Golda Meir, who considered settlement activity the essence of what it meant to be a Zionist, dismissed these proposals. Rather than seeing settlement as a means, veteran leaders tended to view it as an end, and its cessation would betray a fundamental Zionist value. Hence, what should have been a *periodic* value became a *primary* value. After the Six-Day War, the advocates of Jewish settlement in the newly conquered territories used this view to disarm and inhibit Labor Zionist opposition.

One might truly claim that this historical interpretation benefits from hindsight and that Golda and her colleagues represented normative Zionism, which at the time made no distinction between primary, secondary, and periodic values. But such a claim would be beside the point. The task of leadership is to map the future, not to repeat the past. Leadership must be future oriented and not past oriented. The task of leadership is to educate the citizenry that many historical values no longer pertain; that we must invent new ones, suitable to the true needs of the *times in which we live!*

Although its progenitors might have considered a value *primary*, we commit no crime when, in the course of time, and with historical perspective, we redefine it as a *periodic* value. This is the difference between religion and ideology. Ideological values are not necessarily sacred. Ideology is created by the autonomous reason of human beings and may be altered by the same. The young activists, respectful of but not infatuated with the heroic achievements of their elders, perceived this transition; their elders, justly proud of the awesome achievements of their generation but intellectually incapable of transcending their own achievements, could not.

We must also acknowledge that for some segments of the Zionist movement, ideology reflects their religion, and for others, their ideology has become their religion. For the *Mizrahi* (National Religious) movement, the progenitors of *Gush Emunim*, the Land of Israel itself is an ideological value *because* it is a religious value. For some members of the *Achdut Avoda/Kibbutz HaMeuhad* (National Labor) movement, the progenitors of the *Land of Israel* movement, both the land and the settlements were treated as secular sacraments. For Revisionist Zionists, forerunners of the Likud Party, both the land and the state were overlapping Zionist sacraments.

The negative consequences of this policy have become dramatically self-evident. The development towns and immigrant *moshavim* have become a major component of the social/ethnic gap in Israel and contain well more than half of the Jewish population that live below the poverty line. Because these frameworks cannot offer opportunities for young people, many of them leave and resettle in the major cities, often in impoverished neighborhoods.

Poverty and the social gap are thereby perpetuated unto the third and fourth generations. The income gap grows, crime grows, social solidarity diminishes, and the very term Zionism is greeted with sarcasm.

Furthermore, because of the many young people who leave these settlements we have not solved the problem of a Jewish majority in the Galilee. Indeed, we may have exacerbated the problem. The phrases *development town* and *development area* have taken on negative connotations and have become, by definition, unattractive places to live. The middle and professional classes will not move there in significant numbers and locals, if they have any ambition, often choose to leave.

The Jews have not been coming to the Galilee but have been migrating to the cities. The Arabs, on the other hand, have no predominately Arab city in which they would feel comfortable. The traditional village environment, joined to the status of Arab women, results in a high birth rate. Consequently, more Arabs than Jews now live in the Galilee.

This demographic/territorial dilemma has lead to an ugly phrase and an even uglier policy: "Judaizing the Galilee." (I leave the reader to judge what associations this phrase conjures up.) Judiazing the Galilee refers to a proactive policy of trying to attract many Jews to the Galilee.

Because we cannot keep ambitious young Jews in the development towns or *moshavim*, and because we cannot attract the professional and middle classes to these entities, we have invented a new policy—the establishment of small, Jewish, hilltop communities.

This policy has accomplished several things. It gives us a *feeling* that we are really doing something about increasing the Jewish population of the Galilee. This is a total illusion as these settlements seldom have more than several hundred residents. Their small size has compelled us to expend an enormous amount of public money per capita on infrastructure. The proliferation of endless numbers of small settlements has also caused great environmental damage. The continued expropriation of Arab land, which such a policy requires, has exacerbated the alienation of the Israeli Arab population of the Galilee.

Land Day is the yearly commemoration of and protest against the expropriation of Arab land by the state in favor of Jewish development projects. It has become the primary radical expression of the Israeli Arabs and is a direct consequence of this post-state settlement policy. The policy has not Judaized the Galilee but has alienated and radicalized young Israeli Arabs, and they, having *been born* in the "only democracy in the Middle East," have the *Sabra* audacity to demand equal rights and treatment.

We could have avoided this situation by adopting Zvi Kesse's recommendation to concentrate on developing three or four major Jewish population centers in the Galilee. At the same time, we could have cultivated the establishment of a major Arab city of a quarter of a million to half a million residents in the Galilee. The logical candidate would have been Nazareth.

The urbanization of the Arab population combined with a proactive affirmative action education policy for Arab women would have by natural and *enlightened* means greatly reduced Arab birthrates and the perceived Arab demographic threat. Moreover, such a policy would have eliminated the need for state expropriation of Arab-owned land for Jewish projects, would have greatly reduced the scale of illegal building in the Arab sector, and would have greatly eroded the power of corrupt Mukhterism in Israeli-Arab political life. This would have forestalled much bitterness and alienation of Israeli Arabs in recent years.

The consequences of ignoring Kesse's recommendations are numerous. The social gap and consequent alienation within the Jewish population has increased and become a permanent fixture, giving rise to a generation of demagogic politicians and parties manipulating the situation to their own benefit and to the detriment of Israeli society at large. The Jews are losing the demographic battle for the Galilee *and* alienating our Arab citizens at the same time. Zionist symbols have been tarnished, and the moral self-confidence of large articulate segments of Jewish society has been eroded.

If we had followed Kesse's recommendations we would have large and permanent Jewish majorities in both the Negev and the Galilee, the social gap would have diminished, and we would have a more positive engagement with our Arab citizens. Moreover, the moral self-confidence of many Israelis *as Zionists* would have been enhanced rather than eroded and we might have been spared the moral self-flagellation of post-Zionism.

SETTLEMENTS IN OCCUPIED TERRITORIES: 1967–PRESENT

The settlement policies pursued in territories occupied in 1967 are an example of making a bad situation worse, exacerbating the gap between reality and expectation. I do not wish to discuss this subject according to moral, legal, or historical rights standards, I wish to discuss it according to the vital interests of Israel.

I do not believe that the settlements are illegal under international law. No less an authority than Eugene Rostow, former dean of Yale Law School has stated: "Legally, the West Bank and Gaza Strip are unallocated parts of the Palestine Mandate...[and]...the right of the Jewish People to settle in the West Bank under the Mandate has never been terminated....Jewish settlement in the West Bank is...not an intrusion into alien territory...nor a violation of the Geneva Convention. It is...[an] exercise of the right protected by Article 80 of the United Nations Charter...."

More important, however, is equality before the law, a larger universal moral principle and the foundation of democratic civilization. Israel conquered the West Bank from Jordan, which had annexed it in contravention of the United Nations Partition Plan and international law. Only two countries ever recognized Jordan's annexation of the West Bank: England and Pakistan, but Jordan's occupation was accepted and granted de facto sanction by the international community because the territory had no official status under international law.

The same rules must apply to the Jews, according to the principle of equality before the law. If Jordan's occupation and the Jordanian upper-class homes and palaces built in the West Bank after 1948 were legal (or perhaps more accurately not illegal) under international law, then Israel's occupation and building of private middle-class residences must also not be illegal under international law.

Gaza is different, as Egypt never annexed it. It was, however, an unallocated part of the Mandate that the Egyptians ruled as a military occupier disallowing any local Palestinian autonomy or sovereignty, in nonconformance with United Nations decisions and international legality. The international community did not condemn Egypt's and Jordan's disrespect of Palestinian human rights. The status of refugees in Lebanon has been worse than the status of South African Blacks under apartheid, in complete contravention of international law.

Lebanon, Egypt, and Jordan have never been condemned by United Nations resolution for their illegal and immoral behavior toward the Palestinians. The General Assembly and UNESCO never condemned Jordan for destroying more than 40 synagogues and *yeshivas* and turning the Western Wall into a public dump and urinal. Given all this, self-respecting Jews must disallow the right of a politically motivated international majority, unconstrained by constitutional limitations of power, to decide what is legal.

Israel and world Jewry must insist on the objective rules of constitutionality and reject the subjective whim of an international majority swayed by current political fashion in determining what is legal and what is not. Until such international constitutional rules of governance exist, Israel is perfectly within both her moral and legal rights to treat international condemnations with the contempt and cynicism they deserve. Whether it is politically wise to do so is another story.

We must also disallow the false claim that the settlements are the major obstacle to peace. The second *Intifada* broke out after Prime Minister Barak offered a deal to turn 97 percent of the West Bank and Gaza over to the Palestinians (thereby removing more than 100 settlements) and giving the Palestinians sovereignty over land in Israel equivalent to the 3 percent Israel would have kept in the West Bank and Gaza. The major obstacle to peace is still the Palestinian unwillingness to recognize Israel's historic rights in the Land of Israel in general and in Jerusalem in particular.

And what of historical rights? If the Jews have no historical right to settle in Hebron, then the French have no historical right to settle in Lyons or the Scots in Glasgow. This is the most ridiculous objection of all.

The settlements in the territories are not immoral, they are not illegal, they are not the primary obstacles to peace, and they are justifiable in light of the historical rights of the Jewish People. The problem, therefore, is not legal, moral, or historical—the problem is political, and politics are fundamentally a question of *smart* or *stupid*.

The argument for or against the settlements in the occupied territories must be made based on whether they are *smart* or *stupid* in regards to what is good for the Jews. The Jews must ask themselves what value these settlements contribute to the Zionist project in the twenty-first century.

A good case could be made that some of the post–Six-Day War suburbs of Jerusalem and the middle-class settlements contiguous to Israel's pre–Six-Day War borders (such as Alfei Menashe) contribute to Israel's vital interests.

The isolated ideological settlements, on the other hand, have been a tremendous burden on and detriment to all the vital components of Zionist value. They have not contributed economically but rather have been an economic drag. They have not contributed socially, as the vast funds poured into them could have been put to better use expanding educational services and building infrastructure.

They have not contributed security but have been a tremendous burden on the Israeli army, consuming security resources that could have been better used elsewhere. The vast number of man-hours spent guarding settlements has undermined the army's training regime, damaging its preparedness. A more subtle process has been the damaging of the human quality of the officer corps. People who are good at fulfilling the duties of an occupation are not necessarily those who would be good at hand-to-hand combat with the Syrians. Most obvious is the fact that the settlements produce a border more than

1,500 kilometers long, more than four times the length of the border before the Six-Day War. Simple security calculus dictates the following: ever diminishing concentrations of soldiers on ever lengthening lines of defense equals less security, while ever thickening concentrations of soldiers on ever shorter lines of defense equals more security.

The settlements certainly have not contributed politically. Almost every embarrassing political difficulty Israel has experienced since the Six-Day War has been because of these ideological settlements or their supporters, and not a single country in the world has changed its mind regarding the official, legally constituted borders of the State of Israel because of these settlements.

Nor have the settlements contributed spiritually to Israeli society. Indeed, they may have caused a great deal of alienation in many segments of Israeli society, tarnishing the label of Zionist, and weakening the spiritual fortitude and moral certainty of Israel at large. Many Israelis find the settlement subculture abhorrent and resent doing reserve duty because of them.

One cause for increased shirking of reserve duty may be this unwillingness of many otherwise good and patriotic Israelis to guard the settlements. Most important, however, is that by identifying Zionism with the settlements and calling settlement project opponents post-Zionists and even anti-Zionists, the settlers themselves have unwittingly contributed to the spread of that nihilistic post-Zionism now infecting Israeli society. The erosion of Zionist moral self-confidence on the part of large segments of the Israeli public begins with the misguided settlement project.

The question, therefore, is not if the settlers are brave and idealistic but whether the settlement project is smart or stupid, whether it contributes to or detracts from the values, goals, and aims of Zionism as it redefines itself in the twenty-first century.

The British Light Brigade was composed of men who were brave and idealistic beyond measure, but their famous charge was an example of colossal stupidity. General Lee's Confederate soldiers were brave and idealistic beyond measure, but that doesn't mean that Pickett's charge at Gettysburg was smart or that the cause they represented was sublime. I often wonder if Israel's settlement policy is not the political equivalent of the ill-fated British landing at Gallipoli in World War I, upon which the German Admiral De Robeck commented, "Gallant fellows, these soldiers; they always go for the thickest place in the fence." Israel's settlement policy compels Israeli diplomacy to always try to break through the thickest part of the diplomatic fence, the one and perhaps only place where Arab political superiority is manifest.

In political life, stupidity is the greatest sin, not immorality or illegality. Stupidity does the greatest harm to human endeavor. If we were to judge what is pro-Zionist and what is anti-Zionist according to their contribution to or their deleterious effect on Israel's economy, security, society, and overall morale and moral fortitude, we must conclude that the ideological settlements in the occupied territories constitute the most anti-Zionist activity conducted by any group of Jews since the advent of the Zionist project itself.

Ben Gurion once said that we have the absolute right to all the occupied territories but that we also have the absolute right *not* to exercise that right if by exercising it we do serious damage to other vital rights and needs. "Back to Ben Gurionism" should be our motto in regards to the territories occupied in 1967.

THE JEWISH PROLETARIAT AND PEASANTRY

Labor Zionism celebrated the Jewish return to agricultural activity and the creation of an industrial Jewish proletariat. They called this the "normalization" of the Jewish People and perceived it as having inherent ideological value. With the wisdom of hindsight, we now see that both agricultural and industrial work were periodic values at best, important in a particular historical period.

We have pointed out the value of the early agricultural settlements above. We can only reiterate that without them, the Zionist project would not have succeeded and Israel would not exist. Similarly, basic industrial activity in labor-intensive enterprises such as textiles and woodworking played a major role in absorbing the mass immigration following creation of the Jewish State. With a population of 600,000 in 1948, the Jewish State absorbed another 1.5 million by 1965. Basic labor-intensive industry served as the economic and social foundation for this achievement.

But the Israeli and Zionist establishment have celebrated both agricultural and basic industrial activities far beyond the periods they were relevant for. The ongoing health of Israel's economy, society, and environment have suffered.

Because agriculture has been celebrated as a primary value, and even as a metaphor for the return of the Jews to their ancient homeland, policy makers have been loath to take a hard and rational look at what agriculture really entails in twenty-first-century Israel. Israel has no water, and the Jews have no wish to work in a sector with such an abysmal pay scale. Today, water-poor Israel subsidizes the export of water (for that is what you are exporting when you export agricultural products) to water-rich Germany, France, and Scandinavia in order to create jobs for Thai guest workers. And we call this a Zionist policy.

Moreover, the subsidized water is budgeted to those sectors of the agricultural economy under government regulation and dependent on massive subsidies. This deprives unregulated agricultural sectors, which can subsist and profit *without* subsidized water, of the water they require in order to expand their exports. The direct and indirect costs to the Israeli economy of this ideologically motivated water policy are probably equivalent to the yearly contribution of American Jewry to Israel. These resources could have been put to better Zionist use in education and infrastructure. Yet, this policy is justified in the name of faithfulness to the historic Zionist value of Jewish agriculture.

The justifications for labor-intensive industries are no less irrational and their consequences for Israel's economy and society no less detrimental. Ever since the Six-Day War, these industries have continued to survive only because of massive direct and *indirect* subsidies. Even with subsidies, pay scales in these labor-intensive industries have seldom exceeded minimum wage, even for people with years of seniority. These industries form the economic base of the development towns and thus have become major contributors to the deepening social/ethnic gap. One cannot have minimum wage industries and close the social gap; in a dynamic society such as Israel, the gap can only widen as long as such industries exist.

This is because basic labor-intensive industries require a large pool of low-income, low-skilled workers to compete in the global labor market. An historical anecdote will highlight this point. In the mid 1970s a high-tech company wished to open a small factory (60 workers) in a well-known development town. The local textile factory (employing 1,500) threatened to move if the town granted this company a business permit. The factory's owners were afraid of the potential labor options this would open up for the locals, with subsequent upward wage pressure. The development town being, in effect, a company town, was forced to accede to the textile factory's demands. The local residents, having neither big-city employment options nor the wherewithal to commute to large cities, were trapped (and remain trapped) in their residential bubble of poverty.

All the education budgets, welfare programs, and antipoverty projects in the world cannot neutralize this basic negative economic and social dynamic. High-tech industries and sophisticated services need a large pool of highly skilled and hence highly paid workers. Their interest creates positive economic and social dynamics that can help close the social gap.

Yet, even massive direct and indirect subsidies cannot sustain Israel's labor-intensive industries, which, as with other developed countries, are moving to the Third World. Israel is now experiencing desperate demonstrations against closures by workers who long ago became disgusted with conditions and wages in these industries. In other words, these workers want these factories to stay open but would prefer to work elsewhere. Consequently, Israel still has poverty, an even larger social gap, and an added "bonus" of chronic large-scale (up to 15 percent) unemployment in the development areas.

In contrast, the unemployment figures in the nonindustrial, nonpioneering, nonproletariat Sharon area (Kfar Saba, Ra'anana, Herzlia), just north of Tel Aviv, are less than 3 percent. This area is a high-tech hotbed. Its sophisticated service innovation contributes perhaps a billion dollars a year to Israel's export figures. Yet, according to classical Zionist conceptions, these towns have nowhere near the Zionist value that settlements or development towns or near-bankrupt kibbutzim have. According to classic Zionists, the residents of these towns are self-absorbed, egoistic, bourgeois, hedonistic yuppies alienated from authentic expressions of Zionism. The gloomy faithful ignore the fact that these areas produce a disproportionate number of citizens who serve in elite army units as well as a disproportionate amount of economic and professional value and tax revenues that enable the Zionist enterprise to exist.

The crisis of labor-intensive industries could have been avoided by applying the principles of futuristic thinking and simple trend analysis. By the late 1970s it was clear to anyone who cared to analyze the trends that labor-intensive industries had no future in the developed world. Intelligent policy makers in other developed countries began to shed their labor-intensive industries gradually, moving them to Hong Kong, South Korea, and Taiwan and later on to Thailand, Malaysia, and Indonesia, combining this economic policy with a major redirection of the educational system. The gradual process— shedding older workers as they achieved retirement age while not absorbing younger workers—led to radically shrinking these work forces *without social dislocation*. Young people entering the work force were directed to other lines of work, while younger workers were retrained for other branches of the economy.

Israeli policymakers, on the other hand, still infatuated with the ideological myth of the Jewish industrial worker and having no alternative answers for the development towns failed to change course. They too faced pressure from obscurantist labor leaders in the Histadrut, more concerned with their own political power as heads of large unions than with members' long-term welfare. The resultant social dislocation and trauma bear witness to the short-sighted foolishness of perpetuating this periodic Zionist value long after its historical shelf life had expired.

Here, the contradictions of the Zionist Left in particular are laid bare, the contradiction between a Zionist ideology that celebrates the Jew returning to physical labor and a socialist ideology of a decent living wage. These two ideologies have never jibed, do not jibe now, and never can jibe. Unless of course you subsidize this entire "idealistic" project with tax money taken from the hedonistic, bourgeois yuppies mentioned above.

PEACE, PEACE PROCESS, AND PEACE AGREEMENTS

Since Oslo, we have witnessed an infatuation with the instruments of past success at the expense of updated grand strategic focus and intellectual clarity vis-à-vis the peace process. Israel's peace activists have consistently confused the primary value of peace with the secondary or periodic value of a manageable cold war reached by way of peace agreements.

To listen to advocates of Peace Now, one would think that the most important challenge facing Israel is continuous negotiation with the Palestinians and Syrians in order to achieve a peace agreement. The historical success of this particular formula vis-à-vis the Egyptians and the Jordanians is not to be disputed. Indeed, the success was so profound in its implications that we have become infatuated with the *formula* at the expense of possible alternative interim aims.

Since its foundation, Israel's primary grand strategic aim has been to neutralize actual and potential hostile activity toward the Jewish State so that we might develop and absorb as many immigrants as possible. This aim was achieved with Egypt and Jordan by way of a peace agreement; it was achieved, de facto, with the Palestinians, for seven years, by way of the Oslo Accords; it was achieved, de facto, across the Syrian border by way of Israel's military potential. It has not been achieved with Syria's proxy state, Lebanon, or its proxy organizations Hizballah and Jihad and hence not finally with Syria. Given the second *Intifada*, it has not yet been fully achieved with the Palestinians.

Israel's aim is not necessarily peace agreements, but peace and quiet in order to develop. If peace agreements give us peace and quiet, as in the case of Egypt and Jordan, they are good. If the unrestrained quest for a peace agreement gives us an *Intifada*, as in the case of the Palestinians, then this quest is bad.

Contrary to accepted wisdom, Israel has not achieved its primary aim of real peace with either Egypt or Jordan. We have achieved a manageable cold war, a great achievement in itself. The Egyptians have been telling us for years, "We recognize you but we don't accept you." Yet, our fixated infatuation with peace causes us not to notice and to continue to live in an illusion that often endangers the peace process itself.

When Shimon Peres coined the phrase "New Middle East," Israelis greeted it with bemused impatience, but Arabs greeted it with real fear and anger. They interpreted it as a catch phrase for Israeli economic colonialism of the Middle East and another example of the Jewish superiority complex expressed in paternalistic terms. I do not question Mr. Peres' sincerity, but this demonstrates how an unrestrained naiveté and wishful thinking in regards to peace can actually damage the peace process.

Israel's manageable cold war with Egypt resembles the United State's relationship with the Soviet Union during the cold war. It is characterized by a combination of hesitant economic and political contacts and cooperation along with determined economic and political hostility. In our case, this hostility is unilateral, solely on the part of Egypt. We have ongoing communication, we have mutual political recognition, we have incipient economic relations, but we do not have peace. The determined, ongoing, focused hostility of Egypt to Israel's interests in numerous areas is reminiscent of past American-Soviet attitudes or current American-Chinese attitudes. Indeed Egypt's cold war vis-à-vis Israel is even colder than the former American-Soviet or present American-Chinese cold wars. These latter sustained cultural, academic, and scientific contacts. The hostility of Arab intellectuals to Israel and to the Jewish People is so pervasive that these kinds of contacts will not occur for many years. If the American-Soviet cold war was chilly, the Israel-Egyptian-Jordanian cold war is freezing.

This does not negate the tremendous Zionist achievement in producing the two peace agreements and the political and economic spin-offs with other Arab countries they engendered. Indeed, I would call it the greatest Zionist achievement since the establishment of the Jewish State. The peace process, as flawed as it is, is a Zionist triumph and an Arab defeat.

This is because the Israeli/Arab conflict is not symmetrical. The asymmetry is fundamental and substantial. The grand strategic aim of Zionism since the creation of the State of Israel has been to live in peace and quiet in the Middle East, whereas the Arabs' grand strategic aim has been to drive Israel out of the Middle East. The peace process itself becomes a de facto Arab admission of their policy's failure and the success of Zionist policy.

Israel achieved a great deal by way of the peace process. Egypt has been removed from the ring of military threat that once surrounded Israel, thereby improving Israel's strategic position. The peace process enabled Israel to achieve greater global political acceptability that has contributed to its economic development and ability to absorb immigrants. Especially important are the lines of communication the process has opened with Egypt and Jordan. If we had had this communication earlier, we might have avoided the Six-Day War and Yom Kippur War, just as the United States might have avoided the Korean and Vietnam Wars if they had had a relationship and communication with Communist China.

But the relative success of past peace agreements may have blinded us to the essentially different reality we face with the Palestinians and to the fact that the very pursuit of a peace agreement might be dysfunctional to our basic grand strategic aims. Barak's finalistic ambitions at Camp David may have contributed to the outbreak of the second *Intifada* simply because Israel's leaders failed to realize that any Israeli proposal would be all but impossible for the Palestinians and their present leadership (Arafat especially) to accept. In other words, unrestrained pursuit of the peace agreement led to armed conflict that could even degenerate into war.

CHAPTER 6

Reinventing Israeli Grand Strategy

The previous chapter, dedicated to helping us avoid repeating mistakes for lack of grand strategic focus, was a prologue to determining Israel's future Grand Strategy. How might we use conclusions drawn from these historical examples of confusion between primary, secondary, and periodic values in order to rejuvenate our grand strategic imagination?

First, we must realistically and clearly assess Israel's resources and challenges. As in professional policy making, we will use an analytical tool, a SWOT analysis, to identify Israel's Strengths, Weaknesses, Opportunities and Threats.

ISRAEL'S STRENGTHS

The special relationship with world Jewry, especially American Jewry, is Israel's most important grand strategic resource. It is the key to the special relationship with the United States on which Israel's survival depends.

The economic association with both the United States and the Common Market, and Israel's technologically sophisticated economy, underlie Israel's consistent economic and technological superiority over her enemies. Israel's GNP is equivalent to the Egyptian, Jordanian, Syrian, Lebanese, and Palestinian economies combined, and its qualitative economic advantage is even greater: Israel has more companies registered on the NASDAQ than any European country or Japan. All of this derives from Israel's greatest resource, her educated, innovative, and energetic citizenry.

Israel's vigorous democracy, with its independent judiciary, hypercritical media, and ever more demanding citizenry makes the above possible. Although democracy can be annoying, history demonstrates that in the long run democracies have infinitely greater efficiency and survival ability than authoritarian or totalitarian regimes. The point is well made and empirically reinforced by the collapse of the Soviet Union and nascent liberalization of China and authoritarian regimes elsewhere.

As the planet becomes more globalized, with demands for more quality, speed, and flexibility, the relative economic and technological advantages of the world's open societies will only increase. Most important, the special relationship with American Jewry and with the United States depends entirely on Israel being a democracy. If being a democracy constitutes such a vital component of Israel's survivability, we must conclude that Israel is not too democratic, as some would-be patriots would claim, it is not democratic enough.

That all of the above is protected by the fifth most powerful army in the world is a strength impossible to ignore or neglect, even if we enter an era of peace making. Without this strength, peace making is impossible. Israel's military strength created the conditions for peace. Peace is not concluded because of brotherhood and goodwill; it is a product of power and interests. When the power is sufficient, the interest manifests itself. The Arab states had no interest in making peace as long as they could entertain the possibility of destroying Israel. Only when Israel's military power made its destruction far-fetched did peace become a possibility.

ISRAEL'S WEAKNESSES

Israel's most obvious weakness is geographic: it is small and irregularly shaped and therefore tactically and strategically vulnerable. Its total land area within the pre–Six-Day War borders is smaller than New Jersey, and its total population equals greater Philadelphia's. Israel belongs to no international bloc or alliance, which puts her at a great disadvantage in international organizations, especially the United Nations.

Israel is subject to hostile and arbitrary judgments by a majoritarian international community not bound by constitutional limits regarding the unalienable rights of nations. Hostile United Nations resolutions against Israel made by a majority of the member states have gained the status of international law even though they have passed only because of the Arab-voting bloc in concert with the Islamic and Afro-Asian voting blocs. The United Nations has never passed a resolution condemning any Arab action against Israel or obligating any Arab country to fulfill any obligation toward Israel. Therefore, Israel is consistently in contravention of international law, while the Arabs are, by definition, in conformance with international law.

Part of the problem is that Zionism and Israel represent a unique historical phenomenon, and thus even its closest friends often misunderstand it. Every other national liberation movement, whether in nineteenth-century Europe or in twentieth-century Asia or Africa, began with a people speaking its own language within an existing culture, living in its own land, and having its own economic activity. The early Zionists enjoyed none of these preconditions. They had to reinvent Hebrew as a living language, create a new cultural reality, bring the people to their historical homeland, and develop an economy out of nothing. Then, they had to fight their war of liberation. That the Zionist enterprise is unique, and thus so easily misunderstood, is a weakness in a world increasingly driven by perception rather than fact and logic.

Being a democracy and being dependent on the democratic world for its very survival can also be problematic. Israel cannot be as ruthless as its enemies and yet is judged more harshly for lesser transgressions.

The anticipated demographic decline of American Jewry and consequent erosion of its political power may gradually weaken Israel's strongest ally. This makes time an essential component in Israel's grand strategic thinking.

The abysmal standards of Israel's public services and governance are major weaknesses. In science, technology, and some areas of business, Israel is first rate. In certain areas of public services, however, we might be closer to Third World standards. Examples are numerous:

The tremendous water crisis we are now experiencing, despite the fact that Israel has the best water engineers in the world.

The bridge collapse in the 1997 Maccabia Games and the collapse of the wedding hall in Jerusalem.

Israel's extremely high level of workplace-related deaths and injuries (triple the European level).

These examples reflect incompetence, indifference, and contempt for the public, rife at many levels of Israel's government, which may have killed more Israelis in the past 10 years than terrorist attacks. They have certainly alienated and undermined the morale of more Israelis.

ISRAEL'S OPPORTUNITIES

Much maligned globalization might be Israel's greatest opportunity. In a way, it helps neutralize the deleterious effects of not being a member of a particular bloc of nations. It does not, however, contradict Israel's need to become a member of international blocs.

Israel, with its multicultural, multilingual population, can interrelate with other countries and cultures more easily than can its economic competitors. Their cultural and intellectual flexibility makes Israel's citizens a tremendous asset in the era of globalization. The technological and communications revolutions that drive globalization are most suited to the Jewish mentality, culture, and educational ambitions.

Globalization, and its complex multidimensional mosaic of interactions, presents Israel with numerous opportunities, in league with Diaspora Jewry, to form new coalitions with new global players and interest groups. Rising powers such as China and India often find Israel a comfortable economic and scientific partner. Israel's traditional Euro/American orientation has delayed full exploitation of this potential, but now we are seeing the first phases of a more politically diversified Israeli orientation.

Israel might be able to develop a special relationship with India in particular. India has a Moslem minority composing 20 percent of its population and suffers from Moslem hostility over Kashmir. Bin Laden mentioned Kashmir before Palestine in his video speeches. The Taliban regime revealed their radical Islamic contempt for Buddhism and Hinduism in blowing up the giant statues of Buddha in Afghanistan and requiring the Hindu minority to wear a yellow identity patch, a chilling reminder of the yellow patch that the Nazis required the Jews to wear.

China also has a growing and increasingly restive Moslem population and might also one day find itself in the same predicament as India and Israel, namely how to sustain good relations with the Moslem world while dealing with hostile Moslem minorities within their own borders. An imaginative policy would discern significant economic, scientific, and political opportunities for Israel in regards to these two countries.

The fall of communism in the former Soviet Union and the fact that 20 percent of Israel's population speak Russian as a mother tongue also provide opportunities for economic, scientific, and technological cooperation with Russian-speaking countries.

ISRAEL'S THREATS

Persian Gulf Oil

The most obvious threat to Israel's existence is Iranian nonconventional weapon capacity and massive Saudi financing of anti-Israel and anti-Semitic activity. In recent years, these threats have gained new life after a period of relative hibernation.

From the early 1980s up until 1999, relative world market share remained stagnant for the Organization of Oil-Producing Countries (OPEC). Ongoing reductions in the real price of oil further reduced OPEC oil revenues. In 1982, Saudi Arabia had 140 billion dollars in currency reserves, in 1999 it had 130 billion dollars in debt. This general decline in oil revenues in conjunction with other developments had positive consequences for Israel. The debilitating effects of the Iran/Iraq war, the collapse of the Soviet Union, the further erosion of Iraqi power after the first Gulf War, and the consequent weakening of Syria and other radical regimes and movements in the Middle East gave Israel a grand strategic advantage in the 1990s. This helped contribute to a nascent normalization of relations with the Arab and Islamic worlds and improved political relations with the rest of the world until the second *Intifada*.

Rising oil prices in the early twenty-first century and subsequent greater Persian Gulf oil revenues correspond to the rebirth of fanatic Islamic militancy and hostile activity in the industrial West. This is aggravated even more by the decreasing relative portion of non–Persian Gulf oil in the OPEC equation.

Persian Gulf oil is an existential danger to Israel and a strategic danger to the industrial West. It directly finances the nonconventional weapons programs of Iran, and it indirectly finances global terror. Bin Laden's activities would have been impossible without the tremendous wealth of the oil-driven Saudi economy, which indirectly financed the Twin Towers outrage.

The Saudi government quiets their religious fanatics by buying off religious leaders with billions of dollars. This money is distributed worldwide to finance anti-Semitic literature and activity as well as to establish and support the radical Wahabi mosques and schools that nurture and encourage terrorist activity. Saudi Arabia's dominant religious sect is the Wahabi, which produced the Taliban and Osama bin Laden. Saudis in the West are not propagating moderate and enlightened Islam, but a fanatic version indirectly financed by Western energy self-indulgence, as graphically described in an article written by Neela Banerjee ("The High, Hidden Cost of Saudi Arabian Oil," *New York Times*, October 21, 2001).

The growing political power of European and North American Moslems hostile to Israel and the Jews is directly connected to the influence of Persian Gulf oil. With approximately 20 million Moslems in the European Union, many of them attending mosques financed by Wahabi money, and less than 1.5 million Jews, it is a wonder that the European community is not more anti-Israeli.

North American trends remain less extreme than those in Europe, but they bode ill for world Jewry and Israel. Canada will have twice as many Moslems as Jews in several years. The number of Moslems in the United States may have already surpassed the number of Jews. When Moslem organizational and political efficiency, financed by Saudi Arabian money, begins to improve, this demographic development will pose a serious threat to Diaspora Jewish communities, not only to Israel.

Global Governance and Constitutionalism

The lack of a constitutional foundation for global governance may in the long term present the greatest threat to Israel's existence. The global governance network now being created in response to globalization has no constitutional basis for its method of operation. This places unpopular entities such as Israel in mortal danger. Questions of legality are based on popularity, or on membership in some large bloc, and not on the basis of protecting the unalienable rights of an individual country or a minority people against the majority's whim or the winds of current political correctness.

What constitutes this global governance network? It is an amorphous mix that includes the United Nations, the World Court, the European Court, the various national courts that presume to function on a transnational basis, the International Red Cross, and Amnesty International, as well as numerous other *self-appointed* "humanitarian" organizations. The mandates, defined powers, and authority of this network are nondescript at best. They are characterized not by the universal application of first principles (the basis of constitutionality) but more often by the selective application of politically held positions hiding behind the jargon of international law and morality.

For example, Pinochet was arrested in England on a warrant issued by a Spanish magistrate of a particular political persuasion, accusing him of crimes against humanity for his responsibility in the murder of 3,000 of his own citizens. The late president of Syria, Hafiz Assad, was never issued a warrant or arrested, even though Assad murdered more than 30,000 of his own citizens at El Hama, and Syrian dissidents have documented the state murder of another more than 15,000 citizens during his rule. Such disparities demonstrate the subjective arbitrariness of the present global governance legal system.

Pinochet was arrested because he was an unpopular murderer supported by no international power and detested by most of the citizens of his own country. Assad, a far bigger murderer than Pinochet, was not arrested because the Arab League, the Moslem League, OPEC, and most of the Afro-Asian bloc would have supported him, and his arrest would have caused intolerable political damage to Europe.

A politically motivated prosecutor's office in Belgium tried to indict Ariel Sharon in a Belgian court, under Belgian law, on a war crimes charge because of the atrocity committed at Sabra and Shatila by Israel's Christian allies. Sharon had already been cleared of direct responsibility by a distinguished Israeli board of inquiry because he had not planned the atrocity, had not ordered it, and had no intent for it to happen. He was found indirectly responsible and negligent (perhaps even criminally negligent) and as a consequence found himself in the political wilderness for years. Intent is a basic principle of criminal law in countries that consider themselves under the rule of law. The rule of law is a synonym for constitutionalism. In Sharon's case, the question of intent was ignored by parts of the Belgian legal system sympathetic to the Palestinian cause. They in effect became part of the Palestinian propaganda effort during the *Intifada*. Could one imagine this same Belgian system attempting to indict Arafat for dozens of atrocities that he planned, financed, and ordered and which were *intended* to result in murder? Politically correct European public opinion would not have allowed this to happen.

Popularity has become the standard by which international legality proceeds. Constitutions, on the other hand, are constructed to safeguard the rights of the unpopular.

Social Gap and Demographics

The debilitating effects of the social/ethnic gap might also become an existential threat to Israel, especially as it affects demographics. In the nineteenth century, Abraham Lincoln claimed that no people could survive half slave and half free. Likewise, in the twenty-first century, no people can survive half preindustrial and half postindustrial. The combined alienation of the Israeli underclass and resentment of the Israeli middle class at their tremendous tax burden could be a bigger threat to Israel's long-term survival than hostile Arab and Moslem fanaticism. Ignoring or giving lip service to this problem will not suffice.

The demographic challenge of the combined Arab and Haredi birth rates is one negative consequence of the social gap and a danger to Israel's existence as a Zionist State. By 2030, at current birth rates, Israel's Moslem and Haredi communities combined will constitute more than 50 percent of the citizenry of Israel. These two communities are often hostile to the concept of Zionism. Their commitment to the state, therefore, is merely instrumental, limited to what they can get from the state with no concomitant sense of responsibility or citizenship.

ISRAEL'S PEST ANALYSIS

PEST, an analytical methodology, refers to the present and future global political, economic, social, and technological environment. In conjunction with Israel's SWOT analysis, it serves to determine the grand strategic constraints Israel must operate within to achieve her goals. Israel's PEST environment has changed radically since the creation of the Jewish State and few, if any, Israeli policy makers have appreciated the depth and extent of this change.

Israel, when established, was for the most part in harmony with its PEST environment. The establishment of Israel represented a victory for decolonialization and self-determination. Its social experiments such as the kibbutz and Histadrut economy excited the imagination of democratic progressives around the world. Israel's military victories and ingathering of exiles in the face of tremendous hostility after the Holocaust combined the Exodus metaphor with the phoenix metaphor to create a powerful predisposition toward Israel amongst much of enlightened world opinion.

Since the 1967 Six-Day War, however, Israel has become increasingly out of touch with many world political and social developments. We have not perceived the development and unconstitutional direction of the global governance network. We have not noted how the end of the cold war and an ever-growing antimilitarist sentiment in the West, especially in Europe, has made besieged Israel unfashionable. Western geopolitical interests have also begun to turn Israel into an annoying complication in the eyes of many world powers.

When we were a tired remnant of the Holocaust fighting against impossible odds, we were popular. Today, Israel has the fifth most powerful army in the world, and we are in conflict with the much weaker Palestinians. This is not popular. Young Europeans, who have grown up with Israel being tough and, unlike their parents, make no allowances because the once-bullied Jews have finally stood up for themselves, find Israel increasingly unattractive.

We have also become increasingly out of touch with other phenomena that have gained world prominence in recent years. These include multiculturalism and a growing prejudice against countries that appear to be chauvinist and demonstrate an indifferent attitude toward environmental questions. The so-called CNN civilization has changed all the rules of international politics. Military room for maneuver has become greatly limited, now that military activities are accompanied by real-time television coverage.

Globalized communications presents Israel and the Jews with a particular problem. We are no longer dealing with electronic journalism, we are dealing with communications conglomerates driven by profit concerns. Profit follows ratings. There are 15 million Jews, more than 1 billion Moslems, and 200 million Arabs in the world. Potential ratings growth resides with the Moslems and not with the Jews. At the height of the second *Intifada*, for example, CNN introduced its Arabic language Web site. I am not claiming that CNN reporters consciously violate the rules of objectivity. But *all* of these reporters were used in CNN International's commercials promoting this Web site. They all have a subjective interest in the financial health of the company they work for and thus an interest in the success of its initiatives. This self-interest must act as a kind of background "white noise" and must influence the tone of their reporting. If it did not, they would not be human.

In economics and technology, Israel has been a tremendous success and is in harmony with major world trends, as is attested to by its many successes in these areas in the decade before the second *Intifada*.

In other words, a dichotomy exists in Israel's PEST analysis. Politically and socially, Israel is to a significant extent out of harmony with the world environment, while in economics and technology, Israel has become a global success story. Israel must strive to apply its economic and technological attitudes to its own political and social structures. Israel must strive to bridge the radical disconnect between the cosmopolitan mentality and values of its young entrepreneurs and the provincial mentality and values of its politicians and ideologues, as well as large segments of its citizenry.

The dilemma in trying to change attitudes is that what emotionally appeals to one's own citizens often offends external public opinion, and what is satisfactory to external public opinion often appears as pandering to domestic public opinion. Mediocre leadership indeed panders thus by feeding populist social and political slogans that satisfy emotions but are politically and economically dysfunctional. Leadership that aspires to historic stature sees the very nature of its job as constantly reeducating the public and changing attitudes.

STRENGTHENING ISRAEL'S STRENGTHS

The Diaspora

Israel must aim to radically renovate and upgrade Israel-Diaspora relations in order to use Diaspora skills and resources with greater leverage. Israel must stop viewing Diaspora Jews as purely a source of financial contributions and political lobbying and become fully cognizant of the great grand strategic resource it has in world Jewry. Israel must also affirm world Jewry's *inherent* value—it is not just some utilitarian device that exists for Israel's convenience. If we do not radically upgrade and renovate the relationship, this Jewish resource will gradually become enfeebled, to the detriment of the Diaspora as well as of Israel. An imaginative renovation of the relationship would provide Israel with even greater grand strategic resources as well as reenergize the Diaspora, thus helping to reverse many negative trends. This will be discussed in detail in chapter 7, "Reinventing Israel-Diaspora Relations."

The United States

The special relationship with the United States cannot be taken for granted and must also be renovated and upgraded. As previously mentioned, this special relationship did not exist before 1967 and it may not continue unless we work diligently to sustain and improve it. At present, Israel has an excellent relationship with America's political society (Congress, president, and so on) and with certain important segments of America's civil society.

But America is a dynamic society in which certain demographic segments move from weakness to strength as others move from strength to weakness. This reflects the revolutionary demographic changes now taking place in American society. For example, more than 50 percent of California's population is now nonwhite (Black, Asian, and Hispanic). This is a trend in many major states across the country.

We must ask which segments of American civil society are likely to be stronger or weaker in the next 20 years and with which segments does Israel and American Jewry have good, indifferent, or poor relations at present? An honest answer to this question might frighten us if we also include the relative strength of the Jewish community and we remember that the special relationship with America's political society depends on our relative standing in America's civil society. Israel must strive directly and by way of the Jewish community to expand and improve relations with new segments of American civil society.

A good historical example was Yitzhak Rabin cultivating ties with fundamentalist Christians when he was Israel's ambassador to the United States in the 1970s. This initiative angered many Jewish liberals, but in retrospect we see that this was politically appropriate. After the Jewish community, fundamentalist Christians are now Israel's strongest and most devoted supporters in the United States, while Israel's former liberal supporters have declined both in strength and in their level of support for Israel. Fundamentalist Christians were an all but irrelevant, identifiable voting bloc until the 1970s and the advent of television evangelism. Today, the Christian Coalition is an even stronger lobby than the Jewish lobby, and thus ironically a more important ally of Israel. Even though we have serious difficulties with their proselytizing efforts within the Jewish community, we must develop a coherent strategy of interacting with these 70 million Americans who are predisposed to us.

In line with the aim of cultivating new segments of America's civil society, we might ask about Jewish and Israeli contact with the *various* Spanish-speaking communities, which in aggregate have become the decisive voting bloc in states such as Texas, Florida, and California. Are we forming coherent initiatives with the growing Indian community (Hindu and Moslem), with the various Asian communities (Chinese, Japanese, Korean, and others), as well as with the various Islamic communities? What programs and methods are we exploring to improve ties with the Black and Native American populations of the United States? Unless American Jewry can generate creative answers to these questions, its political influence will diminish and Israel's special relationship with the United States might not exist by the year 2020.

The Economy

Israel's technology-based economy has concentrated on North America for investment. Israel must take more initiative in the European Union, our biggest export market. Israel has the potential to perform the same creative role for the European Union that Silicon Valley plays for America. By playing a more important economic and technological role in the European Union, Israel will also improve its political standing and enhance its chances of becoming a permanent voting member.

Israel must radically reduce the bureaucratic drag on its economy and become the most friendly business environment in the world, *without* sacrificing social solidarity. Israel, at present, is one of the most difficult countries in the developed world with which to do business. By liberating itself from bureaucratic drag, Israel can extract greater benefit from the tremendous human potential of its citizens.

Security

The absolute power of the Israeli army must be sustained and even enhanced. More important is a renewal of the military imagination and creativity that characterized it in the past, the intellectual delicacy of conception and execution in its operations. Today, the army is perceived as conventional, and even coarse, in both conception and execution.

Democracy

Israel must become a more dynamic and transparent democracy. It must move from a democracy dominated by its political society to a democracy dominated by its civil society. Israel must adopt a "Bill of Rights" defining limitations of power on the government and the majority vis-à-vis the individual. The unalienable rights of the individual must be clearly defined, protecting him or her against the government, society, and the majority in all activities that do not damage the property or person of other citizens, either directly or *indirectly*.

Citizens' Rights

Israel should revoke the law pertaining to "insulting government workers." It must substitute a law making government workers *personally* responsible, both criminally and civilly, for the efficacy of their performance and liable to both society at large and to *the individual citizen* for damages resulting from incompetence, corruption, or just plain indifference. Citizens must be able to identify those who have done them damage through incompetence, negligence, or arbitrary decision making. Those responsible must be liable to civil suits and to making financial amends to the damaged party. Liability should move from the government, which really means the innocent taxpayer. The citizen taxpayer must become the center of attention, not the comfort and prerogatives of the bureaucracy. The term *public servant* should replace the term *government worker*.

The Courts

Israel should also consider modifying its contempt-of-court laws. The present draconian contempt law limits freedom of expression *outside the environs of the courtroom*. This greatly inhibits public criticism of particular decisions by individual judges. The judge being criticized also judges whether what you say or write is legitimate criticism or constitutes contempt of court. Under present law, if a judge does not like what a citizen says or writes outside the courtroom, that judge can fine or imprison said citizen for contempt of court.

Constitutional democracy is based upon limitations of power: the power of the majority, the power of the government, the power of the bureaucracy, and the power of the courts. In America, the power of the courts is limited by public elections or political nominations, unlimited public criticism, and impeachment by the democratically elected legislature. Executive and legislative prerogatives are *immune* to judicial review except in criminal or constitutional issues. American courts would *never* interfere with executive or legislative appointments and would never publicly question their propriety unless they pertained to criminal or constitutional issues.

Given Israel's particular political culture and mentality, I would not recommend instituting laws of impeachment or holding judicial elections or instituting political nominations, but at the least we should have unlimited public criticism. Israel's judges should be allowed to impose contempt of court punishments only on acts and expressions *in the courtroom*. At present, the Israeli judiciary has a status in contravention of the concepts of balance of power and limitation of power.

The Israeli courts' constant interference into nonjudicial matters, such as the propriety of political appointments, as well as their immunity from free and easy criticism has led to growing public discomfort. Their hyperactivism might boomerang. Segments of Israeli society unfamiliar with constitutional limitations of power might use the arguments of majoritarian democracy to completely subvert the legal system, making it reflect majority opinion at all times. The recent political initiative of a constitutional court is a dangerous example of this tendency to politicize constitutional rights, a tendency that to a large extent is a reaction to the ever-growing interference of Israeli courts into every aspect of society.

WEAKENING ISRAEL'S WEAKNESSES

No internationally acceptable remedy exists for Israel's small size. Not even the United States, Israel's best and most consistent friend, would support annexation of any substantial part of the occupied territories. Constantly improving Israel's ability to quickly respond to a rapidly changing global reality is the only practical means to offset Israel's territorial limitations. We must begin to view Israel not as a nation-state but rather as a city-state serving the "Cosmopolis" of the entire globe. Geographical vulnerability can be offset only by technological superiority, which can be sustained only by being a leading player in the global economy.

Israeli Grand Strategy must include becoming a member of at least one and preferably two international blocs. NATO and the European Union are the most logical and the most important. We might want to team up with Turkey vis-à-vis lobbying to enter the European Union. Turkey is already a member of NATO and is a Moslem country. Israel teaming up with Turkey would help the Europeans to neutralize potential Moslem hostility and thus be more amenable to the idea of Israel becoming a part of the European Union and NATO, especially if this were the price for a radical withdrawal from the occupied territories. In conjunction with a comprehensive peace, we might even propose a Benelux-style entry into the European Union—taking Palestine and Jordan along with us.

The richness and complexity of Zionism and Zionist ideology must be reintroduced into the public debate in Israel, world Jewry, and the world. How can we expect the non-Jewish world to understand us when our own knowledge and understanding of the historical development and ideological variety of Zionism is so deficient? How many Israelis or Diaspora Jews know that *all* the main streams of Zionism were, in one way or another, a reflection of the liberal nationalism that characterized nineteenth-century Europe and were an expression of European Enlightenment values?

The great Italian national leader Mazzini would have argued that unless a nation was united in an independent sovereign state, its members would be unable to command the respect of others and would lack dignity and self-respect. Mazzini's writings reflected a highly developed political liberalism that saw no contradiction between nationalism and universalism or between a collective identity and a radical individualism. Indeed, he saw nations newly liberated from domestic and external tyranny as serving both mankind and their individual citizens. For him, national liberation meant service to all humanity and the self-realization (*hagshama atzmit*) of the individual.

Not one Zionist trend would have disagreed with this view. One of the more famous Zionist tracts, *Rome and Jerusalem*, was written by Moses Hess (an early follower of Marx) as a consequence of the events that led to the unification of Italy in 1859. One of Jabotinsky's heroes was Garibaldi.

It is this original vision of Zionism as being a natural child of future-oriented nineteenth-century liberal nationalism that we Jews should reembrace, rehabilitate, and show to the world rather than religious zealotry on remote hilltops.

EXPLOITING ISRAEL'S OPPORTUNITIES

Israel must fully embrace globalization and use it as a lever to achieve political, economic, and social goals. This requires the cultivation and development of a culture of globalization that begins in our educational system. It means a rejection of the "Nation that Dwells Alone" syndrome and a realization that the success of the Jewish People and Israel depends on the degree to which we can integrate into the new global system. In a deeper sense, it means a thorough reevaluation of classical Zionism, which by stressing the historical necessity of the nation-state cultivated an almost conscious provinciality. Israel as a city-state, a cosmopolitan, technological, and international services node within the global network, must replace the concept of Israel as the nation-state.

Those who question the vision of Israel betting its future on high-tech, financial services, and higher education rightly say that even in the United States only 2–3 percent of the population are employed in high tech and that the rest still work in the old economy. As we have said, Israel should not compare itself to other countries, it should compare itself to other *cities* such as San Francisco or Boston, the greater metropolitan areas of which have the same population as Israel. Both these cities have a much higher proportion of people employed in high-tech, financial services, and higher education than the national average. The other major employer is tourism, the biggest employer of human resources worldwide, which provides numerous opportunities for making an honorable living for those citizens not predisposed to high tech or higher education. Neither city depends on old-economy industry or agriculture.

Boston and San Francisco are city-states serving the global market. They are the proper models for Israel to emulate if it wishes to exploit the unique abilities and temperament of the Jewish People and to create an environment in which twenty-first-century Jews will believe that they are actualizing their human potentialities. Such a model would have meaning for the non-Orthodox, university-trained Jew. It would provide the compelling human added value that the Jewish People require.

By 2050, China will be the largest economy in the world and India will be the second largest. Israel should develop a long-term strategy for building ties with these countries. Additionally, Israel must systematize its contacts with the former Soviet bloc.

We should also be sensitive to the fact that when sub-Saharan Africa finally joins the global order it will become to the first half of the twenty-first century what Southeast Asia was to the second half of the twentieth. Israel is geographically and culturally situated to take advantage of such a positive development. In other words, Israel must move toward a more general global orientation *in addition* to its traditional Euro/American orientation.

NEUTRALIZING THREATS TO ISRAEL

Hostile Islam

Hostile Islamic activity might be neutralized in a variety of ways. First, we might establish direct organizational and individual contact with the more moderate Moslem communities, groups, and individuals in America and Europe. We must avoid painting Islam with one brush. It is as pluralistic as Christianity and Judaism, and with a creative lack of prejudice, Diaspora Jews could actively seek out and engage willing Moslem groups and individuals in civilized discourse.

This initiative must not be tinged with pollyannaish wishful thinking. It could be that certain segments of current Moslem civilization are analogous to German civilization during the Hitler period and that most present-day Moslems are racist fanatics. If this be the case, we are still obliged to reach out to the moderate minority just as progressive Westerners did during the dark days of World War II with the likes of Willy Brandt, Thomas Mann, and Marlene Dietrich.

THE SPECIAL CASE OF GLOBAL GOVERNANCE

The finest legal and judicial minds of the Jewish *and* non-Jewish world must engage in a systematic project to create a constitutional basis for global governance. World Jewry must be at the forefront of creating a constitutional foundation for the legal system of global governance. One historical example will suffice to demonstrate the need for such a Jewish initiative. The United Nations charter guarantees every nation the right of self-determination. This is presented as a fundamental unalienable right of all nations—presumably including the Jews. Yet, United Nations Resolution 194 declares the right of every Palestinian refugee to return to his/her home. This by definition negates the unalienable right of the Jews to self-determination because it would mean the end of the State of Israel, the entity by which the Jews exercise their unalienable right of self-determination. Resolution 194 is in contravention of the unalienable rights of nations, to wit: life, liberty, and a land of their own. The lack of Resolution 194 would not, on the other hand, negate the Palestinians' unalienable rights, which could be exercised in the territories in which the Palestinians are now a majority and soon to be a state.

Yet, no international judicial body has the power to declare 194 unconstitutional. Moreover, there is little hope of an international judicial body dedicated to the constitutional monitoring of international governance without a concentrated intent to establish one. Israel and world Jewry will, therefore, be at a constant disadvantage in any dispute until a constitutional foundation for the legal system of global governance is established.

We must use international academic, intellectual, and judicial frameworks and instruments to wage an unceasing battle against majoritarian world governance. At the same time, we must promote a "bill" of unalienable rights of nations, which no United Nations decision or any other international body could abrogate.

SOCIAL POLICY

In order to ameliorate the problem of our social gap, Israel must become a pioneer in the development of a new welfare policy and program. I will call it a nonaltruistic welfare policy, one dedicated to turning non-taxpaying citizens into taxpayers. It would reject the potpourri of humanistic slogans and poorly thought out programs not held accountable to clearly defined goals. It would also reject the paternalistic and autocratic welfare industry that has grown up around the welfare state. The present welfare system not only fails to help the weaker members of our society, it degrades them, often turning them into obsequious manipulators of the system rather than independent and proud citizens of the commonwealth.

The radical disconnect between the stated aims of these policies and programs and their consequences are apparent for all to see. How does one explain the paradox that Israel's social welfare budgets have risen 50 percent in real terms in the past fifteen years at the same time that the absolute and relative numbers of people living below the poverty line has increased and the social gap has widened?

It can only be explained by critically analyzing the fundamental philosophical assumptions of Western and Israeli welfare policies. The altruistic welfare policies of the Western world have failed. They are in effect a "poverty industry" whose only real beneficiaries are the welfare workers, academics, and politicians.

A nonaltruistic welfare project might serve as an example for the world, an example of Israel doing good by doing well, a concrete manifestation of the ambition for Israel to become a light unto the Gentiles. To advance this project we require an ideological critique of the inverted pyramid thesis that has so distorted social thinking in Israel. The aim must be to turn Israel into a completely bourgeois society and to jettison the proletarian myths that have played such a large role in creating Israel's social gap, as described in the previous chapter.

We require a radical reform of our education and welfare budgets in order to extract extra resources out of existing budgets. We require a radical reform of the entire educational paradigm. This would include such innovations as employing noncertified teachers; subcontracting teaching services to private providers in subjects such as math, languages, and computers; and periodic proficiency examinations to check student progress. The system in general requires greater flexibility. We might explore the possibility of enrolling the high tech sector into the educational programs, making high school diplomas equivalent to technician certification in a variety of areas.

The new economy, rather than the enemy of the social gap, is the *only* means by which we might leverage ourselves out of the social gap. Rather than figuring how to help the human leftovers of the old economy by pouring new-economy tax monies into the same inefficient, counterproductive, and dysfunctional welfare system, we should be thinking of ways to use the new economy itself *as a lever* to raise these people up to a twenty-first century standard of human dignity. The first approach benefits professional populists and demagogues as well as the welfare establishment that makes its living off the despair of those left behind. The second approach is *inherently* (not ideologically) dedicated to returning human dignity to the "leftovers."

This entire concept requires a new Zionist *social* ideology dedicated not to the creation of a workers' republic (Ben Gurion's dream in the pre-state era) but to the creation of a neoaristocratic republic. Such a republic's entire citizenry will be highly educated and will be making their livings in the most sophisticated production and services sectors. The conscious effort to formulate a new social ideology is a necessity in the Israeli reality. For no matter how much Israelis denigrate their old ideologies and ideologues they are still greatly influenced by outmoded social slogans. For the past several decades, third-rate politicians and second-rate academics, manipulating outmoded slogans to gain political, economic, and professional advantage, have dominated Israel's social discourse, as they have in the rest of the Western world.

The only democratic and enlightened way to offset the demographic consequences of combined Arab and Haredi birthrates is to institute massive affirmative action educational programs specifically targeted to Arab and Haredi women. Few women with high school educations have 10 to 15 children. Few women with college degrees have 5 to 10 children.

Diaspora Jewry might consider the possibility of dedicating part of its contribution to educational projects for Arab women and girls. This indirect approach would achieve two things: a Zionist aim of evening out Arab and Jewish birthrates while at the same time disarming the charge that Zionism is racism.

PEACE AND SECURITY POLICY

Israel must resurrect its traditional policy of limited aims and indirect-approach strategy. All-out war as an aim negates statesmanship and intelligent strategy. Strategy aims to win the war, Grand Strategy aims to win the peace, or, in the case of the Middle East, at least peace and quiet. By aiming to win our wars, we may so enervate ourselves, so overdraw on our political, economic, social, and moral capital that in the winning we will in the long run lose. On the other hand, by pursuing a finalistic peace we might inadvertently inspire war.

The second *Intifada* is a case in point. What grand strategic result should Israel have wanted subsequent to the second *Intifada*? The finalistic right-wing answer would be total military victory; the finalistic left-wing answer would be a return to negotiations toward a comprehensive peace agreement. A third, limited-aims answer might have made the consequences of the second *Intifada* so costly that they would effectively eliminate the option of *Intifadas* as a future Palestinian policy instrument. This might coincide with a policy of unilateral disengagement. Israel should also strive to make Syrian and Lebanese enmity toward Israel as unattractive as possible by a combination of means.

A strategy of limited aims and indirect approach dictates that Israel's tactics should be as discreet as possible. Israel should make every effort to avoid photogenic responses to terror attacks. Low-key operations against the economic interests of corrupt Palestinian and Syrian officials would be more effective. Photogenic F-16 and helicopter gunship rocket attacks *immediately* after a terrorist atrocity draw media attention away from the original terror attack and draw instead condemnation of Israel. To the extent that innocent civilians are also killed, we, by our own hands, destroy the moral high ground we are trying to occupy with regard to terror. Discreet operations enable plausible deniability, are not photogenic, and therefore are not media attractive. They also could highlight the corruption of the Arab regimes without distracting from the original terror attack.

Israel has two noncontradictory options. First, a unilateral withdrawal to defensible borders and the creation of an Iron Wall defense against an Arab world that still appears determined to destroy Israel as a Jewish State, albeit by more sophisticated means than in the past. The aim of this approach would be to achieve a long-term de facto arrangement during which a Palestinian state would arise and we would unilaterally withdraw from militarily worthless parts of the West Bank. This would mean rejecting a millenarian foreign policy and replacing it with a more realistic, Realpolitik foreign policy of limited aims.

Such a policy would reflect George Kennan's advice to Harry Truman regarding American policy toward the Soviet Union following World War II. To paraphrase within the context of the Middle East: long term, patient but firm and vigilant containment and neutralization of Arab and Islamic military, political, and economic hostility until which time the Arab world finally accepts Israel. We might also add, long term, consistent, disciplined, and prudent Jewish opposition to Arab military, political, and economic interests until the Arab world finally accepts Israel. Such a policy would realize that Arab acceptance of Israel will be achieved in phases.

The peace agreement with Egypt may have neutralized Egypt's military hostility, but it left room for ongoing Egyptian political and economic hostility. Certain aspects of Egypt's political and economic hostility have become gradually blunted as a consequence of Egypt's own political and economic interests. These include, amongst others, the Egyptian establishment's fear of Moslem fundamentalism and political instability in the region. Egypt's need for good relations with the United States, for tourism as well as the potential sale of Egyptian natural gas to Israel encourage moderation.

If the primary goal of real peace (not peace agreements) appears unachievable at present, our primary grand strategic aim should be to achieve a controlled, manageable nonviolent cold war with as many Arab countries and entities as possible. Conflict management would have to replace conflict resolution as the focus of our energies.

Secondly, in the long run, a properly thought out peace arrangement would be the ultimate antidote to Israel's security problems. If and when a peace agreement seems possible, Israel should make part of the territorial price it pays dependent on becoming a member of NATO and a member of the European Union. It cannot be stressed enough that Israel must strive to become a member of at least one international alliance or bloc. Such an achievement would be a more significant contribution to Israel's long-term security than a few kilometers of occupied territory. The special relationship with the United States is not a substitute for becoming a member of a bloc. Indeed, the special relationship can only be sustained over time if Israel succeeds in ending its international isolation.

We must realize that America's patience as the lonely defender of Israel is not infinite. We must also realize that America's external geopolitical interests are in great flux and that the internal egoistic interests of American politicians are also in great flux. These shifting interests might one day coincide in a way gravely dangerous to world Jewry and Israel, unless world Jewry and Israel create a more imaginative Jewish policy. The next chapter discusses some possibilities for such a policy.

CHAPTER 7

Reinventing Israel-Diaspora Relations

A Jewish Grand Strategy must revolve around a revitalized Israel-Diaspora relationship. The driving force behind this new relationship should be the Diaspora and not Israel. The Diaspora should take a larger responsibility for addressing the grand strategic challenges of Jewish survival. This approach would replace the present character of Israel-Diaspora relations in which Diaspora efforts and resources are directed to the social problems of Israel as a supplemental force in education, welfare, and immigrant absorption.

Israel is so preoccupied with the daily physical struggle for survival that it lacks the spare intellectual and spiritual energy to deal with long-term fundamental survival questions of a pan-Jewish and not just Israeli character. Israel lacks even the time or energy to deal with its own quality of life problems.

This division of labor between Israel and the Diaspora will be the fundamental subject of this chapter, with the stress being placed on the role of the Diaspora. We use the terms *Diaspora* and *American Jewry* interchangeably throughout because American Jewry constitutes 80 percent of the Diaspora and will often be the particular Diaspora performer in our discussions. We do not, however, discount the potentially productive role that European Jewry and other small Jewish communities could also play.

The slow deterioration of Israel-Diaspora relations over the past several decades is a perfect example of the loss of grand strategic focus that derives from perpetuating a previously successful arrangement well past its time. Inertia is not constructive in the fight for survival. A new relationship must be as concerned with Diaspora interests as those of Israel. We cannot ignore how Israel's problems affect Diaspora Jewry. The second *Intifada* had both psychological and security repercussions for many Diaspora communities and triggered a new wave of anti-Semitism in Europe.

Israel-Diaspora relations are not in crisis—it might be less dangerous if they were. They are in a state of fatigue, of boredom. A true crisis, by its very nature, would compel us to a reenergized engagement around clearly defined issues with the clear goal of developing coherent solutions. The present enervating fatigue and boredom is the natural outcome of the objective and subjective evolution of the relationship.

TOWARD A NEW PARADIGM

The dominant Jewish paradigm since the creation of the State of Israel has been a highly efficient Diaspora fundraising apparatus transferring money to Israeli institutions dominated by Israel's political society. The sums have been diminishing in real terms in relation to Israel's GDP and their relative impact on Israeli society. This is a positive indication of Israel becoming a mature, developed economy, and society. This would not have occurred without the Diaspora financial contribution, but as we have already pointed out, the success of a particular framework in ameliorating a problem changes the very nature of the problem. Thus, the framework becomes increasingly anachronistic, and even dysfunctional, and eventually part of the problem instead of the solution.

This traditional financial relationship has had little if any effect on most of Israel's citizens for the past several decades. Many informed Israelis would even claim that the contribution relationship has become dysfunctional to the healthy development of Israeli society. It constitutes, they assert, an indirect subsidy to the monopoly power of Israel's political society to the detriment of the development of Israel's civil society.

This calls for a new paradigm wherein these relatively small sums go directly to Israel's civil society with the aim of improving Israel's quality of life. Achieving greater leverage would increase the efficiency of Diaspora contributions.

The traditional Israel-Diaspora relationship was a tremendous historical success, but success breeds satisfaction with the forms, structures, values, and subcultures that made it possible. Self-satisfaction is a certain recipe for failure, as demonstrated by Israel's triumphant success in the Six-Day War, which led to a self-satisfied arrogance throughout the entire Jewish World and resulted in a lack of preparedness for the Yom Kippur War.

The economic histories of IBM, the Swiss watch industry, and the American automobile industry have demonstrated the universal dangers of self-satisfaction. Long considered paragons of success, they almost collapsed during the 1980s because of their inability to adapt to the rapidly changing environment that they themselves had created. The phrase "reinventing the corporation" was coined in order to highlight a new organizational cultural value: the ability to change, adapt, and innovate in real time. Speed, flexibility, and initiative have replaced order, consistency, and loyalty as the cultural primaries of the modern organization. The old saying, "if it ain't broke don't fix it," is no longer germane. The new slogan is "if it works well make it work better—before it stops working well." Waiting until something stops working well may be too late. It certainly will make reform and reinvention more difficult. Both Israel and Diaspora organizations must internalize these new principles.

The story of Japan might be a good analogy to Jewish organizational life and Israel-Diaspora relations. The ongoing crisis of Japan in the 1990s and into the twenty-first century traces directly to the extraordinarily successful Japanese methods during the four decades following World War II. These methods generated one of the great economic success stories in history, but they became anachronistic in the new era of global communications and Internet. Inability to shed the extraordinarily successful methods of the past constitutes the very foundation of Japan's present crisis.

I suggest that the classic Israel-Diaspora relationship resembles Japan's story in terms of its early fantastic success and its current inadequacies. The organizations and institutions that constituted this relationship made the creation of the Jewish State possible and sustained and nourished it in its first several decades. An unintended, but no less important consequence was the creation of the most organized, dynamic, and self-confident Jewish community in Diaspora history. Diaspora Jewry, especially American Jewry, has benefited no less and perhaps even more than Israel from the traditional institutional relationship that developed.

FROM POLITICAL SOCIETY TO CIVIL SOCIETY: THE NEW RELATIONSHIP

Heretofore, the Diaspora has related to Israel primarily by way of Israel's political society, either directly with the Israeli government or indirectly by way of Israel's political representatives in the Jewish Agency. The various levels of Israel's political society have mostly mediated person-to-person and community-to-community projects such as Project Renewal. The Diaspora's principal relationship has been with Israel's political society and only secondarily with Israel's civil society. Reversing this order would create a more balanced and symmetrical relationship, as organized Diaspora Jewry is by definition a civil society.

The Diaspora originally interacted almost exclusively with Israel's political society because Israel had no real civil society during its first decades. Today, however, Israel possesses a rich variety of volunteer, self-help, and citizen organizations that offer numerous opportunities for a wider, deeper, and richer Israel-Diaspora relationship.

Ironically, Diaspora Jewry can take some credit for the development of this civil society. Project Renewal, the New Israel Fund, and increased Federation emphasis on involving contributors in specific projects rather than dunning them for a generic contribution are some Diaspora initiatives that have helped nourish this civil society and have laid groundwork for the new relationship suggested here.

The goal should be to deepen Diaspora contact with the rich tapestry of Israel's civil society, which has reached a level of maturity whereby it can engage Diaspora Jewry's civil society as equals without the mediation of Israel's rather tired and drab political establishment.

World Jewry *needs* to do this. Israel is still world Jewry's window to the world and thus world Jewry's reflection of itself. As Edward Alexander wrote in the *Congress Monthly*: "American Jewry, like French or Brazilian Jewry, is held together today not by study of Torah, not by synagogue attendance, not by Jewish Studies programs, but ... by its devotion to ... the state of Israel. To millions of American Jews, Israel provides, precisely as Zionism claimed a Jewish state would, a center of national feeling; a model of courage, resilience, and faith; a lodging for the organized memory of Jewish national consciousness" (September/October, 1987).

In other words, Israel is the concrete instrument by which all Jews interrelate with world civilization and the showcase through which the Gentiles perceive the Jews. Most Jews take pride in Israel's achievements in desert reclamation; its military exploits (such as the Entebbe operation) and the fact that other small, successful countries and aspiring undeveloped countries often see Israel as a model to emulate. Even serious Palestinian intellectuals (off the record, of course) will tell you they see Israel as a model for their embryonic Palestinian State.

Conversely, most Jews feel shame and dismay at Israel's foibles and mistakes. If Israel is the showcase that world Jewry shows the world and her actions affect world Jewry, it becomes a moral obligation and an absolute right for world Jewry to interfere with Israel.

FROM TOTALITARIAN TO LIBERAL DEMOCRACY

Diaspora Jewry does not require the approval of Israel's political society in order to cooperate with Israel's civil society in radical reform projects that will directly and indirectly affect all of world Jewry. American Jewry, especially, has the right and the *obligation* to assist Israel's march from majoritarian to constitutional (liberal) democracy because such a development is necessary for its own long-term communal survival.

Totalitarian Democracy is a phrase coined by Israeli scholar Professor Yaakov Talmon in his classic book of the same name. A common synonym is majoritarian democracy. It refers to democracy rooted in the French Revolution, a democracy that celebrates "the will of the people" and its concrete expression as manifested in the leaders of the people. It often condemns as undemocratic those who do not acknowledge the monopoly of the general will of the people and the majority regarding legitimacy of political activity, and who do not relate to that will exclusively by way of its democratically elected representatives.

Liberal democracy on the other hand, is rooted in the English and American Revolutions and recognizes the debilitating influence of conformist majorities and its negative influence on elected representatives. Liberal democracy limits the power of both majorities and democratically elected representatives by granting individuals and minorities unalienable rights to freely pursue their aims as long as these aims do not harm another's property or person. America's political culture might be weak in comparison to other countries, but its civic culture is superior because of this worldview. In simple terms, this approach *sanctions and celebrates* the unlimited freedom of association and action completely independent of any political establishment—democratically elected though it might be.

Israeli politicians, influenced more by the Continental rather than the Anglo-Saxon model, have often used the majoritarian argument to intimidate Diaspora Jews. This attitude has inhibited Diaspora civil initiatives and the development of many potential projects and relationships. Diaspora Jews, overly impressed by the self-confident surety of Israeli politicians, and unschooled in the philosophical principles that underlie modern democratic societies, were made to feel guilty about "going behind the backs" of Israel's democratically elected officials. They were reminded repeatedly that Israel is a sovereign democratic state and not a colony of the Diaspora and that they would do well to pay proper respect to its institutions and its leaders.

Diaspora leaders were not knowledgeable enough to respond that Israel is a democracy composed of free men and women, and therefore Diaspora Jews, as free men and women, have an unalienable right to associate, interrelate, and act with any segment of Israel's population without obtaining permission from political operatives.

This situation must end. It is by way of Israel's civil society that the Diaspora civil society can make its most important contributions to Israel and consequently to itself. Politicians will be involved only when the two civil societies decide they are necessary. Neither liberal democratic civil society should acknowledge the right of politicians to censor their activities.

FROM THE FINANCIAL TO THE HUMAN RESOURCES CONTRIBUTION

That Diaspora financial contributions to Israel characterized Israel-Diaspora relations was a necessary phase of the relationship, and in the pre-state era and early years of statehood such contributions produced astounding results. This approach, however, has now run its course.

Not only is the Diaspora financial contribution of declining importance to Israel's economy and dysfunctional to the development of Israel's civil society, it has also become dysfunctional to Diaspora life—concentrating on the wealthy few to the detriment of the community at large. Many Diaspora Jews feel neglected by Jewish organizations and alienated from organized Jewish life because they do not have large sums to give and are thus marginalized or even ignored. Diaspora Jewish life has become a plutocracy that may threaten the survival of Diaspora communal life.

The emphasis should now change from monetary contributions to Israel's political society to human skills contributions to Israel's civil society. This would be of greater benefit to Israel and would also enable Diaspora organizations to widen the base of Jewish activity. It would attract individuals and groups alienated from Jewish communal life. A chronic weakness of Diaspora Jewish life since the State of Israel began has been a dearth of activities that interested significant kinds and numbers of Jewish professionals and academics and could best use their skills in meaningful communal involvement.

The basic operating principle of this new approach should be to strive to leverage declining Diaspora Jewish power into ever-increasing Jewish power. We can do that in two ways:

Create coalitions around issues and projects that bear directly on long-term all-Jewish security, have a wider general non-Jewish appeal, and can engage large groups of heretofore unaffiliated Jews in projects of benefit to the Jewish People. We will call these *National-Universal Projects.*

Develop coalitions with Israelis around issues and projects that bear directly on the health and efficiency of Israel's economy and society and can involve large groups of heretofore inactive Jews in projects that benefit Israel and the Jewish People. We will call these *National Projects.*

Let us envisage some possible projects and how they might benefit both Israel and the Diaspora.

THE JEWISH ENERGY PROJECT (A NATIONAL-UNIVERSAL PROJECT)

Energy is a Jewish issue. The greatest threats to the Jewish People are Iran's nonconventional weapons development and growing hostile Moslem populations in Europe and North America. Underlying these threats are Persian Gulf oil revenues. This dictates that the Jews formulate a coherent Jewish energy policy aimed at creating political alliances and economic instruments dedicated to slowing, eventually stalling, and ultimately *reversing* the growth of petroleum use worldwide.

Worldwide consumption of crude oil is projected to grow by 40 percent by the year 2020 if the consumption growth rate of the past several decades is sustained. Most of this supply increase will come from Persian Gulf countries, which have the largest proven reserves and those cheaper to develop than known and potential reserves elsewhere. Even if the real price of oil does not increase or even declines slightly, these militant anti-Jewish countries will benefit from a stupendous increase in financial and hence political and military power. As a consequence, we may expect increasing support for terrorist organizations, anti-Semitic propaganda, and a heightened rate of development of nonconventional weapons of mass destruction.

A Jewish energy policy would present Diaspora Jews with numerous opportunities to develop alliances with assorted pressure groups and economic entities thus widening the peripheries of Jewish power. It would also give organized Jewish communities an excellent opportunity to open up lines of communication with heretofore unaffiliated and alienated Jews, enlisting them in activities of benefit to the Jewish People. Following is an incomplete list of allies American Jewry might recruit around a project dedicated to making North America energy independent within the next 10 to 15 years:

Environmentalists. The American Jewish lobby could join forces with elements of the environmental lobby to push for alternative energy and conservation measures on federal, state, county, and local levels. Such an alliance would be attractive to large groups of environmentally sensitive young Jews who are at present alienated from any kind of Jewish activity or identification. If we packaged this activity in traditional Jewish concepts such as *tikkun olam*, we might also even interest them in their own tradition.

Family Farmers. Farm the wind, not wheat. Even with billions of dollars in subsidies, family farms in the American grain belt are on the verge of bankruptcy. Grain belt states alone have enough wind power to supply all of America's electricity needs. The Jewish lobby could be a catalyst for the creation of a coalition of family farmers, environmentalists, and Jewish communities to promote a policy wherein the *one-time* federal subsidy to build windmills, capable of providing a steady income for family farmers, would replace the *ongoing* subsidy of unprofitable grain. This would make both environmental and economic sense. It would also help nurture the development of allies in non-Jewish Middle America.

Retrofit America. The aim of this program would be to reduce per capita household consumption of energy to the levels of Sweden or Germany. It would mean lobbying for tax write-offs for energy-saving home improvements and appliances. Allies would be industry and home improvement giants such as General Electric, Hewlett Packard, Westinghouse, Home Center, Home Depot, and many more. These industries could mobilize a lobby of millions of voters directly or indirectly employed by them.

Small Oil Producers. The United States contains hundreds of thousands of capped low-production wells that can only be profitable if the price of oil hovers around at least twenty dollars a barrel. These wells are for the most part owned by middle-class families, small businessmen, and farmers. Uncapping these wells costs thousands of dollars and would only be worthwhile with long-term price guarantees. The Jewish lobby could join forces with these small producers to lobby for a federal price support system that would guarantee the real price oil, much like the grain price support. Such a program would begin to release hundreds of thousands of barrels per day in the short term and up to 1 million barrels a day over the next several years. In comparison, the much more environmentally sensitive Alaskan Natural Wildlife Reserve (ANWR) would produce 600,000 barrels a day *at its peak* and would take at least 10 years before it pumped its first barrel. Once again, the Jews would be cultivating valuable allies in Middle America and in the environmental community.

Organized Labor. The above policy would produce hundreds of thousands of well-paying industrial and sophisticated service jobs over a long period of time, and thus we could enlist organized labor in support. This could be a major factor in reestablishing organized Jewry's traditional alliance with organized labor.

Veterans and National Security Organizations. Energy is the preeminent grand strategic resource of the industrial world. Yet, for more than 30 percent of its energy needs and 50 percent of its petroleum needs, the industrial world depends on unstable countries such as Saudi Arabia, Kuwait, Venezuela, and Nigeria, or hostile countries such as Iran and Libya. This security lapse should be causing a great deal of concern amongst veterans and national security organizations. The Jewish community might, therefore, have a good chance of enlisting these essentially conservative organizations in support of the above energy policy. It should be remembered that the interstate highway system, the Internet, and even the Emancipation Proclamation were implemented under the security rubric and that the security rubric is always an easier political sell than any other. Richard Nixon had an almost perfect record on civil rights legislation, not because he believed in brotherhood and justice but because the issue was tremendously damaging to America's image at the height of the cold war.

Educators. One might envision a Twin Towers energy project promoted throughout the school districts of the United States. Uniting the social studies and science departments, it would encourage school children to surf the Internet and engage in other research to find low-cost energy conservation measures that *they* could install in their schools and at home. An entire system of Twin Tower clubs could be established and could piggyback on existing youth programs such as Boy Scouts, Girl Scouts, and 4H. Children are by nature idealistic, and the combination of patriotism and environmentalism could galvanize them and create an irresistible grassroots movement. Such a project would enable Jewish teachers, a large and neglected segment of the community, to finally assume their rightful position in the Jewish community.

The two million Jews of Europe, including Russian Jewry, could promote their own version of a European energy independence project. This policy might include components such as preferential tax treatment for natural gas over petroleum; banning all single-hulled tankers from European ports; preferential license treatment for hybrid, fuel cell, or natural gas automobiles; tax penalties for conventional internal combustion cars, and subsidies for underground coal gasification. Their allies might include the following groups:

European Environmentalists and Green Parties

European tourist and fishing industries, especially those segments gravely damaged by catastrophic oil spills as well as accumulated oil pollution.

Old Economy areas with large coal deposits. These would include England, Germany, and many Eastern European countries, such as Poland and the Ukraine. Coal liquefaction and gasification projects in these areas would combine energy, environmental, economic, and social goals.

Organized labor. As is the case in North America, the above policies would create and sustain well-paid union jobs.

Russia. Russia's *known* natural gas reserves are greater than the oil reserves of Saudi Arabia (40 percent of the known natural gas reserves in the world), and it is her ambition to become the chief energy supplier to Europe and Japan. The fulfillment of this ambition should also be a Jewish interest, as it would replace Persian Gulf oil on the European and Japanese markets. Natural gas supplied by pipelines is environmentally friendlier than oil supplied by tankers. If the Jewish community directly allies itself with Russian oil and gas interests, we might influence the Russians to lessen their technological support for Iranian nonconventional weapons programs. We might persuade them that an alliance dedicated to help Russia replace Saudi Arabia as the largest energy exporter in the world would be more to their interests than an alliance with the ayatollahs.

The above might also help regenerate good will in Europe for issues of Jewish concern, including Israel. The South African, Australian, and some Latin American communities could pursue similar smaller scale initiatives. Clearly, Diaspora Jewry could leverage its limited power by building coalitions around projects of universal interest that have direct benefit for the Jewish People and that could attract new groups of young Jews into active Jewish life.

REINVENTING ISRAEL'S PUBLIC SERVICES: A NATIONAL PROJECT

Israel can potentially become the most efficient country in the world, a country with the most rational public services possible, a country Swiss, Swedes, and Singaporians visit for ideas about improving their public services. This project would exploit Diaspora Jewry's substantial human resources in management, organization, and legal advocacy in order to improve public administration and services in Israel.

It would run as an organizational consulting firm. Its aim would be to join forces with Israeli civic groups demanding Western levels of return for their tax monies. Israeli citizens are weary of the waste, inefficiency, and corruption of their public institutions and would appreciate skilled allies in their campaign for greater accountability. Anecdotal evidence in newspaper reports and the annual state comptroller report indicate that such a project would probably harvest out of the system hundreds of millions if not billions of dollars a year of unnecessary expense. We are speaking about a scale of savings much greater than the present annual financial contribution of the Diaspora to Israel. An added bonus would be the upgrading of Israeli citizenship and civil society, as well as a broader base of Israel-Diaspora interaction.

Theoretically, Israel has the private management and organizational skills to do this on its own, but Israel's managerial and organizational classes are too dependent on Israel's political society for their livelihood to risk provoking it. Also too few Israeli professionals have the financial wherewithal to contribute their skills pro bono. Israel's political society plays lip service to Israel's growing civil society but fears and resents it. Israel's evolving civil society has been gradually eroding political society's monopoly on power. Despite its supportive rhetoric, political society is fighting a rear guard action to slow this trend.

Israel's political establishment would most likely attack such an initiative as interference in Israel's internal affairs. We have dismissed their right to do this, but we must be aware that while this is no longer an ideological problem it remains a tactical problem. Because of this, any Diaspora involvement must be requested by local Israeli citizen groups. This tactical consideration would dictate where best the skill contribution could be made.

The first stages of the human resource contribution will probably *not* be made in those segments of society that need it the most, but those that have highly developed civic organizations and an articulate citizenry sophisticated enough to realize the benefits of such a relationship. The strategy would be to establish a beachhead amongst the strongest segments of society and work outward. The aim would be to build success until needier, less-organized parts of the society could approach the Israeli civic groups and request assistance.

Let us envisage the stages by which we might implement such a program. It would be most logical to begin with local councils and small towns with substantial numbers of residents from English-speaking countries. These are people with similar standards and expectations regarding public administration, with whom American Jews would most readily interact. They could form the core of the civil population that turns to the Diaspora organization for assistance. This core would enlist the support of national organizations such as the English-Speaking Residents' Association (ESRA).

Organizations such as these might eventually supplant the Jewish Agency/ WZO as the major conduit of Diaspora skill contributions. They could also enlist other Western immigrants as well as veteran Israelis who desire Western standards of governance. This organizational stage could be financed by the Diaspora organization, if necessary.

From this beginning, activities would expand into local councils and small towns without substantial English-speaking populations, and finally to larger cities such as Beersheba, Haifa, Ramat Gan, Petah Tikvah, followed by major cities such as Jerusalem and Tel Aviv.

Alternatively, the project might concentrate on public institutions, such as universities, and make continued flow of Diaspora contributions conditional on a stringent organizational review and subsequent reorganization. Proper management of these organizations would save more money than presently contributed. The various Diaspora "Friends" of Israeli institutions should be dissuaded from continuing financial contributions that often allow these institutions to ignore the need for organizational reform by papering over their inefficiencies with Diaspora money. Continued contributions must be conditional on reform. In their sincere desire to assist Israel, Diaspora Jews have unwittingly provided a security blanket for many of the inefficiencies in Israeli society in the civil service and in nongovernmental organizations.

These initiatives would not be an offense against Israel's sovereign democracy but a qualitative contribution to it. As institutions become more efficient, they become more transparent and more accessible to citizen supervision and critique. Seeing that they can create change encourages citizens to be more active and makes them better citizens. The slogan of this campaign might be, "Help Israel Save a Billion Dollars a Year in Operating Expenses."

ISRAEL DEMOCRACY PROJECT: ANOTHER NATIONAL PROJECT

This project would be an adjunct to the management consultant project outlined above. Israel is a political democracy in name but with an authoritarian civil service in practice. The standing joke amongst English-speaking Israelis is that it is neither civil nor does it give service. The average citizen pays a tremendous price in energy and maddening frustration trying to combat the petty injustices of a Kafka-esque bureaucracy. The management consultant project would correct much of this, but it remains serious enough to warrant a special initiative.

This project would exploit the substantial legal advocacy resources of Diaspora Jewry in order to transform Israel's civil service into one determined to serve its citizens. This project would support Israeli citizen's advocacy organizations, and itself function as a citizen's advocacy organization, with a budget and legal staff that would respond in real time to the petty injustices and arbitrary behavior of Israel's bureaucracy. The effect on the morale of the country would be tremendous.

Diaspora Jewry should also join with enlightened Israelis to actively promote real equality before the law, which is in practice constantly violated by the arbitrary behavior of the Israeli bureaucracy. Advancing women's rights and the right of habeas corpus would also attract many Diaspora Jews.

Diaspora Jewry must also participate in Israel's constitutional debate, using affirmative action principles to justify certain statutory favoritisms such as the law of return. American Jews, especially, can bridge the false dichotomy between being a Jewish State and being a democratic state by actively exploiting the Jewish roots of much of the American concepts of constitutional democracy.

Most important, however, this project would deal with the question of constitutional global governance. No other political entity in the world has been such a victim of arbitrary concepts of justice and outrageously exaggerated comparisons as has Israel. This part of the project, like the energy project, would be a national-universal project. Its primary task would be to help neutralize a threat to Israel's survival, but its consequences would be of essential benefit to the entire world. It would throw the moral pretensions of organizations based upon majoritarian democracy into serious question. It would entail a massive critique of international law and precedent from a standpoint of foundational first principles and would strive to establish a basis for a *planetary constitutional democracy.*

However, this project must be conducted without prejudicing the legitimate right to criticize Israel's civil rights record, which would be shooting ourselves in the foot. To be a strong and robust country in the twenty-first century, we must radically upgrade Israel's civil and human rights standards in many areas. This requires an atmosphere of radical criticism.

THE SPECIAL ROLE OF THE ISRAELI DIASPORA

The Israeli Diaspora, which by now comprises 15–20 percent of North American Jewry as well as several other Diaspora communities, must assume a special role in redefining Israel-Diaspora relations. Expatriate Israelis understand better than other Diaspora groups the needs and weaknesses of Israel. They are therefore less likely to be impressed and intimidated by possible protestations from Israel's political society.

Heretofore, the Israeli Diaspora has been the stepchild of Jewish life, often condemned and boycotted by "official" Israel and looked upon askance by Diaspora Jews. In the eyes of official Israel, they were *yordim*—people who descended from Israel, in contradistinction to *olim*—people who ascended to Israel. Emigration from and immigration to Israel is not just the sociogeographical phenomenon it is with other nations; traditionally, it has had explosive moral implications. For official political Israel, *yordim* were often pictured as traitors or as weaklings. This was not the case, of course, for civil Israel, whose sons and daughters they were.

The attitude of native Diaspora Jewish communities toward these Israelis has been ambivalent at best:

The fact that they had left Israel, often for good reasons, complicated communal and fundraising activities and confused Diaspora emotions. Israel is more idealized by Diaspora Jews than by Israelis. The very existence of Israelis who left Israel challenged strongly held conceptions.

The fact that they were Israeli in every way—that is, rough like the Israelis in Israel—annoyed Diaspora Jews no less than the Israelis in Israel annoyed them.

The *yordim* often did not participate in Jewish communal and institutional life. They often kept their distance and did not trouble to hide their condescension. For many Israelis, Diaspora Jewish life is but a pale shadow compared to their Israeli experience. They did not camouflage this attitude and earned the resentment of many Diaspora Jews.

Official Israel actively dissuaded the Diaspora communities from enlisting them. When they were enlisted, it was for practical reasons.

This approach to the Israeli Diaspora must undergo a radical transformation. In the future, the Israeli Diaspora must become the militant bridge between Israel's civil society and the Diaspora civil society. They must become the unapologetic militant ally of reformist forces in Israel. This is a role native Diaspora Jews have been loath to play and feel uncomfortable with.

The Israeli Diaspora must also begin to assume a greater leadership role in the social and cultural life of the Diaspora community. For the non-Orthodox Jews especially, they are the most Jewish Jews. They offer a living model for a secular Jewish culture that is alternative to Orthodoxy and an often shallow Diaspora Jewish life.

In short, the Israeli Diaspora might fulfill the most Zionist pioneering function of the twenty-first century by assuming a leadership role in Israel-Diaspora relations. The law of unintended consequences may have turned the most maligned group in Jewish life into one of the most important players in the battle for Jewish survival.

CHAPTER 8

The Future of Arab-Jewish Relations

Any robust policy must have clearly defined first principles to effectively sustain itself over time. Our first principle pertaining to our relations with the Arabs should be what is good for the Jews. In its modern context, this means what is good for Zionism. I have defined Zionism as the collective option for individual Jews in Israel or in the free Diaspora to integrate into modern life without sacrificing their Jewish identity. I do not define Zionism as the attempt to recreate the Kingdom of David, reconstruct the Temple, with attendant animal sacrifice, or construct a settlement everywhere the patriarch Abraham once rested his head.

We should want peace because it is good for the Jews, not because self-appointed humanitarians will love us or because it will relieve accumulated Arab stress at being consistently defeated by the lowly Jew. I identify myself with the first generation of Jews without inherent guilt; I do not open my eyes in the morning and say, "We are guilty," and then ask of what we are guilty.

I want peace because killing Jews will stop, Israel's economy will prosper, tourism will rejuvenate, unemployment will decrease, our democracy will grow stronger, and the standards of our civil service will approach European levels. I do not want peace in order to win the Nobel Prize or to go to heaven.

I do not consider peace the most important thing in human affairs. Survival is more important, security is more important, liberty is more important, justice is more important, freedom is more important, dignity and honor are more important, and constitutional democracy is more important. I am not willing to sacrifice any of the above in order to achieve peace.

I am for a peace that increases Israel's security, its international political status, and its economic strength, thus enabling Israel to close the social ethnic gap. I believe in taking calculated tactical risks in order to achieve the above. I do not believe in taking strategic risks, calculated or otherwise.

I know that in order to achieve peace, we must take into consideration the Palestinian concern for security, national liberty, justice, dignity, and honor. I also affirm that we Jews have not always paid proper respect to Palestinian concerns about these issues and that many Jews in Israel and the Diaspora have nothing but contempt for the human aspirations of Palestinians. I dissociate myself from these people, not in order to gain international praise but because to achieve peace we must recognize and accommodate, to the best of our ability, legitimate Palestinian aspirations. And peace is good for the Jews. No rational person wants something unless it is good for him.

Any call for Jews to sacrifice or even risk sacrificing their vital interests in the name of peace should be rejected. Self-sacrifice is the most grotesque form of human sacrifice, and human sacrifice has been erased from human civilization for centuries.

THE PEACE PROCESS AND SETTLEMENTS

These views explain why, despite the second *Intifada*, I affirm the Madrid/Oslo process as being the greatest Zionist achievement of the 1990s. As discussed above, I reject the ideological settlement project in the occupied territories as being anti-ethical and damaging to Zionism. Israelis and Diaspora Jews should not support the peace process and oppose the settlements in order to please world opinion or placate the Arabs. We should support the peace process and call for the dismantling of the ideological settlements because these positions are good for the Jews.

The Madrid/Oslo process raised Israel's international political standing and strength for a crucial decade in its history. Although this standing has eroded in the wake of the second *Intifada*, the Madrid/Oslo achievement helped contribute to the robust economic growth of Israel throughout the 1990s (4–5 percent per year).

Israel's economy is export driven, and during the decade of the 1990s, 60 percent of Israel's export growth was to countries and markets we had not traded with prior to the Madrid/Oslo process. This economic growth was a major reason for the relatively successful absorption of close to one million immigrants from the former Soviet Union. These immigrants supplied close to 50 percent of Israel's technical manpower needs during the 1990s. Their availability was another major reason for increased foreign investment in Israel's technology sectors, which, despite its inherent volatility, is the basis for future economic growth.

Another positive consequence of the Madrid/Oslo process was the de facto demise of the Arab boycott, which had been losing its effectiveness as Israel's relative economic power grew and the relative economic influence of Arab oil power waned. The boycott's demise removed the final psychological barrier to international investment in Israel and led to large foreign investment in

Israel in the 1990s. The resurrection of the Arab boycott was seriously discussed at the height of the second *Intifada*, but nothing came of it because Israel's economic status had already evolved to a higher level. That Arab factors were even considering renewed economic warfare against Israel is, however, of concern and compels Israel and world Jewry to reconsider its position in regards to the Arab world.

The Madrid/Oslo process was, therefore, a major contributor to Israel's economic growth by one-third and its Jewish population growth by 20 percent during the 1990s. Madrid/Oslo has been good for the Jews, notwithstanding the failure to achieve a finalistic peace or the subsequent outbreak of violence. We had seven years of violence before Oslo, several years of violence during Oslo, and there is no logical reason to assume that the second *Intifada* could have been avoided if we had not concluded Oslo.

The worst thing that could be said about Oslo is that it provided Israel with an opportunity to realize strategic Zionist aims while opening Israel up to severe tactical challenges that, while murderous and intolerable, do not present any real strategic dangers to Israel's existence. On balance, Oslo has been a Zionist triumph.

The existence of the ideological settlements forecloses options for interim (unilateral) separation from the Palestinians or a final settlement with the Palestinians. Either option would be beneficial to Israel and the Jewish People. These settlements constitute a Zionist Gordian knot that we are constantly trying to untie, with endless bypass roads and tunnels and overpasses as well as costly security arrangements that divert Israel's military power away from areas of better use.

A perverse logic is at work here. Many Israelis and Diaspora Jews assume that because the settlements are so obnoxious to the Arabs they must be good for the Jews. The notion that the settlements might be both obnoxious to the Arabs and totally stupid and dysfunctional to Jewish interests (completely independent of our relations with the Palestinians) has not been a serious part of Israel's public debate.

Anything so deleterious to Zionism, to our relationship with Arab countries and the world should be vigorously combated on purely Zionist grounds. A first step must be the unilateral removal of minisettlements located in a sea of hostile Arabs. Such a step would create maneuvering room for Israel, enabling it to take unilateral steps if future negotiations with the Palestinians do not bear fruit. Ironically, these settlements serve the Palestinian political cause because they limit Israel's freedom of action, making it dependent on Palestinian agreement.

PRINCIPLES FOR FUTURE JEWISH RELATIONS WITH THE ARAB AND MOSLEM WORLDS

Jewish relations with the Arabs must be fair but firm, with an unconditional demand for reciprocity. What we must demand from ourselves regarding the

Arabs we must demand from the Arabs regarding ourselves. Without fairness, we will not achieve peace. Without firmness, we will not survive. The radical Israeli hawks and doves are both wrong.

Firmness refers not only to military firmness, but to a robust *reciprocal* moral standard. Israeli Left attitudes in particular have often been paternalistic and forgiving. Because peace means so much to so many Israelis, we have often overlooked corruption, incompetence, and racism in Arab countries as well as in many self-governing bodies of Israel's own Arab citizens.

This must cease. We must adopt a policy of zero tolerance for Arab corruption and racism as well as their dismissive contempt for legitimate Jewish rights. A great moral failure of the Israeli Left has been its ultrasensitivity and criticism of Jewish contempt for legitimate Arab rights and concerns, as it studiously overlooked the much greater Arab contempt for Jewish rights and concerns—indeed, contempt for the Jews per se.

Toward the Arab and Moslem world in general, we must become proactive unapologetic lobbyists to end direct and indirect international funding to countries, projects, and educational systems that propagate anti-Semitic propaganda and that implement racist policies. This includes countries with which we have diplomatic or consular relations. We must become proactive in helping to publicize attitudes toward women in these countries. We must demand of the world and of ourselves a single standard. We may not succeed, but at least we will expose these social norms and help neutralize the insufferable posture of moral superiority of Arab propagandists, which puts so many Israeli and Jewish spokespeople on the defensive. We must force the Arabs to explain their behavior and actions rather than the present situation, wherein the Jews are constantly forced to explain theirs.

CAN ISRAEL BE A JEWISH AND DEMOCRATIC STATE?

Israel is a Jewish *and* a democratic state. Democracy for Israel is not just some abstract ideal that "tough-minded Realpolitik" is all too ready to sacrifice in the name of survival; it is an absolute necessity of survival. Israel would in no way earn the support of the United States and of American and European Jewry if we ran Israel like the other Middle Eastern countries. We must reject the claim of Jewish extremists that either we are a Jewish state or we are a democratic state and that as long as we are at war we cannot afford the luxury of democracy. It is precisely because we are at war, and require powerful democratic allies, that we must remain democratic.

We must also reject the attempts of Arab intellectuals and Jewish post-Zionist intellectuals to de-Zionize and de-Judaize the state by changing the national anthem, *HaTikvah*, and removing symbols such as the Star of David and the menorah. We must emphatically and unapologetically reject the demand that Israel become a state of all its citizens *instead* of a Jewish state. Israel can and *must* be both. It can and must be both a Jewish and a democratic state. If either of these components is removed from the equation, neither Israel nor the Jewish People will have a future.

The Importance of Symbols

The Arab nationalist and post-Zionist attack on the Jewish symbols must be nipped in the bud. The demand to remove the Star of David from the flag and the menorah as the national symbol and to replace *HaTikvah* must be rejected, as insufferable *chutzpah* on the part of the Arabs and Jewish intellectuals who demand it. This demand does not reflect superior moral and democratic values, it reflects the residual historical contempt of Christianity and Islam (wrapped in a cloak of politically correct postmodern leftism) for any Jewish pretension at political equality. It also reflects the obsequious self-hate of deracinated Jews, which has been a historical consequence of that contempt.

England, Norway, Finland, Denmark, Sweden, Greece, Iceland, and Switzerland are all democratic countries, and *all* have Christian crosses in their national flags. Most have an official state religion. England and Denmark are structural theocracies: the queen is head of the Anglican Church in England, and the Parliament has ultimate control of the Lutheran Church in Denmark. These countries' national mythologies, coats of arms, and holidays are not ethnically neutral; they reflect the dominant ethnic group, even while these countries give absolute freedom and equality to all their citizens, whatever their ethnicity. In this sense, Denmark is the country of the Lutheran Danes *and* of all its citizens, and no Jew or Moslem residing in Denmark or deracinated Danish intellectual would dare demand the removal of the cross from the flag (which according to Danish legend, King Valdemar the II received from heaven in 1219).

India is the largest democracy in the world. Its flag has an ancient Hindu symbol, the Dharma Chakra, at its very center, just as the Star of David is at the center of Israel's flag. The state emblem of India is a representation of the top of a pillar built by Asoka, a Hindu who converted to Buddhism, just as the state emblem of Israel is a Menorah. Some 20 percent of India's population is non-Hindu and non-Buddhist, with more than 150 million Moslems and close to 20 million Christians, whose rights as citizens are also constitutionally guaranteed. Could one imagine these non-Hindus having the effrontery to carry on a public campaign to change the symbols of India?

India's non-Hindus justifiably fight to translate their formal constitutional rights into equal treatment in practice. Israel's Arabs should also fight to translate their formal constitutional rights into equal treatment in practice and not constantly accuse the Jews of racism because we desire one geographically insignificant state on the face of the planet whose national symbols are Jewish. In so doing, the Arabs would earn the support of many Jews. As it is, it is psychologically difficult to fight for the equal civil rights of people who deny you equal national rights.

Israel's democratic model is Denmark, not the United States. Denmark should be a light unto the Jews, and we should strive to equal Denmark in its treatment of its non-Lutheran, non-Danish population.

We certainly do not want as our models Pakistan, Algeria, Libya, Mauritania, or Tunisia, all of which contain the Islamic crescent in their flags, a fact that for some reason does not excite the indignity of European, Moslem, or deracinated Jewish intellectuals as being racist.

The Law of Return

And what of the Law of Return? How can a country that pretends to be democratic have a basic immigration law that favors one ethnic group over all others? Is this not a racist law by definition? In an imaginary world of absolutes, it might be thus defined. In the real world of imperfect, empirical, historical context, it is the antithesis to racism. In this real world, the Law of Return is a humanistic response to racism.

In its original formulation, the Law of Return guaranteed a safe haven for anyone who would have been exterminated as a Jew by Hitler. This included numerous individuals who had no self-definition or even self-knowledge that they were at least one-eighth Jewish, and who were by definition not even Jews according to Jewish tradition, which makes it a real stretch of the imagination to call this a racist law. Especially consider that it came in response to the so-called civilized world's failure to offer safe haven during the Nazi period. The countries of the West closed their borders, sentencing hundreds of thousands if not millions of Jews and others to death. For so-called intellectuals and humanists to attack as racist this most human and humane response to colossal moral failure is an example of moral and intellectual dishonesty of immense proportions.

But the Law of Return also has moral and historical justification independent of the Holocaust. It is an example of political affirmative action, which should not in itself offend politically correct postmodernists. The Jews suffered for 2,000 years because they had no safe geographical/political haven in which they had demographic, political, cultural, and economic hegemony. Zionism was born well before the Holocaust and is not dependent on the Holocaust. Zionism is dedicated to correcting the condition of collective Jewish political disenfranchisement by creating and sustaining a Jewish state in which the Jewish People could guarantee, by their own efforts, with or without outside approval, their demographic, political, cultural, and economic hegemony. The Law of Return is an integral and necessary part of this guarantee, and its basic moral assumptions are similar to various affirmative action laws and programs in the West. When a minority is discriminated against over a long historical period in a vital arena of human activities, they must be allowed to claim certain privileges to repair the damage for a defined time.

The Law of Return fits this definition and is, therefore, morally justified and by definition not racist. It is rather a mechanism to correct the racist inheritance of thousands of years of anti-Semitism. The legitimate question is for how long. Is affirmative action to be indefinite in time?

I would be willing to assuage Arab sensitivities on this issue by agreeing to put a retroactive sunset limit on the Law of Return. The law would be applicable for 100 years, a period of time equivalent to 5 percent of the 2,000 years during which the Jews were disenfranchised of collective sovereignty. This would mean that by 2049 the Law of Return would be invalid and Israel would adopt the naturalization laws of Europe or the United States. Given the present demographic trends of world Jewry, this gesture toward the Arabs would be of little practical consequence to the Jews.

JEWISH ATTITUDES TOWARD ISRAELI ARABS

In regards to Palestinian Arabs of Israeli citizenship, we must adopt a creative policy based upon justice and equality before the law, nondiscrimination in the job market, and equal access to *public* budgets. I stress public because when a substantial portion of Israel's development budgets are filtered through the Jewish National Fund and the Jewish Agency and are for the Jewish population only, any claim to equality becomes but a pretense. We then become open to the accusation that the Zionist project is inherently racist.

We must, however, be unapologetic and self-asserting regarding the fact that Israel is a *Jewish* state. What should the Jewish response be to Israeli Arab leaders and intellectuals who call for a de-Judaizing of Israel? The Jews must clearly declare that Israel's democratic nature permits any Israeli citizen to call for the destruction of the Jewish State by way of erasing all of its Jewish symbols. In turn, however, that same democratic nature enables Israel's Jewish citizens to treat as unworthy of cooperation those who fail to recognize the Jewish national right to a state founded on Jewish symbols and Jewish culture.

Israeli Arabs should always have equal rights and privileges under Israel's democratic form of government and should not be discriminated against in Israeli courts or in regards to public budgets. Those Israeli Arabs or leaders who support the notion that Israel should cease to be a Jewish state, however, should not expect active civil or political cooperation from self-respecting Jews. For self-respecting democratic Jews, Israel's Arab citizens have four options:

1. To fight for equal implementation of laws and budgets within the framework of the Jewish State. If this is the chosen option, many democratic Jews will be their active partners.

2. To continue to call for the destruction of the Jewish State, in which case respect for Arab rights will be completely passive and formal and Israeli Arabs will forego active cooperation from Jewish civil or political society. The status of Israeli Arabs

who embrace such a position will be much the same as Louis Farrakhan's Nation of Islam or the Aryan Brotherhood in the United States. Freedom of speech and assembly, yes, acceptance and cooperation, no.

3. *Voluntary* emigration from Israel if its particular Jewish character is so obnoxious to them. This is an accepted option: many English speakers have moved from Francophone Quebec, not because their constitutional rights have been damaged but because they felt uncomfortable and not completely at home in French culture and society. Others have remained, adapted, and compromised. This same democratic option holds for those of Israel's Arab citizens who cannot stomach the thought of living in a Jewish state. This option is in no way comparable to the controversial "transfer" policy advocated by certain segments of Israel's radical right wing. No Israeli Arab would be encouraged to leave the country. Voluntary emigration, on the other hand, is an option for every citizen, Jewish or Arab. Indeed about a half million Jewish citizens have emigrated because various aspects of Israeli society are obnoxious to them. This same option is open to Israel's Arab citizens.

4. To receive complete (not cultural) autonomy in areas presently under Arab council jurisdiction. Those Israeli Arabs who opt for autonomy will cease to be Israeli and will lose the right to vote for Israel's Knesset. They will vote for their own Arab agency, with its own flag, symbols, and hymn, which will generate its own educational and development budgets and coordinate with the Jewish State by way of a common *development authority* modeled on the New York Port Authority. This coordination will deal with issues such as access to Israel's highway, water, electrical, and sewage systems and the fees the Arab agency will pay to the state for its share in their use. The Knesset, as the sovereign legislative body of the state, has the authority to pass laws rescinding Israeli sovereignty over areas with a substantial Arab *or Jewish* population. I stress Jewish because it is clear to many Israelis that in the near future, whether through peace or unilateral withdrawal, the Knesset will be forced to rescind sovereignty over most of East Jerusalem and/or the Golan Heights. Another alternative for Israeli Arab communities or as individuals would be annexation to the Palestinian state, even in areas noncontiguous to the Palestinian state, thus becoming Palestinian citizens. If groups or individuals of Israeli Arabs opt for either one of these two options, the Jews will respect their choice— just as Slovakia's decision to separate from the Czechs was respected. None of this will prejudice the constitutional rights of those Arabs who choose to remain citizens of the Jewish state.

A CAUTIONARY ABOUT JEWISH MORAL ARROGANCE

Israeli Jews must beware of adopting a pose of moral superiority. The moral gap between the Palestinians and Israelis is sometimes not as great as we Israelis would like to pretend. For example:

1. What if lynchers of Israeli soldiers during the second *Intifada* had in the past been systematically beaten and humiliated while under Israeli administrative detention? Or if the relatives of some of them had died under questioning while under administrative detention? Could we sustain the same level of moral indignation?

True, Israeli police, despite chronic accusations of brutality, would not have permitted a similar event if the situation had been reversed. This moral superiority we might claim, but we have all witnessed Jewish mobs in the past that, but for the Israeli police, were capable of committing mindless acts of violence. An ultra-Orthodox woman from Jerusalem was put under *herem* by her community for preventing a Jewish mob from lynching an Arab after a terrorist attack.

2. How can we claim that we Jews have a higher respect for human life than the Palestinians when the monumental gravesite memorial to the murderer Baruch Goldstein was erected and stood for years as an attraction to nationalist Jewish fanatics? True, Israel conducted an objective, public, and transparent inquiry that led to the eventual dismantling of the memorial. The Palestinians have never done that, and this might be our claim to moral superiority. Yet, scores of Israelis condemned both the inquiry and the dismantling and still praise Goldstein's atrocity.

3. How can we condemn Palestinian swinging-door justice for individuals accused of terrorist activity against Israel when President Chaim Herzog pardoned the Jewish Underground members who planted bombs that killed and mutilated Arab officials as well as Israeli soldiers? Or when settlers kill Arabs and receive light sentences? True, Israeli media, academia, and citizenry roundly condemn these phenomena, which supports a claim of moral superiority but not the chronic self-righteous pose assumed by certain Israelis.

4. How can we condemn Arab contempt for Jewish human rights when Israeli authorities and many Israeli citizens have adopted a wink-and-a-nod tolerance for the thuggery, bullying, and constant humiliation of Palestinians by certain segments of the settler population and individual soldiers? True, unlike the Palestinians, we have a free media and a vigorous civil discourse that exposes and condemns such behavior as contrary to our societal norms, and this is our claim to moral superiority. Yet have we shown any substantive initiative to stop these practices?

5. Can we truthfully claim that Israel's Arab citizens are equal before the law or in regards to budgets, public attitudes, or job market? We, who scream about discrimination against the Jews everywhere in the world, should look at ourselves. Growing Israeli Arab radicalism festers in a conducive environment of structural discrimination.

Despite the above, a superior social and cultural moral norm is evident in the fact that many devoted Zionists write so openly and critically about Israel's violations of human rights and dignity while almost no parallel voices speak on the other side. We are aware that the very claim to cultural superiority invites the wrath of politically correct multiculturalists, we nonetheless claim this for Israel.

JEWISH COMPLIANCE WITH ARAB CORRUPTION, SEXISM, AND RACISM

Whenever the call for equality of budgets for Arabs is raised in Israel, we usually see a spate of Jewish-authored articles describing in great detail the astounding corruption and administrative incompetence of Israeli Arab municipalities. These imply that before more money is funneled into the Arab sector we should guarantee higher standards of public behavior and transparency vis-à-vis public budgets dedicated to the Arab sector.

The facts that these articles uncover and the call for higher standards are correct, and it would not damage any Israeli progressive's credentials to publicly condemn these phenomena. Nor would it damage the nationalist qualifications of Arab intellectuals to also publicly condemn these phenomena. The fact that they do not devalues the impact of their moral indignation about Israeli discrimination.

Zero tolerance for these phenomena, as well as for the status of women in the Arab sector, are moral imperatives. Excusing, explaining away, or overlooking these negative phenomena in the name of brotherhood and intercultural understanding and tolerance is politically correct multiculturalism gone wild.

But once again, it behooves the Jews not to adopt a stance of moral superiority. We encouraged and nurtured the traditional corruption of the Arab sector. Let us name it *mukhtarism*, after the traditional name for local Arab leadership, the *mukhtar*. We made the traditional corrupt leadership of the Arab communities our conduit to our Arab citizens rather than encourage the development of modern concepts of citizenship and civic behavior and status of women in the Arab community.

This system was first developed by the center left *Mapai*, the progenitor of the Labor Party, and later inherited and enhanced by the center right Likud Party. Its rationale was that such a corrupt society would be more malleable and given to manipulation and thus less militant and troublesome. We feared that by encouraging modern standards of citizenship we might give birth to a local Arab leadership. Such a leadership might take seriously Israel's claim to being the only democracy in the Middle East and thus might become more inconveniently militant about pursuing Arab rights.

Mukhtarism never troubled the radical right, with their racist tendencies toward the Arabs. They hoped to let them fester in their own incompetence; the more incompetent they were the better it would be for the Jews.

The radical left, supported by primitivist anthropologists and infatuated with anything non-Western, has historically gone out of its way to excuse away these practices, claiming that Israel has no right to interfere with the cultures of other peoples. The Left has consistently overlooked the fact that their position has been inherently racist and contemptuous of Arab culture. They have also ignored the fact that their position violated their own sacred principles in a variety of areas and exposed them to the accusation of hypocrisy and double standards.

How, for example, could the Israeli Left excuse the gross corruption of the Arab sector while vigorously attacking the gross corruption of the Haredi sector? Additionally, how can they justify, excuse, explain away the status of Arab women? To do so is to accept by implication the Arab cultural norm that Arab women are "their women" (that is, the property of the men, who rule Arab society) and not "their own persons" (that is, have ownership over themselves). All this while viciously attacking similar attitudes in ultra-Orthodox Jewish society and in general adopting a militant feminist position on all things in Jewish society. The Israeli Left has advocated zero tolerance for injustice to women in the Jewish sector and optimal patience for injustice to women in the Arab sector "because we cannot interfere in another people's culture."

This has led to a situation contrary to the interests of the Zionist project. The inferior status of Arab women has produced a serious demographic challenge to Jews in Israel. The inferior level of Arab public administration and services has resulted in bitterness, which has indirectly contributed to radical tendencies in Israel's Arab citizens.

The irony is that, despite our best efforts to prevent it, a new militant Israeli Arab parliamentary leadership has arisen. Their attitudes are semi-modern but cynical and bitter, with no great desire to encourage higher standards of citizenship in the Arab sector. Rather than engage in critical analyses of the effects of *mukhtarism* on Israeli Arab society, which might reflect a genuine concern for Israeli Arab welfare, they cynically exploit its consequences for their own political agenda in order to build their own political power. In other words, the Israeli Arab parliamentary lobby, rather than alleviating Israeli Arab distress, by a *combination* of internal reform and external lobbying, has an interest in exacerbating this distress to generate the extremism necessary for their real agenda: support for Arafat's dream of a Greater Palestine.

Indeed, we might ask if the very term *Arab intellectual* is not an oxymoron. The definition of an intellectual is one who engages in critical analyses of one's own culture. Where are the Arab intellectuals who are criticizing the *mukhtarism* of Israeli Arab society? Where are the Arab intellectuals in the Arab world who are criticizing the corruption and racism of all the Arab regimes? In Israel, they are simply quiet. In the rest of the Arab world, you find such Arab intellectuals in exile, in jail, or in the cemetery!

THE FUTURE

Future policy should incorporate the following:

1. Affirmative action programs for Israeli Arab women in every area of Israeli life: education, advancement in public positions, hostels for battered Israeli Arab women, boarding schools for Arab girls being "socially abused" by their fathers by being kept out of school, and so on.

2. Recognition of a Palestinian state and a total rejection of United Nations Resolution 194 calling for the repatriation of Palestinian refugees to their original homes. Accepting 194 would be tantamount to the suicide of the Jewish State.

3. Moral reciprocity with Egypt: nonacceptance of their public contempt and their anti-Semitic activism, and unilateral removal of their ambassador from Israel.

4. Striving for a universal Jewish-Moslem rapprochement. This might be attempted and achieved under the auspices of the European Union.

5. Total rejection of double standards in regards to the norms of governance in the Israeli Arab sector as well as in Arab countries.

6. Reevaluation of the Israeli Arab job market. This means the active enlistment of skilled Israeli Arabs in public sector positions.

Such a policy would integrate Jewish self-esteem with social justice for the Arab population and would reflect the fact that Israel is not only a Jewish state but also a democratic state with concern for all its citizens.

CHAPTER 9

The Future of Ethnic Relations and Israeli Culture

This chapter analyzes factors that have created some of Israel's residual communal resentments, their consequences, and what we can do to invent an alternative future for ethnic relations and Israeli culture.

HISTORICAL-CULTURAL BACKGROUND

Oriental and Sephardi Jewry were the dominant numerical and cultural forces in Jewish life until the end of the European Middle Ages. Ashkenazi Jewry was a minor numerical and cultural force, outside mainstream civilization and thus outside mainstream Jewish civilization. Historically, the centers of Jewish creative dynamism have been either in or on the fringes of world civilization centers, and the level of Jewish culture has reflected the society in which the Jews live.

Jewish history has followed world history, from south and east to north and west. From the Middle Ages onward, the Ashkenazi star ascended and the Sephardi-Oriental star descended. By the nineteenth century, the Ashkenazim had reached numerical and cultural superiority. By 1825, Jews in the world numbered about 3.25 million, 80 percent of whom were European.

By this time, Ashkenazi cultural developments had surpassed those of the Sephardim. The Hasidim, the Gaon of Vilna, and Mendelssohn had no parallel in Sephardi-Oriental development, just as earlier the Rambam and Saadya Gaon had had no parallel in Ashkenazi development. During the nineteenth century, Ashkenazi Jewry went through a period of extraordinary cultural ferment and demographic growth. The Reform and Conservative movements, the neo-Orthodoxy of Rabbi Hirsch, the Mussar movement, the Jewish

Enlightenment (*Haskala*), Zionism, Bundism, Hebraism, Yiddishism were all primarily products of Ashkenazi Jewry. They had no parallel in the Sephardi-Oriental communities, just as the premedieval and medieval intellectual and social ferment of Sephardi and Oriental Jewry had had no parallel in the early Ashkenazi communities.

After the Jews were expelled from Spain during the Inquisition (1492), the Sephardim experienced a schism. The "western" Sephardim who moved to France, Holland, England, and America eventually assimilated almost completely. They ceased to be a significant factor in Jewish history. Some individual western Sephardim, such as Moses Montifiore and others, became prominent in Gentile society and used their influence to help Jewish communities in distress. The "eastern" Sephardim, who moved to the Ottoman Empire (Yugoslavia, Bulgaria, Greece, and Turkey), preserved a dynamic aesthetic Ladino culture and engaged in vigorous economic activity but failed to sustain the intellectual dynamism of their early history. By the nineteenth century, the culture of Oriental Jewish communities reflected the static Islamic societies they lived in.

Ashkenazi society's cultural and intellectual ferment prepared Ashkenazi Jews for their encounter with modern civilization; Sephardi and Oriental society did not. Ashkenazi Jews were greatly involved with the creative outburst of nineteenth-century Europe. Sephardi and Oriental Jews were less so.

DEFINING THE PROBLEM

The ethnic problem in Israel is essentially psychological. It stems from culture shock, cultural dismemberment, and a resultant poor self-image. An Israeli doctor of Iraqi origin, interviewed on Israeli television, gave the reasons he left Israel and came to the United States. His answer was revealing: "In New York, I am a Jew, in Israel I am an Iraqi." This is a significant statement. It says that the way society views you has a lot to do with the way you view yourself. We tend to internalize the impressions others have of us and develop characteristics that other people expect us to possess.

The great American Black leader Roy Wilkins once said, "It doesn't bother me that the Whites think we are inferior, it bothers me that we think we are inferior." In other words, the American Black internalized the view White America had of him; he developed characteristics expected of him and began to view himself as he was viewed. The situation of the Iraqi Jewish doctor was similar. Jews as Jews may be disliked and even hated, but Gentile society sees them as intelligent and inclined to success. They are *expected* to be intelligent and successful. The Jews internalized this expectation. This might be one reason why Jews have been relatively successful. Iraqi Jews in Israel, on the other hand, were expected to be somewhat backward, were treated that way, and consequently began to behave as if it were their natural lot to be backward.

Israeli politicians and Zionist functionaries are fond of quoting statistics showing how the standard of living of Oriental Jews has risen since their arrival in Israel. In regard to health care, nutrition, education, and housing, they are for the most part correct. But in stressing the material aspect, they miss the point. From the psychological perspective, Oriental Jewry's standard of living has often gone down.

In their countries of origin, Oriental Jews were members of the middle classes. They had a definite place in society and performed necessary tasks. They had their own culture and judged themselves by the criteria of that culture. They might have been second-class citizens and certainly suffered discrimination—despite romantic myths regarding the benevolent relationship between Jews and Moslems—but they were still subjects in control and not objects being controlled. Similarly, Eastern European Jews, while suffering persecution, saw themselves as subjects and not objects. The Chinese poor in America also see themselves as subjects while the Blacks, on the other hand, often see themselves as objects. This may be one reason why the Chinese have been more successful than the Blacks, even though the discrimination they encountered was no less virulent.

This is why the Blacks sent the White liberals home. The Whites, with all their good intentions, treated Blacks as objects to be helped and not as subjects with their own lives, values, and culture. The agenda of the Black revolution has been to transform Blacks from objects into subjects. This is the thread connecting the various Black organizations and strategies. The message of Black Power was to "do it yourself," under your own power. Likewise, the Zionist Pinsker, in *Auto-Emancipation*, said that the Jews must do it themselves. White liberals cannot do it for us, Enlightenment progressives cannot do it for us, an international revolution of the proletariat cannot do it for us— *we must do it ourself if we are to be truly free.*

However, due to a convergence of social and historic circumstances, the Oriental Jew was prevented from doing it himself. As many Israeli social commentators have noted, Oriental Jewish immigrants were often treated as objects. They became overwhelmed by the confusion of their new society. They felt powerless and became passive and dependent. One researcher reported that, when describing their journey to Israel, Oriental Jews would use the active voice—what they did. Yet when describing their experiences in Israel, they would use the passive voice—what was done to them.

YEMENITE JEWRY AS AN EXAMPLE

The Yemenite Jews were the poorest and most persecuted of Oriental Jews. Because law forbade them to testify against Moslems, they were subject to arbitrary justice. They could not ride horses, camels, or donkeys in the cities so as not to be higher than a Moslem. They were permitted to do so in the rural areas but were obliged to dismount every time they passed a Moslem.

Because the Moslems believed that orphans were children of Mohammed, Jewish orphans were forcibly taken from the Jewish community and raised as Moslems. As in other Middle Eastern countries, infant mortality was more than 50 percent and eye and skin diseases were common. Clearly, their formal legal status and material standards improved when they came to Israel.

Yet, psychologically, they were worse off. In Yemen, they were part of a culture they had created, that gave them an outlet for their creative imagination and was part of their everyday lives. In Israel, that culture has been treated as "folklore" and "exotica," something to be "preserved," to be shown at folk festivals. Not a living culture, reflecting the creative dynamism of a certain group, but a cultural museum piece, while in their everyday lives they are expected to assimilate and live according to a completely different culture.

Yemenite Jewry constituted almost the entire skilled working class of Yemen. They were metal workers, carpenters, shoemakers, and such. The word *expert* was a synonym for Jew. In Yemen, they were central to the entire national economy and were most valuable members of society. In Israel, they became a social problem to be solved, the objects of welfare specialists, on the margins of society. In Yemen, for all their suffering, they were social subjects; in Israel, for all their material progress, they became social objects.

What is true for the Yemenites is true for other Oriental Jewish groups as well. After being in the middle of society for centuries, even though a technologically primitive and often cruel society, Oriental Jews now found themselves in the lower social strata, even though a technologically developed and humane society. This is especially pertinent because, in Yemen, for example, position was preeminent for the Jews and they would often take a cut in income to attain a more prestigious craft.

CULTURE SHOCK: THE CULTURAL RIFT

Substantial academic research identifies culture shock as a partial explanation for failure. One famous research project compared several hundred cases of sets of North African Jewish brothers—one who went to Israel and one who went to France—with results unfavorable to Israel. In almost every case, the French brother had been more successful. We may speculate about possible reasons. During colonial rule, the French co-opted many North African Jews into French culture. Many North African Jews became French citizens and were instrumental in spreading French culture in North Africa.

When North African Jews said they came from southern France, it was not because they were ashamed of their origins, as some smug Ashkenazim would have it, but because it reflected a certain reality. Numerous North African Jews were in varying degrees already French because France viewed Algeria as part of southern France and administered her as such. Thus, when many North African Jews moved to France, it was as if they were moving to a different area in the same country. The language, customs, bureaucracy, educational system, social mores, economy, and mentality were already quite familiar to them.

They arrived just as France was entering a period of sustained economic growth and becoming a consumer- and service-oriented society. Thus, the petit bourgeois North African Jews held onto their economic habits. Like their Ashkenazi brethren a century earlier, the North African Jewish petit bourgeois maintained their traditional occupations with simple upgrades. Indeed, by performing the mercantile and service tasks they had always performed, they rapidly established a solid economic foundation in France. Being Jews, they were disliked, but by virtue of being Jews, they were expected to be educated and successful. Thus, their self-image was preserved and even enhanced.

In comparison, North African immigrants to Israel confronted an unfamiliar variation of European culture, with a mentality, life style, and expectations foreign to them. The only unifying force was the commonality of Jewishness.

Israel possessed an undeveloped nonconsumer economy whose mercantile sectors were already overcrowded with the Ashkenazi petit bourgeois. This situation required that the North African Jews switch to manual labor in industry, agriculture, and the lower services. Cultural antipathy to physical work, however, caused great strains. Oriental Jews often would boast that they had never had to do physical work. Juxtapose this social attitude to the fact that more than 34 percent of Oriental Jews in Israel had menial jobs (janitors, semiskilled laborers, and such) as opposed to 12 percent of the Ashkenazi Jews, and one can comprehend the sense of humiliation and fall from station.

Certain aspects of European romanticism that glorified physical work influenced the European founding fathers of Zionism. Tolstoy and his Zionist disciple, A. D. Gordon, had a great impact on the early Zionist worldview and contributed to the creation of the Jewish peasant/worker myth. The Oriental Jews had no parallel Tolstoyan-Gordonian myth of the glories of physical labor.

Oriental Jews underwent a complete change in life style in a society that they did not understand. And unlike their brethren in France, they were seen as primitive and backward Asiatics to be raised to the level of European civilization. North African Jewry is composed of many subgroups, some of whom were completely untouched by the French influence. Few of this latter group went to France, most came to Israel and shaped the public image of all of North African Jewry, to the discomfort of the Frenchified North African subgroup.

North African Jews were lumped together and seen as primitive. Being labeled as objectively incapable of raising themselves, the task fell to the humanistic and socialistic Ashkenazi elite, who were only too glad to demonstrate their altruistic social values and humanitarianism by exposing these "unfortunates" to the glories of Western civilization. The Ashkenazi *halutzim* perhaps had a subconscious motivation to exaggerate Oriental Jewry backwardness: they needed to justify their own active "humanitarian" part in overcoming it. In their anxiousness to help, they destroyed the most valuable possession any individual, especially the Oriental individual, possesses—his or her self-respect. Viewed as welfare cases, Oriental Jews often became welfare cases.

The breakdown of the Oriental family caused by the trauma of interacting with Western culture caused many of the problems. The more modern but still unprepared son became head of family, while the traditional father was relegated to a secondary and thus humiliating status. The father might try to exercise authority without real authority, and the son would give superficial, ceremonial respect to his father while circumstance forces him to guide his father like a child. Is it any wonder that such families had such a difficult time competing in Israel, often becoming dysfunctional?

Despite all this, most Oriental Jews no longer fit the above stereotypes. Perhaps only 20 percent of Oriental Jews can still be defined as hard-core poor. Most have raised themselves to middle-class status, in the face of tremendous odds, through sheer hard work and initiative.

Those who do make it materially do not resolve the psychological tensions inherent in the social-cultural gap. The majority of Oriental Jews are materially successful but have not fully assimilated Western values and conceptions. Their material success in many cases, leads them to feel with even greater intensity the psychological disconnect of the social-cultural gap. They are in constant contact with the Ashkenazim socially, in the workplace, and even in marriage. They are, therefore, liable to be ultrasensitive to differences in cultural attitudes.

Much Eastern European *halutzim* antipathy toward Oriental culture can be attributed to a more general phenomenon. The frontiers of a given civilization are often less tolerant of other cultures than their cultural centers. Those on the frontiers usually suffer from a lack of cultural self-confidence regarding their own cultural identity, The cultural centers, on the other hand, are usually characterized by a self-confidence bordering on cultural arrogance.

This may explain the early East European pioneers' contempt and patronizing attitude toward Oriental music, whereas the highly cultured French so easily absorbed and embraced Mediterranean and Oriental motifs in their chanson and pop music. This is analogous to the political jingoism of the former American Panama Canal colony or the demonstrative patriotism of small-town America, as opposed to the easy-going, cosmopolitanism of big-city America, which is more self-confident about its Americanism.

Israel's social gap, therefore, is the problem of those who have made it. It is not the material problem of the 20 percent hard-core poor, it is the cultural problem of 100 percent of Israel's society. Israel's ethnic tensions are more a cultural rift than a social gap.

ZIONISM

Israel as a product of Zionism adds another dimension to the problem. Ben Gurion said, "The Zionists don't make *aliya* and those who do are not Zionists." Most of those who had been coming to Israel were largely unaware of modern Zionism and had come for traditional values.

As explained before, Zionism is the modern national liberation movement of the Jewish People that developed in Europe in the nineteenth century on a background of particular conditions. This Zionism derived from the traditional yearning of Jews for Zion throughout the ages. Modern Zionism, however, is a movement and ideology that arose in response to the specific problems of European Jewry. This movement analyzed and proposed solutions for the condition of European Jewry in a ruthless critique of European Jewry and its Gentile environment. Its aim was to effect a cultural, political, psychological, and social revolution of European Jewry. This meant rebuilding the Jew from within. The Jew as a subject must first change himself and by doing so change his environment—as Pinsker suggests in his essay *Auto-Emancipation*. Jewish life was mercilessly criticized in a way that, if done by a non-Jew, would have been termed anti-Semitic.

The Zionist elite were Ashkenazi Jews, steeped in Ashkenazi culture, who felt the need and the right to make this critique. The fact that people who were part of the criticized culture and society made this critique gave Zionism its great authority. The critique was not only accurate, it came from within, commanding attention and effecting substantial change.

The same critique could not be applied to Oriental Jewry. Their environment was significantly different, and they related to that environment in a different way. Zionism was an import, not homegrown. It touched heartstrings and excited enthusiasm, but usually in terms of the traditional yearning for Zion and not because of the relevance of modern Zionism's analysis for Oriental communities. Portions of the Zionist critique were relevant for all Jews, but it contained no integrated conception of the particular Oriental Jewish situation. It is paradoxical that while Oriental Jewry played only a minor role in the history of the Zionist movement and ideology, Oriental Jews played a major role in the Zionist enterprise itself—the State of Israel.

There *were* Oriental Zionist movements, but no Oriental Zionist ideology dealt in self-criticism. Oriental intellectuals pursued no fundamental, soul-searching attempt to criticize the values and mind sets of Oriental Jewry.

This was because Islamic culture lacked the tradition of self-criticism that had flourished in European culture since the Renaissance. Moreover, Oriental Jewish realization of their own inadequacies regarding modern society took place in a Jewish rather than a Gentile environment. This may have hindered self-criticism. For although fearful of it, Jews have had a basic contempt for Gentile public opinion. This is not pertinent in an all-Jewish society, in which the "others" are also Jews whose opinions command respect. Despite the alienation many Orientals feel toward Israeli society, it is still a Jewish country that by definition stimulates love and attachment. While many North African Jews in Israel feel discrimination and are less well off, research shows that they still feel more identified with Israeli society and feel less prejudice than their more successful North African Jewish counterparts in France.

This represents a complex combination of attachment to and alienation from—an honestly felt "we" the Jews, and a just as honestly felt "we" the Orientals and "them" the Ashkenazim. The attachment makes society's negative perception all the more serious and disturbing. The alienation inhibits self-criticism. Being part of a society and also concerned about its opinion heightens the sense of alienation and makes self-criticism more difficult.

Thus, the attempt to rebuild Oriental Jewry came from without—from an Ashkenazi-dominated society. It was resented, resisted, and misunderstood; it was wide of the mark and used means completely foreign to the Oriental tradition and mentality.

ON TRADITION AND MODERNITY

The problem is not one of East versus West, but of traditional versus modern. The breakdown of tradition amongst Oriental Jews in Israel had also occurred amongst European Jews a century earlier with the spread of technology and science. In America, especially, the breakdown of traditions occurred at an astonishing rate.

Those Jews who adapted to the new society progressed. The Orthodox reactionaries who failed to adapt and remained in the ghettoes of Bnei Brak and Williamsburg did not progress to the same degree. The poverty of Ashkenazim in Mea Shearim is no less than that of Musrara, the North African Jerusalem slum, but the Ashkenazim managed to keep their traditional social forms intact while the Orientals did not. A major reason for this was Ashkenazi domination over religious institutions in Israel until the advent of the Shas Party. Thus, even the security of their own traditions was closed to the Oriental Jew, dependent as these traditions were on religious forms and expressions. The tremendous success of Shas bears witness to the residual need of many Oriental Jews for an authentic Oriental cultural expression with the power to compel attention and respect.

Even if they wanted to remain traditional, Orientals were often required to transfer from their own premodern tradition to an Ashkenazi premodern tradition. The latter was as foreign to them as Mars in its language, customs, food, and intellectual approach to Judaism. The stories abound in Israel of Oriental children in Ashkenazi *yeshivot* being beaten because they did not learn Yiddish, refused to eat gefilte fish, and to dress in kaftans. And even if these stories may have become exaggerated over the years, they reflect a great resentment in the Oriental community that contributed to the creation of the Shas Party.

The generally easier-going and down-to-earth approach to religion of the Oriental-Sephardi rabbinate aroused suspicion amongst the Ashkenazi rabbinical establishment, who either bullied or patronized their Oriental colleagues into submitting to Ashkenazi norms of religious observance. Oriental youth, prevented from functioning in a traditional religious framework, and still unable to integrate into modern society, fell into a pseudomodern Levantine street culture. Substantial numbers were absorbed into the more tolerant modern orthodoxy of Bnei Akiva. But Bnei Akiva itself was an outgrowth of European cultural developments and joining also entailed a significant alienation from family roots.

We should avoid being overly romantic and recognize that the breaking down of traditional culture is a necessary phenomenon. Traditional cultures are more than aesthetic expressions of dance, song, and dress. These by themselves are simply folklore. A culture is more inclusive and extensive. It is a mindset, a mentality, and a way of looking at the world. Traditional cultures, Eastern *or* Western, are *always* inadequate to the needs of a dynamic technological society. The romantics who try to preserve them end up losing them in any case, with only poverty remaining. But this breaking down can either be disintegration or an evolution into something new. Many Oriental Jews have experienced more disintegration; the Ashkenazim have experienced more a combination of disintegration and evolution.

The West modernized first, as modernity is a natural outgrowth of the internal developments of Western culture. Modernity and westernization overlap. For most Third World countries, modernization and westernization are one and the same thing. This is culturally unpalatable, and sometimes the Third World vomits up its westernization, as in recent convulsions shaking the Moslem world.

THE EFFECT OF RHYTHMS AND STANDARDS OF PROGRESS

The rhythm of modern society at the time a traditional culture encounters it has a lot to do with the ability of that culture to integrate. When the Ashkenazim confronted modern society, both the rhythms and standards of that society were much lower than when the Orientals encountered it. Also, the West was still largely traditional and much less secular than today. Their historical-cultural preparation, their tightly knit nuclear families, and the psychological benefits of encountering Western society in a Gentile and not a Jewish form aided the Ashkenazim in their meeting with modernity. The economic opportunities of a still primitive economic system that made few demands on technical skills but responded well to energy and initiative were also an advantage.

The masses of East European Jews were just as "primitive" when they came to America as were the Orientals when they came to Israel, yet conditions in the

West allowed them to make rapid economic progress. Orientals, on the other hand, encountered modern society when its rhythms and sophistication were light years ahead and when respect for tradition had all but vanished. We can liken this to jumping onto a moving train just as it is leaving the station or trying to jump on the same train as it roars through the station at 150 miles an hour.

Again, we deal with stereotypes. Colonialism had already obliged substantial elements of Oriental Jewry to begin their own modernizing process. Here, the admixture of tradition with modernity lessened the shock and allowed for a gradual and digestible absorption of modern values. In this way, large elements of North African, Iraqi, and Egyptian Jewry, as well as the Sephardim of the Balkans, had already begun their own process of internalizing Western and modern concepts.

In a colonial setting, Jews and other minorities for several reasons almost always identified with the imperialist power. The democratic imperialist powers preached, and sometimes practiced, equality under the law. Also, their policy of divide and conquer led them to make a point of giving due process, and even favorable treatment, to minorities persecuted under the previous native regime, in order to co-opt them. This made the modern culture of the imperial power more accessible to the Jews than to the non-Jewish native, and the Jews quickly reinforced their middle-class status by identifying with the imperial power.

It must also be noted that historically the Jews tend to identify with the more vigorous culture when given a choice between two non-Jewish cultures. Thus, in the Middle Ages, the Spanish Jews identified more with Islam than with Christianity. After the European Enlightenment, Central European Jews identified more with German culture than with Slavic culture. After the Bolshevik revolution, Russian Jewry was at the forefront of the Russification of non-Russian provinces of the Soviet Union, and after French colonization the North African Jews were at the forefront of the Frenchification of North Africa. In the twentieth century, Israel identified with Western and not Middle Eastern culture.

Substantial numbers of Oriental Jews were prepared for their encounter with modern civilization. The success of North African Jews in France and Iraqi Jews in Ramat Gan, Israel demonstrates this.

THE SPECIAL PROBLEM OF THE ORIENTAL INTELLIGENTSIA

One problem of developing an Oriental elite into an organized Oriental leadership is the very openness of Israeli society. Successful Oriental Jews assimilate well into Israeli society. Israel's relatively high rate of intermarriage between European and Oriental Jews attests to the fact that when the two groups interface as equals, personal prejudice is almost nonexistent. Yet, it is precisely here that Israeli cultural prejudices are demonstrated: what occurs is not a true integration of two cultures but often the individual assimilation of the Oriental.

A dynamic of expectation in regard to behavioral patterns causes successful Orientals to conform to the behavioral patterns of the dominant culture. This prevents them from going back to their roots as an agent of reform within Oriental society. Instead, they often live the life of a "black" Ashkenazi, the representative Oriental *of* Ashkenazi society, and are lost to the Oriental community as a positive force. The Zionist nature of Israeli society has prevented this phenomenon within the Israeli Arab community. Consequently, Israeli Arab intellectuals have had more impact on their community than Oriental intellectuals have had on theirs.

Contrast this to the situation of Eastern European Jewry in a similar stage of development in the nineteenth and early twentieth centuries. Their intelligentsia was often prevented from integrating into general society. As a consequence, they often turned back to their communities. First-class minds became teachers within the Jewish community. They became agents of change and objects of imitation. Their failure to assimilate forced them to become the cultural property of their communities. Thus, another psychocultural event helped prepare the Ashkenazi Jewish masses for their coming encounter with modern civilization.

GENERAL CULTURAL ATTITUDES

The value of a culture must be judged empirically and not a priori. It must be judged in relation to both its adherents and to the human community at large. Every culture is of intrinsic value to those who belong to it, but not of intrinsic or equal value to those who do not. Mongolian culture is as significant for a Mongolian as Chinese culture is for a Chinese. Libyan culture is as significant to a Libyan as Egyptian culture is to an Egyptian. Afghani culture is as significant for an Afghani as Indian culture is for an Indian. Estonian culture is as significant for an Estonian as German culture is for a German. But to a nonmember of any one of these cultures, Chinese, Egyptian, Indian, and German cultures are of extraordinary importance, while Mongolian, Libyan, Afghani, and Estonian cultures are but marginally significant. We may say, in this context, cultural pluralism yes, multiculturalism no. Every group has the right to celebrate its own culture. This does not mean that every culture has the same *universal value*.

It has been the affliction of humankind to confuse the universal impact a major culture has on the course of human events with the specific value every culture has for its own adherents. This confusion leads to the cultural arrogance that precedes political and economic imperialism, as well as the historical stupidity that leads to the radical relativism of multiculturalism.

The nineteenth century European conservative, liberal *and* socialist outlook engendered an attitude of cultural superiority. Marx himself had the utmost contempt for non-Europeans and welcomed every imperial conquest as introducing the very civilizing developments that would make the eventual world revolution inevitable. Herzl, in contrast, compares most favorably to Marx in this regard. He foresaw an independent Egyptian state as well as an alliance between an independent Black Africa and the Jewish State.

ISRAELI CULTURAL ATTITUDES

This attitude transposed itself to Israel. The Ashkenazi Zionist elite believed it their responsibility to uplift their more unfortunate Oriental brethren, to assume the "white man's burden." Unfortunately, they confused bestowing the advantages of technology, democracy, and science—the universally significant contributions of the West—with uprooting the entire cultural foundation upon which these people based their psychological well being. Every culture is legitimate in the eyes of its adherents, and forced acculturation can often cause culture loss rather than culture gains. Deculturation has, therefore, become the biggest threat to the stability of Israeli society. If a culture does not gain respect, the more profound elements of that culture will wash away, leaving a slimy residue of nondescript attitudes that are but a mixture of the worst of East and West: the quintessential Levantine.

Except for the development of coffee, Yemenite history has made little impact on anyone outside of Yemen. German culture, on the other hand, has affected the entire human race, whether they are aware of it or not. Yet, for immigrant Yemenite Jews, the epic poems of Shalom Shabazi were more important than German music, philosophy, or science. Their family and relation to their social environment were more important than Freud, Marx, or Einstein.

Many aspects of Oriental society are unacceptable to modern individuals. Attitudes toward women and some perceptions of honor have no place in modern society, and we should not even pretend to tolerate them. To accept the intrinsic value of all cultures for their adherents and to respect that fact when dealing with peoples is by no means the same as turning into a fawning White liberal, enthusing over every aspect of the exotic no matter how grotesque.

Different cultural attitudes affected perceptions of the Land of Israel itself. Oriental Jewish Zionism was essentially Biblical and messianic with only the thinnest overlay of modern Zionism. Many Orientals came to Israel, the Holy Land, and expected to live a biblical lifestyle. They did not anticipate the semihysterical technologically intense society that Israel grew up to be. Some saw their *aliya* to Israel as part of the advent of the messianic period. Israel was pictured as the Garden of Eden in which God would provide and no one would have to work. Imagine the trauma of seeing the land as it was, living in refugee hovels, and being asked to do the most menial work. During the short time of a plane ride, they descended from the highest messianic expectations to the lowest reality. The Ashkenazi immigrants were more pragmatic in their approach and did not suffer the cultural and psychological dislocation of their Oriental brethren.

HISTORICAL ANALOGIES

Cross-border cultural admixtures have been at the root of material progress and political vigor throughout history. Cultural pluralism and openness is a prerequisite for material progress and prosperity. The so-called Golden Age of Islam was a 400-year period, from the mid-ninth century until the sack of Baghdad by the Mongols in 1256, when Islam was a cultural crossroads, open to all the major cultures of the world from East and West. Islamic culture was really an admixture of the Greco-Roman tradition, by way of Byzantium and Alexandria, and the Persian and Indian cultures of the day. The so-called Arabic numerals were really invented by the Hindus some 3,000 years ago. Their greatest mathematical triumph was the invention of the zero. The Arabs built on Hindu mathematics to create algebra and algorithms, as they built on Greek geometry to create the elegance of Islamic architecture.

When the Arabs turned their backs on the world following their final "triumph" over the Mongols in 1260 and the Crusaders in 1291, their scientific and cultural progress all but ceased. It has not yet begun to renew itself, even though individual Moslems and Arabs have made significant contributions to humanity as members of Western societies. The "defeated" Crusaders, and the international trade that followed their misadventure, opened Europe up to outside cultural influence. They brought back to Europe Arab mathematics and the Greek philosophical/scientific tradition, which the Arabs had saved. The latter was a major contribution to the rebirth of classical humanism, which resulted in the Renaissance.

Arab mathematics represented a reintroduction of quantitative forms of thought into Europe, a necessary step toward the Scientific Revolution. Copernicus, Galileo, Bacon, Descartes, and Newton would not have made their contributions but for the Arab intellectual contribution. Consider the fate of Western civilization had it decided to be culturally pure and rejected all foreign influences

Europe then took the compass, gunpowder, and iron foundering from the Chinese and combined them with the Arab inheritance to create a social, cultural, economic, political force that began to conquer the world. The conquest of the Americas generated a tremendous surplus of gold and silver that indirectly contributed to the rise of modern investment banking as well as commercial projects to invest in. Conquering the New World introduced new agricultural products such as corn and potatoes, which resulted in population growth and expanded commodity trading in Europe.

Holland, a former Spanish colony, became the commercial and cultural crossroads of Europe. The ethnically and ideologically neutral nature of commerce made Holland a refuge for Jews and intellectuals persecuted elsewhere and helped Holland become the wealthiest and most civilized country in Europe.

Spain, on the other hand, went in the opposite direction. It instituted the Inquisition and threw out first the Jews in 1492—gutting commercial activity—and then the Moslem Moors in the early sixteenth century, gutting agricultural activity. The diminution of commercial activity eventually led to a massive flight of American silver and gold bullion from Spain to Holland in the form of investments. No real investment institutions and opportunities remained in Catholic Spain.

Spain also experienced no Renaissance, no mercantilist/commercial revolution, no Scientific Revolution and no Enlightenment. Rather, a commercial counterrevolution and anti-Enlightenment took place. In the context of European civilization, the Spanish became a nation that dwelt alone. They turned their backs on the global developments they had helped to bring about and suffered the consequences.

Only in the past 30 years has Spain begun to recover from its centuries of obscurantist darkness, while Holland remains one of the most civilized countries in the world. We can see parallels to this in our own time. Saudi Arabia's tremendous oil wealth has enabled it, for a time, to turn its back on world development and norms and reinforce its medieval social structure, as did Spain 500 years ago. Saudi Arabia has been ruled by a theocratic monarchy that ignores modern standards of civil rights (especially of women). It is suspicious of foreign influences and does not engage in real industrial, agricultural, and commercial development because it has always had oil to fall back onto, just as Spain depended on its bullion. As with Spain, this is beginning to have disastrous economic and social consequences for the Saudi people. The Saudi per capita income has been halved in the past two decades. Like Spain, Saudi Arabia has been exporting its capital in the search for investment opportunities unavailable at home. Like Spain, Saudi Arabia has moved from tremendous currency reserves to tremendous foreign debt. To offset this, they must open their economy and their culture. They must reform their entire political system. Like Spain, they appear unable or unwilling to do this in any significant way.

England's economy benefited greatly when it gave refuge to Protestant Huguenot craftsmen fleeing French persecution in the seventeenth century. The intertwining of cultural openness and economic development is self-evident throughout history. Likewise, when Idi Amin expelled thousands of Indian merchants and professionals, their loss was a major factor in Uganda's 30 years of subsequent economic malaise. In England, however, these refugees have made an impressive economic contribution. We see the same lack of wisdom almost repeated in Fiji, where indigenous Fijians wanted to toss out the Indian business class. If they had succeeded, Fiji would have been set back 50 years. Racism and discrimination are a sure formula for backwardness. Just look at the American South before the success of the civil rights movement. The liberation of southern Blacks from the yoke of Jim Crow helped integrate the South into America's continental economy and accelerated its economic growth. Paradoxically, this benefited the southern White even more than it did the southern Black.

There is a lesson here for Israel's advocates of being a nation that dwells alone and "no matter what the Goyim think." If they gain the upper hand in Israel's cultural consciousness, Israel will almost certainly regress into poverty.

The United States is the quintessential open society whose entire economic, commercial, scientific, and technological history is based on vast migrations of peoples of different cultures. The United States became the scientific capital of the human race as a consequence of the Nazi conquest of Europe. The European scientists and engineers who flooded into the United States before and following World War II culminated a historical process dependent upon the inventiveness and energy of immigrants. From Scottish steel maker Andrew Carnegie to Swiss chemist Pierre Dupont to German inventor Charles Steinmetz (the wizard of Westinghouse) to the Jew Albert Einstein to the Italian Enrico Fermi, America's material and moral progress has relied on an open society.

Consider that while the United States opened itself to the world and to immigrants, the Soviet Union closed itself off from the world and developed a xenophobia that put tens of thousands of foreign residents into forced labor camps. This self-inflicted cultural claustrophobia drove much of their home-grown scientific and cultural talent to look for ways to escape to the West.

THE CULTURAL HISTORY OF ISRAEL

Israel's cultural history has developed in a different direction. The pioneering stage was closed and suspicious of outside influences. When I arrived in Israel in the late 1960s, Israel's cultural menu consisted of classical music and what is called "Land of Israel" music, which is almost completely derivative of Russian and Ukrainian folk music.

All other music was held suspect by the political and cultural establishment. "Salon music" (popular dance music) was a pejorative signifying cultural decadence. The fighting ability of an entire generation raised on such shallow fare was a constant concern. The adverse attitudes toward popular Western culture were so extreme that the Israeli government dedicated several sessions to debate the question of entrance visas for the Beatles. The visa request was eventually denied in order to protect the youth from their destructive influence. The extraordinary achievements of the salon-music generation during the Six-Day War dispelled such silly notions. In hindsight, the Six-Day War and its political and economic aftermath may have been the turning point as Israel developed a much more open, self-confident, and pluralistic culture.

This "bolshevik" cultural attitude was particularly apparent in regards to Middle Eastern music. Up until the 1980s, this music was denigrated as "cassette music" because it was usually self-recorded on cheap radio/tape cassettes because the major Israeli record companies would not record such culturally inferior fare. Another term was "Central Bus Station" music, because the Oriental music cassette shops were mostly located at the Tel Aviv Central Bus Station. Oriental Jewish music was designated one or two hours a day on the Israeli radio and was always defined as folk music. Once a year, an Oriental Jewish Music festival and contest appeared on television. This was as far as the cultural/media establishment of Israel was prepared to go in recognizing the cultural legitimacy of more than 50 percent of Israel's Jewish population. Arab music was totally taboo and limited to the Arabic language broadcasts only.

The enforcement of these cultural norms was fierce. As a volunteer on a kibbutz after the Six-Day War, I once turned on a radio station transmitting Arab music. I thought that in order to understand the Middle East I should at least make an attempt to understand its culture. A young kibbutznik walked into my room, without knocking, of course, and angrily turned off my radio: "We do not listen to such garbage here." Later, a female volunteer tried to enter the dining room wearing a beautiful Arab dress. She was denied entrance because she was inappropriately dressed. Both of these events occurred on a progressive, peace-loving, workers-of-the-world-unite kibbutz—the ultimate reverie of the Left. The Israeli Right was much more tolerant of Oriental Jewish culture; Oriental Jews were their natural constituency.

To be fair, these attitudes quickly changed in the six years between the Six-Day and Yom Kippur Wars. In the early 1970s, Israeli women were au courant if they wore Arab dresses, and Israeli fashion in general adapted many Middle Eastern motifs. The official keepers of the Israeli cultural gate, however, discriminated against Oriental music until the late 1980s–1990s. Today, thankfully, it is part of the Israeli cultural mainstream, and Oriental musical motifs have become an integral part of mainstream Israeli popular music.

Before the Six-Day War, Israel was a cultural province, and its technological exports totaled about 17 million dollars a year. Today, Israel's cultural menu is probably one of the most diverse in the world, and its technological exports total more than 11 billion dollars a year. Innovation is a cultural characteristic and cultural openness and technological innovation are two sides of the same coin. Israel has become an interesting cultural and technological center.

But cultural openness does not mean cultural relativity. A hierarchy of cultural values exists and a *metacultural* base must serves as a cultural backbone. In the United States, the metacultural backbone is the Constitution, a set of basic values to which all subcultures declare loyalty. The difference is profound between cultural pluralism and multiculturalism.

THE FUTURE

All this is past tense. The question remains, what will be the future of Israeli society? Will it be demographically Oriental and culturally Western, or will Israel emulate the United States and constantly create and recreate its cultural life while paying scant attention to the sources of its cultural raw material? Do American musicians really care if their cultural raw materials are Scots-Irish, Black, or Hispanic?

Musically, at least, the future is now. Current Israeli music is already a mixture of classical East and West, modern pop and ethnic. One can hear music in Hebrew with Latin and Arabic motifs wrapped in the driving beat of modern pop.

Admixtures such as these will continue to develop, driven by a combination of technology, communications, and cross-border migrations of peoples carrying different cultural baggage. It is interesting to note that countries or regions with the highest percentage of immigrants are the most technologically and culturally dynamic. Technological progress is a cultural attribute and technological progress is a consequence of cultural openness and pluralism. This has given Israel its qualitative edge over its enemies. Any attempt to make Israeli culture monodimensional will have serious consequences.

Cultural pluralism posits that the richer and more varied the cultural mix, the healthier the cultural ecology will be. Healthy cultural ecologies produce economic and technological dynamism because they introduce a multiplicity of viewpoints into the creative mix. In this sense, cultural diversity is a vital survival tool for humanity. With it, we can adapt to economic and technological environments now changing in real time. The greater the number of viewpoints, the greater the chance that someone will come up with the solution for a vital problem.

Individuals who cultivate within themselves a plurality of cultures also have a much better chance of survival. For example, I am Jewish, American, Ashkenazi, Israeli, Middle Eastern, European, and a world citizen. I am all these at once; this enables me to be. Such should be the attitude of cultural discourse in Israel and the Diaspora in the twenty-first century. This would be a healthy model for all residents of Earth in the twenty-first century. To the extent that Israel can make this cultural attitude a norm, Israel will truly be a "Light unto the Nations."

Multiculturalism is contrary to the above. It says there are no objective cultural values, values are subjective constructs. Therefore, to speak of values in terms of some objective moral and ethical standard is foolish and misleading. All values are subjective, and culture is an ideology that reflects these subjective values. There is, therefore, no hierarchy of cultural values. All cultures are created equal and should be treated as equal. Multiculturalists see rationalism as a Western ideology, not an objectively consistent value. Nonrational societies and cultures are equal to rational societies and culture; rationality has no prerogative over irrationality; there is no objective thought, only subjective feeling.

Taken to its extreme, a consistent multiculturalist would deny the *Universal Declaration of Human Rights* because there is no such thing as a universal concept of human rights, and therefore the universal declaration must be cultural imperialism. The rights stated in the declaration are based on Western civilization values as first formulated during the European Enlightenment: the sanctity and preeminence of the human individual, possessing certain natural unalienable rights by the very fact of being a human being.

The former prime minister of Singapore and the present prime minister of Malaysia have denigrated this "Western ideology" and have raised the flag of "Asian Values." This vague term celebrates the collective over the individual and the wisdom of the patriarchal leader over the judgment of the individual citizen, and is geared to justifying authoritarian rule.

This debate is especially relevant for Israel, as the Arabs have constantly claimed that Israel is a foreign Western implant and should integrate itself into the region, that is, reject the West and integrate itself into the Middle East. Let us examine this claim in greater detail. It is the discipline of specificity that uncovers the absurdities of multiculturalism as it applies to Israel's future.

Should Israel aspire to the judicial system of Iran or the judicial system of England?

Should Israel aspire to the civil service of Egypt or the civil service of France?

Should Israel aspire to the rights of women in Saudi Arabia or the rights of women in Sweden?

Should Israel aspire to the technological level of Yemen or the technological level of the United States?

Should Israel aspire to a Third World standard of living or to a Western standard of living?

Should Israel aspire to a welfare society or to a subsistence society?

When one becomes specific and avoids vague generalities such as "For peace Israel should become less Western and more Middle Eastern," one uncovers the fundamental intellectual dishonesty of this demand.

There *is* a hierarchy of values. A culture that implements the death penalty is inferior to that which has rejected the death penalty. A culture that cuts off the hands of thieves is inferior to a culture that imprisons them. A culture that places the state above the individual is inferior to a culture that places the individual above the state. A culture that denies women equal rights is inferior to a culture that grants women equal rights. A culture that stresses the past is inferior to a culture that stresses the future. A culture intolerant of criticism is inferior to a culture that encourages criticism.

So, what is the future of Israeli culture? Cultural pluralism yes, multiculturalism, no. We must strive to create a metaculture that is "Western," that reflects the principles of the *Universal Declaration of Human Rights* and contains subcultures that do not contradict these basic Western metacultural values. We must engender an endless proliferation of aesthetic cultural expressions that draws raw materials from every human culture on the planet but remains anchored in Western concepts of rights and social and economic organization. We must be constantly inspired by the variegated cultural traditions of the Jews as we have developed over the past 4,000 years and as we *will continue to develop* into the future.

A cultural vision based upon reconstructing past cultural achievements is a prescription for ruin. We live in the future and not in the past. We require a space age Jewish cultural attitude that will cultivate romantic yearnings for the future instead of fossilized yearnings for the past. We will examine some notions of what these might be in chapter 11, "The Future of Jewish Identity."

CHAPTER 10

The Future of Jewish-Christian Relations

Any full discussion regarding the future of the Jewish People must attempt to lay new foundations for our relationship with the Christian world. Paradoxically, the present seemingly benevolent attitude of Christianity poses the greatest threat to Jewish identity in the twenty-first century. Christian-inspired inquisitions, pogroms, and holocausts do not threaten Jewish survival, but vague liberal "acceptance" and the seductive power of *uncritical* ecumenism do. The New Age bromide, all "religions" are really the same, challenges the future of Jewish existence.

I place religion in quotation marks for accuracy. Judaism, like Confucianism, is as much a life system, an attitude to life on Earth, as it is a religion in the sense the Christians use that term. This difference indicates the difficulties we have in inventing a new language in discourse with the Christian world. Historical circumstance has forced us when debating with the Christian world to use Christian concepts, not the least of which are *God* and *religion*.

This has tended to subvert how Jews see their own tradition. Viewing their tradition through Christian eyes has made them easy prey for other religions and life systems. The result is that most Jews, including many Orthodox, are ignorant of the essential particularity of their own tradition.

This has put the Jews at a disadvantage when they try to explore the Jewish tradition. I prefer to speak of Jewish tradition, Jewish worldview, or Jewish ideology, instead of Jewish religion, as I believe they convey a truer sense of Jewishness.

The future of Jewish-Christian relations must be based upon a reaffirmation of Jewish integrity. It must be contingent upon the end of Jewish apologetics. The Jews, as the threatened minority, must draw clear lines regarding the ideational differences between Christianity and Judaism. Ecumenism does not mean the blurring of precise analytical inquiry for fear of offending or provoking those with a different view of life.

Ecumenism does not mean we have to compromise or shade our view of the world in order to be socially acceptable or immune to physical threat or implicit political intimidation. This requires a twenty-first-century reaffirmation of the Enlightenment principle of total separation between church and state. Enlightenment principles are not the enemy of modern Jewish identity and survival, as some neo-Orthodox thinkers now claim, they are a prerequisite for continued Jewish identity and survival.

Ecumenism should be a political and not a religious arrangement between peoples with different worldviews. It should simply mean good planetary citizenship based upon the same principles as the American republic: freedom of inquiry and freedom of conscience. These principles require that we do not murder one another or otherwise harm one another because we have different views of the world.

We can and should cooperate with Christians and adherents of other faiths and philosophical outlooks as responsible citizens of our respective countries and of the planet. Jews cannot avoid delineating certain basic differences between the Jewish and Christian approach to life out of fear. The ecumenical blurring of differences is endangering our survival by engendering Jewish indifference to the potential, particular value of the Jewish tradition. Some Jews thus become receptive to the "Jews for Jesus" or "Messianic Jews" who claim one can believe in Jesus as the Messiah and still be a Jew.

This discussion contains an inherent problem. Answering the question of who or what is a Christian is no less difficult than answering the question of who or what is a Jew. I will try to be as precise as possible in ascribing particular beliefs to Catholics, Protestants, or Evangelicals when appropriate. I am also mindful that most present-day Christians, of whatever denomination, are indifferent to doctrinal issues and are content to conduct respectful relationships with Jews outside a theological frame of reference. I would hope, therefore, that what follows does not in anyway inhibit or damage the fruitful Christian-Jewish cooperation of the past 50 years.

JUDEO-CHRISTIAN ETHIC: MYTH AND REALITY

The first step in establishing a healthy relationship is to clarify the similarities and differences between the Jewish worldview and the Christian worldview. With clarity comes understanding, and with understanding comes mutual respect.

Judaism and Christianity are in general agreement about many macroethical guiding principles regarding the essence and meaning of human life. In the microethical, the moral living of life on a *daily* basis, we discover significant differences.

Jews and Christians accept the Ten Commandments as the foundation of morality. So do the Moslems. The Buddhists, Confucians, Shinto, and various animistic religions also have a foundational macroethics similar to the monotheists. Human beings must live in society to survive. To do so, they must not murder one another, steal from one another, lie about one another, and so on. For this practical reason, all great religions and philosophical systems have similar foundational macroethics. If we were to stop here, we would not be speaking about the Judeo-Christian ethic, we would be speaking about the Judeo-Christian-Moslem-Buddhist-Confucian-Shinto-Animist-Stoic-and-so-on ethic.

Christians and Moslems accept the Jewish maxim that human beings are created in the image of God, are equal in his eyes, and inherently valuable as individuals. This macroethic is particular to monotheistic religions. Here, we would be speaking about a Judeo-Christian-Islamic ethic.

If human beings are valuable in themselves, their lives are valuable and have meaning. If they are created in the image of God, they have natural rights that no earthly power can obviate. The individual has sanctity for having been made in the image of God. In its secularized form, the concept of individual sanctity has served as the basis for resistance to tyranny.

During the European Enlightenment, the secularized expression of equality before God led to concepts of equality before the law. The secularized expression of natural rights led to natural rights theories of politics and society, which led to the concept of unalienable rights, which gave impetus to the American Revolution. Carl Becker in his classic book, *The Heavenly City of the Eighteenth-Century Philosophers*, describes how the foundations of our modern secular civilization derive from the internal evolution of Christian Europe.

The governmental requirements of Imperial Rome, with its mosaic of cultures and social norms, gave birth to the concept of "universal" natural rights, which took precedence over the cultural mores of specific peoples and obligated all peoples. A secularized Christian Europe, under the influence of "in the image of God" truly universalized this by applying it to *all persons* not just all peoples. This European Enlightenment contribution to human civilization is the source of the Universal Declaration of Human Rights, the United Nations Charter, and all of international humanitarian law.

Judaism and Christianity both agree that the human drama is played out on a historical stage and that human beings have a historical role to play of cosmic significance, although the particulars of that role differ. Christian historiography is based on Jewish historiography, and here we find a particular Judeo-Christian ethic.

Both Judaism and Christianity have more positive attitudes toward human work and human enterprise than other traditions. Both see nature as something provided by God for human use and not something sacred in itself. Pagans see nature as sacred in itself; monotheists see human beings as the objects and purpose of God's sacred creation. Monotheism is a prerequisite for humanism.

It is no accident, therefore, that the Industrial Revolution occurred in Christian Europe, which affirmed the intrinsic value of work and viewed nature as utilitarian to humankind. It did not occur in India, China, or ancient Greece or Rome because societal norms denigrated those who did physical work or engaged in commerce. It also did not occur in cultures that sanctified nature and set "her" above humankind.

More technological innovation and adoption of technology from other cultures occurred during the European Middle Ages than in the entire history of pagan Greece and Rome combined. These innovations and adoptions included the iron plow, the horse collar, the stirrup, the horseshoe, the three-field system, the windmill, the flying buttress, primitive clocks (developed by Benedictine monks for prayer time), and others.

Modern historical research speaks about the medieval agricultural revolution, a consequence of the iron plow, the horse collar, and the three-field system, and the medieval industrial revolution, a consequence of the windmill. Both engendered the commercial revolution, a major factor in the Renaissance. This in turn engendered the Scientific Revolution, the Enlightenment, and mercantilism, which eventually led to the Industrial Revolution and industrial capitalism. Culture precedes economy and technology, and modern Europe and its North American offspring were created on the foundations laid by medieval Christian Europe.

A worldview that values *all* human beings as human beings may not actively encourage innovation but will allow innovation that lessens physical drudgery and thus increases human spiritual potential. A worldview that sees the lower classes as inferior humans or less than human cannot develop the cultural norms that encourage innovation. Thus, the Industrial Revolution occurred in Western Europe, which had ended slavery and serfdom and had raised the commercial and mechanical classes to a kind of lower nobility, and not in Czarist Russia where 90 percent of the population were serfs. Just as the Industrial Revolution occurred in the free-labor American North and not in the slave-holding South.

MICROETHICS: THE BIG DIFFERENCE

At the microethical level, where most human beings live, *Judeo-Christian ethic* is a conjoining of words devoid of any real meaning. The rationale behind the Jewish position on abortion reveals this, as does how the Jews would have justified a decision to separate Siamese twins, thus killing one of them, or the Jewish and Christian perspectives on altruism versus egoism.

Jews justify abortion when the fetus threatens the life of the mother, not because it views the life of the mother as intrinsically more valuable than the fetus, but rather on the grounds of self-defense. This is in accord with the Talmudic dictum, "He who comes to kill you, arise and kill him first." In the Jewish tradition, self-defense is a moral obligation, not only a moral right, even as it pertains to an unborn fetus. Such argumentation is foreign to the average Christian and yet a concrete expression of a first principle of Judaism: the unconditional right to our own lives. This Jewish principle, mirrored in the Anglo-Saxon tradition of human beings having property over their own lives, may be one reason why Jews have found English-speaking Christian countries most amenable to a civilized Jewish existence.

Another example of significant microethical differences based on this right of self-defense is the case of the Siamese twins born in Malta and taken to England for treatment. One twin had no chance of survival even if separated, the other twin did have a chance to survive if separated but would have died if not separated. The parents were Catholic and wanted the courts to forbid the operation and let God's will be done. The Catholic clergy supported the parents, even though both babies would have died. The English courts and English doctors agonized over what to do and spoke in terms of "murdering" one baby to save the other and finally approved the operation by way of a utilitarian rationale. The Jewish approach would have been, in its very essence, different. The baby who had no chance to live threatened the life of the baby who might live. The viable baby had the right to defend itself against the unviable baby. Lacking the ability to do so on its own, its guardians must exercise that right for the baby. The other baby had no such right, because its twin did not threaten its life. In the light of Jewish tradition, this was a case of the unalienable right of self-defense and had nothing to do with murder.

The Christian ideal is to be Christ-like, to constantly ask what would Jesus have done. What Jesus did was to sacrifice himself so that humanity could be purified of sin and be saved. The Christian ethical structure is based upon the most famous case of altruism in human history, someone unconditionally giving up his life for others. I would not presume to challenge the spiritual and therapeutic power of the crucifixion story for believing Christians or the positive role it played in civilizing barbarian Europe. I would only say that it cannot be accommodated into a Jewish belief system. A Jew cannot be a Jew and be *for* the Jesus of the crucifixion story.

Human sacrifice is anathema to Judaism, and Jews would view unconditional self-sacrifice as the most incongruous form of human sacrifice. Judaism forbids one to engage in reckless altruism that threatens one's life.

This Jewish ideal is demonstrated by a famous Talmudic case: *"Mayim Le Shtaim"* (water for two). A modern version of this story would go like this: Two individuals have to cross a dry desert. Their very survival depends on each of them taking two full canteens of water, the minimum needed to survive the crossing; anything less than two full canteens means certain death. At the point of no return and after they have each consumed one canteen, one of them discovers that he forgot to fill his second canteen. Question: "What is the moral obligation of the individual who remembered to fill both canteens?" Remember, if he shares his remaining canteen with his forgetful friend, he, too, will surely die. Now, a believing Christian, whose personal ideal is to be Christ-like, will almost certainly share his remaining water and pray to God that they both will be spared. In other words, he will risk sacrificing his own life in order to be like Christ, placing his very life in the hands of fate and faith. The rabbis who discussed this case, however, concluded that not only was the responsible person not morally obligated to share his water with the irresponsible person, it would be a moral transgression if he did so.

In the Jewish tradition, a responsible person has no moral obligation to risk sacrificing his life because an irresponsible person has placed himself in danger. We have no obligation to sacrifice our lives as a condition for justifying our lives. If our very existence causes suffering to other beings, we have the moral obligation to try to ameliorate that suffering, but we have no obligation or *moral right* to sacrifice ourselves in order to relieve that suffering.

The very *method* of debating moral and ethical dilemmas reflects radical differences between Jews and Christians. The Talmud deals with specific cases of real people in real situations and expects the reader or student to infer the principles out of these specifics. In regards to human life, the Jewish tradition places the concrete before the abstract—microethics before macroethics. The Christian tradition, on the other hand, grounded as it is in Greek philosophy, is more likely to stress the abstract principle and try to conform the concrete situation to it—macroethics before microethics.

SUPERFICIAL ECUMENISM

Judeo-Christian ethic has become a fashionable phrase in recent years through superficial ecumenism, which hides underlying and perhaps subconscious considerations of both Christians and Jews. I believe most Christians use this phrase for two reasons: one positive and one negative.

Positive: Since the Holocaust, Christians have recognized how Christian anti-Semitism contributed to the greatest crime in human annals. This realization truly horrified them as human beings and as honest Christians because it endangered the foundational bedrock of Christianity as a religion of love and not of hate. By stressing the common ethical bond, they sincerely wanted to demonstrate the greater similarities of the two religions thereby heading off manifestations of anti-Semitism amongst their own coreligionists in the future. They also wanted to demonstrate their own goodness as manifested by their tolerance and broadmindedness. It was a sincere attempt after the fact to make amends.

Negative: The Jews for Jesus and Messianic Jews use this phrase as a strategy for breaking down Jewish resistance to their proselytizing efforts by way of Jewish symbols. Thus, "Our ethical view of the world is the same, we are not asking you to give up your Jewish culture, all we are doing is adding on Jesus who himself was a practicing Jew. You are not losing anything, or changing anything, you are only gaining spiritual added value."

Belief in Jesus as personal savior and the feeling of being born again, liberated from past sins, has tremendous psychological appeal and therapeutic value for those who have led a life characterized by troubles and or sociopathic behavior. Therefore, this method of arguing and strategy of proselytizing have had some success in the Jewish community, especially as the Christian communities using this strategy are often Israel's biggest supporters. This deflects objections from Jews who deplore the phenomenon but who love Israel and are loath to alienate any Christian elements that support her.

The Jews, on the other hand, have been seduced into using the phrase *Judeo-Christian ethic* because, after the past's extreme anti-Semitism, the phrase offers a warm security-blanket refuge. It signifies acceptance into Christian society and provides an ideological shield against future hostility. I have even been told that the Jews originated the phrase to emotionally co-opt their Christian fellow citizens for self-defense.

Ecumenism holds different meanings for Jews and Christians, whether they are cognizant of it or not. Christians join ecumenical organizations to show how good and full of brotherhood they are. Jews join as part of a more general Grand Strategy of self-defense. As long as we belong to the same brotherhood organizations and speak of Judeo-Christian ethics chances are "they" won't kill us or destroy our property. Some Jews will take issue with this interpretation, preferring to believe that Jewish ecumenism is motivated by the same "pure" altruistic reasons as the Christians, but are they being honest with themselves? The reader must reflect on the truth of this interpretation.

JEWISH VERSUS CHRISTIAN PRINCIPLES

Judaism has been characterized by several major principles that clarify some differences with Christianity.

The War against Idolatry

The worship of anything that can be conceived of in a material or bodily sense would be considered idolatry for Jews. Judaism is a celebration of the fact of existence. Life itself is positive for the Jew: "and you have chosen life." The basically positive force underlying life, we call "God." We sanctify that force, pay tribute to it, and worship it. The very attempt to define or materialize or personalize that force would be idolatrous for the Jew.

One of our problems is the word *God*, an inadequate three-letter Anglo-Saxon word that the Jews have borrowed from the Christians by dint of the fact that we speak European languages. In fact, God is the proper name for an ancient, pagan Anglo-Saxon god.

The Hebrew equivalent is Elohim, which implies a fundamental force underlying our material world that governs and moves our material world.

Another Hebrew word for God is *Yahweh* (sometimes written "Yehova"), translated as the proper noun *Jehovah* by Christians. Orthodox Jews are forbidden to even pronounce the word and substitute *Adonoi* (my Lord).

There is, therefore, no Jewish theology—"God knowledge" in Greek, only a Jewish way of behaving—*derech eretz* in Hebrew, *Yiddishkeit* in popular Yiddish terminology. Jewish "doctrine" is preoccupied with the earthly behavior of human beings as a supreme value *in itself* and as the key to the world to come, *not* the true nature of God and getting this right in order to enter the world to come.

The Unmediated Individual Apprehension of God

This is not a personal relationship with God, impossible according to the Jewish conception of God's indefinable nature, One cannot have a personal relationship with something that is not a person and that by definition is beyond definition.

What cannot be defined cannot be mediated, neither by a rabbi nor a priest nor Jesus. When Evangelical Christians speak about a personal relationship with God, they seem to be speaking about a personal relationship with Jesus—the person part of the triune Godhead.

A Jew might have an intimate "relationship" with his own idea or sense of what God might be. He might even "appeal to him," "praise him," "talk to him," "argue with him," or even "reprimand him," but a Jew cannot have a personal relationship with God, because God is not a person.

This does not mean that Jews throughout the ages have not yearned to "know" or claimed to "know" God. It only means that normative Judaism has no official position on the matter and is historically suspicious of movements and individuals who claim mystical communion with God. As a religious Israeli scholar once said, "The false messiah is one who comes," that is, one who declares himself or allows himself to be declared.

Jews as a social collective use communal prayer and normative modes of worship to celebrate and sanctify the force the Christians call God. Jews do not establish a collective connection; they perform collective celebrations. Catholics require the mediation of the priest for seven sacraments and during the mystery of the Mass establish a direct communion with Christ by consuming his symbolic blood and body; Protestants require the mediation of a minister or pastor for two sacraments; Jews do not require a rabbi for any sacraments. One can be an ultra-Orthodox Jew without ever having contact with a rabbi. A rabbi is not a clergyman; he is more like a well-informed spiritual consultant with greater knowledge and capable of giving advice on confusing religious issues. Jews have acceded to the concept of rabbi as clergyman as one way to obtain respectful treatment at the hands of Christian society, which grants special status to clergy.

The Inherent Inability to Positively Define the Concept of "God"

The phrase *I believe in God* is troublesome for Jews who truly understand the essence of Judaism, even though belief in the existence of God is the first of the 613 commandments. To utter that sentence, they would first require a clear, *objective* definition of what God is and then clarify what they mean by belief. Both tasks are by definition impossible. In the Jewish tradition, any *positive* definition or description of God *limits* God.

The entire Jewish tradition discourages speculation and discussion about the nature of God, even though there is no specific prohibition, and some Jews have done so throughout the centuries. Historical Christianity, on the other hand, in its various formulations, seems to have been preoccupied with the nature of God and the proper definition thereof. Moses says to the "voice" emanating from the burning bush: "They (the People of Israel) will say unto me what is his name? What shall I say unto them?" And God replies, "I will be what I will be [an indefinite formulation, implying incompleteness and future tense in translation]...say unto the children of Israel: 'I will be' hath sent me unto you...this is my name forever...my memorial unto all generations" (Exodus, p. 67, Jewish Publication Society Bible).

The proper Jewish "naming," in translation, of the concept the Christians call God is just one of many rubrics Jews must address as a rational defense against the more sophisticated proselytizing attempts of some segments of present-day Christianity. For this task, we would do well to refer back to Maimonides's negative theology,— that is, what we cannot say about God—as an alternative to Christian "positive theology," the attempt to positively define God. Indeed, most observant Jews refer to this force as *HaShem*—the name. What has no real name is called *HaShem*. Christians talk about the God they worship, while Jews worship what cannot be talked about. In this case, does the claim that "we all worship the same God" have any real meaning? And why should this be an issue at all in regards to how we treat one another as human beings?

A Stress on Right Action Rather Than Right Belief

Jews most often ask "do you keep the commandments?" and only rarely "do you believe in God?" How to act, not belief, is the defining characteristic of the Jew. No matter what the differences between the various trends of Judaism, all would agree that Judaism is a commandment- and act-centered system. Jews dispute about what acts and which commandments—not about which beliefs.

A classic Jewish story exemplifies this tradition. A yeshiva student approaches the head of the yeshiva in an attitude of trepidation and distress. "Rabbi I have a terrible problem." "What is your problem, my son?" "I no longer am able to believe in God." The rabbi ponders this astounding news and responds: "All right, but what has that to do with *Yiddishkeit?*" In other words, what has that to do with being a good Jew? Would such an answer be possible for any believing Christian?

Some Christians often seem to instill right belief with ethical value and content. For Jews, belief has no inherent ethical value; behavior is everything. Many Christians believe Jesus has monopoly power over the world to come. Only by way of him will you enter the Kingdom of Heaven. Jews would find offensive the concept of monopoly power over anything having to do with God.

Christian belief is theological (that is, concerned with knowing and how to know God—what some Protestant denominations call "being right with God"). Historically, intra-Christian sectarian disputes have most often centered on the proper description of God. Many Christians believe that if you have this wrong, you will not have salvation. Some fundamentalist Protestants even say that Mother Teresa, while a good person, did not know God in the right way (was not right with God) and therefore would not go to heaven. The Catholic Church, for its part, has just reaffirmed the doctrine of *the exclusivity* of the Catholic Church as the way to heaven because that is the only way to right knowledge about God.

Granted, many present-day Christians, Catholic or Protestant, would not ascribe to either view and would view it as an archaic leftover totally irrelevant to their spiritual life as Christians. Be that as it may, both these views have played a major role in how Christians view Jews and how the Jews view themselves. The inertia of these perspectives still plays a major role in Western civilization, especially as it pertains to Christian-Jewish relations.

Jews, on the other hand, make no exclusivity claims whatsoever in regards to the world to come. Normative Judaism says that any human being who does not violate the "Seven Commandments of Noah" will have a place in the world to come. I mention this because Judaism is most often accused of being a "tribal" religion reflecting a provincial outlook on life as opposed to the cosmopolitan approach of universal Christianity. Yet, which view is provincial and exclusive, and which is universal and inclusive, and which view would be most suitable for the tolerance necessary to sustain a democratic and free society?

Preoccupation with right belief is a dangerous game and has totalitarian implications. In its religious formulation, it resulted in the Inquisition and witch hunts. In its secular formulation, it resulted in the guillotine and gulags. The sincere advocates of right belief cannot tolerate tolerance or a live and let live attitude. They are morally bound to save the souls of the "blind" by any means possible. Missionaries must liberate others from darkness, and ideologues must liberate them from their false consciousness.

The Moral Sovereignty and Autonomy of the Individual

The essence of Judaism is that people have absolute responsibility over their own lives. Unlike Christians, Jews cannot blame an outside force (the

Devil) for bad behavior or look to an outside force (Jesus) to sanction or forgive behavior. *Bar mitzvah* is the Jewish coming of age as an adult responsible for his or her own behavior.

To be an adult means to exercise autonomous reason and to take absolute responsibility for the rest of your life. Both autonomous reason and absolute responsibility are, of course, ramified through a filter of normative social interaction. Human beings do not dwell alone, they live in society. The trinity of human survival is reason (the primary survival tool of the individual), society (the primary survival tool of the collective), and property (without which neither society nor the individual can survive). *Real life*, in this world, consists of the ongoing attempt to ameliorate the inherent tension between these three components of human being.

Judaism, therefore, is a social, in-this-world tradition and not a transcendent, otherworld tradition. In the Jewish tradition, what is moral or immoral has to do with relations between people and not with relations with God. You can only be immoral to (hurt) people. You cannot be immoral to God. God cannot be hurt by our actions. You cannot do God good, and you cannot do God evil. Indeed, Maimonides's negative theology would say that God is beyond such concepts. If any concept could reflect Nietzsche's term *beyond good and evil*, the Jewish concept of God would.

Rules of morality and ethics are for human beings. In this regard, Judaism would probably be closer to Confucianism or Buddhism than to Christianity or Islam.

Catholics are forgiven their sins (against God and against man) in confession; Protestants are forgiven or cleansed of their sins (against God and against man), literally, born again, when they are saved. On Yom Kippur, Jews are forgiven only for their transgressions against God. They are not and cannot be forgiven by God for sins against other human beings. Only the human beings you have sinned against can forgive you, not God. And even they are not obliged to forgive you until and unless you have requested forgiveness at least three times.

The Jewish God may have the power to be an absolute monarch, but "he" has chosen to be a constitutional monarch who rules over autonomous individuals who have certain unalienable rights—*even vis-à-vis God*. The concept of limitations of power—which lies at the root of constitutional democracy—has its beginnings in the story of Abraham's relationship with God.

This autonomy and these unalienable rights are demonstrated early in the Bible when Abraham pleads for Sodom and Gomorrah and calls God to task for not living up to his own concept of justice. God relents to Abraham's protestations about due process for those who might be innocent. In other words, Abraham wins his argument with God. In another story about Abraham, from the oral tradition, Abraham is speaking with God when he sees three strangers approaching. He excuses himself from God's presence, explaining that his primary obligation is to offer his fellow humans hospitality.

In the same tradition, Eli Weisel relates an event that occurred in one of the Nazi concentration camps. Ultra-Orthodox Jews put God on trial for breaking his covenant (contract) with the People of Israel by permitting the Nazi injustice to take place. They found God guilty and then went out to perform their afternoon prayers. This story, easily accessible to the Jewish spirit, is probably incomprehensible to most Christians.

Then there is the remarkable Talmudic story of Rabbi Eliezer trying to convince his colleagues of the justice of his position by calling on God. When a heavenly voice indeed declared that Eliezer was right, Rabbi Jeremiah, representing the opposition majority opinion, responded that the "Torah was given to us on Sinai, and hence we have no need to pay heed to a heavenly voice." In other words, when sages are discussing a point of law, God has no place in the discussion. These stories reaffirm the moral and intellectual sovereignty of the human individual; meaning there are no easy outs in appealing to God and hoping God will tell you what to do. What in the fundamental Christian worldview could accommodate the ethos that underlies these stories? Do these stories reflect a Judeo-Christian ethic?

Acausal Ethics

Nothing does more violence to basic Jewish values than acausal ethics. The concept that another being has died for us and cleansed us of our sins, that we are now "saved" (forgiven) by an act of grace unrelated to personal behavioral merit, is foreign to the entire Jewish worldview. Simply stated, one cannot be a Jew and believe in Jesus as one's personal savior. Such a belief would be antiethical to everything the Jewish tradition represents. If the Jewish messiah comes to save the Jews and all other humans (not simply individuals who believe in him) as *a consequence* of our behavior, his coming is conditional, not unconditional. This renders Jews for Jesus an oxymoron. How one can even speak of a Judeo-Christian ethic when belief in Jesus as the Son of God and every man's potential personal savior is the central tenet of Christianity, is beyond understanding.

OTHER DIFFERENCES

Many other fundamental differences arise between Judaism and Christianity. These relate to life on this earth versus life in the world to come, to attitudes toward miracles, to bodily satiation versus bodily denial, and to differing concepts of spirituality. These require entire books to deal with them properly. Such books include *Judaism and Christianity—The Differences*, by Dr. Trude Weiss-Rosmarin. This compact, clearly written book should become required reading for all Jews and a basic text for every Jewish education program.

Another outstanding and more extensive book is *Where Judaism Differed*, by Rabbi Abba Hillel Silver, which should also become required reading for all

Jews. These books should be on every Jewish bookshelf. They should serve as the primary Jewish references for debate and discussion with Christians of all persuasions (Catholic, Protestant, or Evangelical), as well as secular post-Christians and intellectual Jews who have unknowingly inherited Christian prejudices against the Jewish worldview.

WHAT JEWS FIND OFFENSIVE

Jews must be forthright in telling Christians what we find offensive. Jews are no longer cowering in ghettos, afraid of offending Gentiles and triggering pogroms. Israel exists; a proud, independent American Jewish community steeped in the principles of the American Constitution exists. A European Jewry integrated into European society exists. European Jewry is now capable of creatively challenging the Christian roots of European post-Christianity to the mutual benefit of Europe and the Jews.

Let our individual and communal posture reflect this reality in the twenty-first century. Let us behave with a little more honor, dignity, and intellectual honesty when discussing in public forums what we really believe about ourselves and about others. What ethical implications accompany the strategy to convert the Jews by way of Jews for Jesus? We must tell our Evangelical friends that we view the strategy to assail Judaism from within by using Jewish symbols as unethical.

In America, every group has the legal right (under the Constitution) to practice and promote its beliefs. These same constitutional rights are also valid for citizens of the European Union. This also pertains to the Jewish members of Jews for Jesus as well as their evangelical Christian supporters. The question is, does this legal right give them the *ethical* right to violate the fundamentals of truth in packaging? When one "buys" the Jews for Jesus or Messianic Jews as a legitimate expression of Jewish identity, it is akin to buying a box of cornflakes and getting a box of laundry soap. If truth in advertising pertained to religion as it pertains to soap and cornflakes, Jews for Jesus and their Christian supporters would be committing a punishable criminal offense.

For most Jews, this missionary strategy exceeds the boundaries of common decency and neighborly behavior and grossly violates the ecumenical spirit of mutual respect that most present-day Christians profess and genuinely want to develop. We Jews must invite our Christian friends to honestly confront this radical disconnect in their behavior toward the Jewish community.

Let us ask our Christian friends the following question: How would Christians feel if Orthodox Jews organized Christian converts to Judaism into the Original Church of the Brotherhood of Israel and sent them back into the Christian community using Christian symbols and church-style services to convert confused Christian youth to Judaism? What if they told the youth that the converts would still be members of the Christian community? One can only imagine the ferocious response to this "underhanded Jewish sneaki-ness" and implicit innuendo harking back to classic anti-Semitism.

It is true that Jewish cultural expression is pluralistic and that religious belief and practice are not the supreme criteria of Jewish peoplehood. More than a century ago, however, the *agnostic* Jewish historian Simon Dubnov wrote, "If we wish to preserve Judaism as a cultural-historical type of nation, we must realize that the religion of Judaism is one of the integral foundations of the national culture and that anyone who seeks to destroy it undermines the very basis of national existence...the exit from Judaism by acceptance of the Christian religion means exit from the Jewish nation."

Even most Jewish "atheists" would agree with this. Messianic Jews and Jews for Jesus represent a kind of spiritual transvestitism, to which those who are afraid of the surgical knife of complete conversion adhere. It may be difficult for Christians to understand, but most members of the Jewish community would see a Jewish "atheist" who eats pork on Yom Kippur as still being a Jew. While a Jew for Jesus who keeps kosher and *lays tefillin* but who believes in Jesus as his personal savior would not be considered a Jew.

SUBLIMINAL AND SUBVERSIVE ATTACKS ON JEWISH IDENTITY

Post-Christian secular society has inherited from its presecular Christian roots a subliminal and more invidious background music that implies the prim-itiveness of Judaism and remains essentially anti-Jewish. Innumerable negative images of Judaism that endanger Jewish identity have insinuated themselves into modern post-Christian secular civilization. Examples of these are

1. The expression "Talmudic thinking" as a pejorative
2. The story of Jesus and the moneychangers as a legitimate purifying act in defiance of a degenerate and corrupt religious establishment
3. Tribal Judaism versus catholic (universal) Christianity
4. Legalistic Judaism versus Christian love

The inertia of this Christian view of Judaism continues in secular academic scholarship. Modern secular literature, history, and philosophy texts abound with such subtle pejoratives. These concepts are cultural and psychological guerilla warfare against the poorly schooled modern Jew. They predispose him against his roots and against a robust reevaluation of these roots.

The historeosophic project of Arnold Toynbee is one of the more extreme examples of this ubiquitous phenomenon. Toynbee, relying on grotesque misrepresentations of Judaism inherited from Christianity, called the Jews a "fossil" whose historical relevance had ended with the appearance of Jesus and Christianity. This was presented as an objective historical analysis but was in fact a secular version of the Christian myth that with the advent of Christianity, Judaism ceased to perform a vital role in human history.

Such is the intellectual fare several generations of our twentieth-century, university-trained Jews have ingested. This works on the subconscious mind of young Jews, alienating them from their Jewish identity. The Jews have been remiss in developing ways and means to combat these subliminal attacks on the Jewish psyche, partly because combating them is like combating a false rumor. Where does one begin?

Also, we are loath to address this issue for fear of offending the Christian community. We must be forthright in dealing with this problem in a serious way, which may lead to comparisons and interpretations unfavorable to Christianity. This would create a serious Jewish *political* problem. We still live in a Christian and post-Christian environment and have a vital interest in cultivating good relations with Christians of all denominations.

How do we assert our cultural/spiritual/intellectual integrity in repelling the assault of some Christians against our very cultural being without offending potential Christian and post-Christian allies and weakening our political position? Israel's biggest supporters in American civil society are the 70-million-strong Evangelical communities, the very communities that fund the various manifestations of the Jews for Jesus or Messianic Jews. This is a difficult strategic dilemma, but the difficulty does not free us from our moral obligation to deal with the issue.

Talmudic Thinking versus New Testament Thinking

Talmudic hairsplitting is a recognized pejorative even in secular debate; signifying a tortured, artificial style of argumentation. The Jews call this process *pilpul*, from the Hebrew word for pepper, because it sharpens the mind.

Yet, if we were to critically examine Christian dogma and exegesis, we could conclude that New Testament thinking should replace Talmudic thinking to indicate tortured, twisted, artificial logic. Scores of *Christian* intellectuals and scholars have been documenting this for years. A future Jewish educational project might be to prepare popular handbooks showing how some Christians have misinterpreted the Old Testament. Trude Weiss-Rosmarin's book has numerous examples of this phenomenon, but it might be more politically wise to compose an anthology of Christian comments.

Such a project would obligate the Jews to reevaluate their own attitudes toward concepts like *pilpul*, which is often used as a pejorative even in Jewish circles. *Pilpul* is designed solely to train the minds of practitioners never to accept face value and always to seek new ways of thinking. Its misuse by ignorant rabbis to confuse and control the unschooled has given it a bad name. In point of fact, *pilpul* anticipated today's creative-thinking workshops, which train people to developed their lateral (associative) thinking by connecting and integrating concepts that appear unrelated.

Pilpul is an exercise to deepen and widen one's ability to think analytically, critically, synthetically, and creatively. It generates new ways of looking at problems, which prompts innovative solutions. Judaism has no final doctrine, because human thought is unending in its ability to conceive and reconceive and thus allow no final word on anything. This is what makes human beings "in the image of God." Maimonides, recognizing the evolutionary character of the human mind, went so far as to say that the Torah itself must be reinterpreted in every generation.

While *pilpul's* intent is to sharpen the mind, New Testament argumentation intends to prove the truth of Christianity. It forms a cornerstone of the Christian faith and belief system and claim to cosmic exclusivity. It is not an exercise—it is a foundation stone of the entire Christian enterprise and belief system. Yet, during the past 100 years of critical *Christian* scholarship, scores of Catholic and Protestant scholars have questioned the veracity, the factualness, and even the intellectual honesty of much New Testament argumentation and exegesis. Many churches, however, act as if these researches and conclusions do not exist and continue to preach the Gospel as if it were unchallenged truth.

For a remarkable description of this phenomenon, read *Jesus Son of Man* by Rudolf Augstein, founder and publisher of the German magazine *Der Spiegel.* Mr. Augstein, a non-Jew, has conducted secondary research into what Catholic and Protestant scholars during the past 100 years have been writing about the veracity of traditional Christian dogma. He documents their discoveries and highlights their reticence in bringing these discoveries to light and severely criticizes what he construes to be intellectual dishonesty. His work has great relevance for Jews who want to reevaluate their tradition as it has been filtered through Christian eyes.

Jesus and the MoneyChangers

In his first inaugural address, Franklin Delano Roosevelt referred to driving the moneychangers from the temple. He was using this turn of phrase as a metaphor for the control that American plutocrats had over the temple of American democracy. The image was immediately accessible to all Americans who even had a passing acquaintance with the New Testament. It is one of the most striking images of the entire Christ story and is universally recognized as a purifying and revolutionary act.

It is also a story that reinforces images of the Jew as a moneygrubber willing to pollute his own holiest of holies for profit. The entire Jesus moneychanger story is seen through the retroactive filter of a medieval view of the Jews. Jews have trouble dealing with this story because, at first glance, it seems like a noble and just revolutionary act of Jesus, and uneducated Jews have flashes of shame that such goings on were part of the temple activity. This comes from seeing the story through the eyes of Christian norms, beliefs, and expectations. Seeing the story from both a Jewish and a modern point of view might change one's perspective.

First of all, we must relate to the Christian concept of the temple as a quiet, dignified place of prayer and meditation being polluted by filthy commerce; a kind of medieval gothic cathedral, which people enter in quiet awe. In fact, the temple was an Oriental temple. Anyone who has visited the Far East or viewed documentaries about it will recognize the noise, tumult, crowds, people hawking wares and religious artifacts, animals walking around, women nursing, and perhaps even people willing to change money. This also reflected the ambiance of the European cathedrals during the Middle Ages.

Norms of behavior and taste change over time. Compare the atmosphere of a modern theater to that of Shakespeare's Globe Theater.

Jews made pilgrimage to the Temple three times a year. These pilgrimages represented most of the income of permanent residents of Jerusalem. Jews came from long distances, often with their families. They were dirty and tired and wanted nothing more than to rent quarters, eat a meal, and go to the ritual baths, not only for ritual purification in preparation for the sacrifice but also for refreshment. They often had currency not in use in Jerusalem and thus had to change money before paying for services. They preferred to use the moneychangers who had stalls within the Temple walls rather than those outside because the Temple officials supervised them according to the commercial laws of Judaism and thus fairness was guaranteed.

They stood in a moneychanger's line, dirty, and hungry, with impatient wife and children waiting for them. The line moved slowly. No electronic board posted the relative currency values. Every transaction required argument and negotiation. Sometimes, one moneychanger had to ask a colleague about an unfamiliar currency. He had to weigh the currencies, check the purity of the gold or silver. Time bore heavily. Thousands of pilgrims waited in dozens of lines. All of a sudden, there appeared a strange individual who turned over all the tables. Mayhem ensued. The moneychangers, legitimate businessmen performing a necessary service, saw their wealth rolling on the ground, the tired pilgrims and their families were dismayed, and all were furious.

In the meantime, the townspeople who had prepared every spare corner of room and courtyard to rent to the pilgrims stood and waited and wondered why so few had appeared to rent space. Suddenly, they saw furious groups of pilgrims heading to the outskirts of the city to sleep in the open. Upon inquiry, they were informed that somebody named Jesus turned over the tables of the moneychangers and that this is the last time they are coming on pilgrimage. The stomachs of the residents sank in despair; they saw their present and perhaps future income disappear. The story would surely spread throughout the Jewish world. The ire of the Temple officials, of the moneychangers, of the residents, and of the pilgrims was great.

How does this story look now? Would one want to use this story metaphorically to justify an action? How would one feel if this happened to him? Jews must engage in such an examination of numerous issues to clarify to essential differences with Christianity.

Jewish "Legalism," Parochialism, and other Misrepresentations

Christianity, since its inception, has presented itself as a religion based on love, in opposition to the dry formalistic legalism of the Jews. The technical term for the extreme expression of this belief is *antinomianism*. The literal meaning is "against the law" and, as defined by the *Random House Dictionary*, "maintains that Christians are freed from the moral law by virtue of grace as set forth in the gospel." The *Encyclopedia Britannica* defines it as "a doctrine according to which Christians are freed by grace from the necessity of obeying the Mosaic Law."

Mainstream Catholicism and Protestantism have resisted extreme conclusions regarding the practical implications of this radical interpretation of grace over works doctrine. But antinomians can justify their position by appealing to sources as authoritative and varied as Paul, Augustine, and Luther.

From the book of Romans to the Montanists, Marcionites, the Spiritual Franciscans, and various popular pietistic movements up to and including Luther, antinomianism runs like a thread throughout Christian history and can justifiably claim that it is a legitimate child of Christianity. Even today, one will find *some* fundamentalist church people claiming that because they have already been saved they no longer have any fear of hell no matter what misdemeanors and sins they might commit in the future. This is not the dominant view, but its very existence in modern Christian discourse demonstrates the residual power of antinomianism and the spiritual smugness and moral arrogance it is capable of producing.

If one is saved by the grace of God and not because of moral worthiness, being saved is an absolute and cannot be retroactively revoked. As Jews, would we be justified in asking if these Christians are more righteous or just more self-righteous?

Why, if antinomianism has such a rich Christian pedigree, is it so severely attacked by Christian churches and theologians? To live in human society, men need laws to govern their behavior. Therefore, the early Church quickly began to create a body of canon law to govern the behavior of men while on earth. Later, Calvin wrote his authoritarian *Institutes*. Ironically, "antinomian" Christian law is often less tolerant and less loving than "legalistic" Jewish law, perhaps because in Christian law, loss of God's grace, not sin against another human being, is the primary transgression (see the Epistle to the Romans). Loss of God's grace is much more terrifying than crimes against men, no matter how horrible.

A useful joint project for both Jews and Christians might be to compare canon law as well as the laws of other Christian denominations with Jewish law in terms of its tolerance and liberalism and compare the actual behaviors of each based on Christian love and Jewish law. A one-on-one comparison on many issues might dispel the myth of loving Christianity versus a dry, legalistic Judaism. Christians require the law just as much as Jews, and Jews are instructed to act with love just as much as Christians. Dispelling these historical stereotypes might benefit both traditions. It would certainly provide a sounder foundation for a healthier Christian-Jewish dialogue.

In regards to universal Christianity versus tribal Judaism, we might compare the Christian approach of Jesus's monopoly power over the world to come—with the Jewish approach of the Seven Laws of Noah and ask which is more universal and which is more provincial. Which is better geared to living a civilized life in a pluralistic democracy?

FUTURE RULES OF JEWISH-CHRISTIAN RELATIONS: MUTUAL *DERECH ERETZ*

The encounter between Christians and Jews requires a new set of rules, and the Jews must take the lead in setting them. Our principles must be firm, our policy must be resolute, but our strategy and tactics must be informed with the principle of *derech eretz*—good manners. We still live in a Christian and post-Christian world. We still require good relations with and allies amongst our Christian and post-Christian neighbors. Indeed, as pointed out above, our biggest quarrel appears to be with the segment of the Christian community that is Israel's biggest supporter in the United States, the Christians with whom we hope to build alliances on numerous issues important for the Jewish people.

The Jews face a dilemma. We cannot afford to offend our strongest supporters, yet we cannot avoid letting them know how much their proselytizing activities offend us when these are packaged in the Jews for Jesus or Messianic Jews packages. The majority of decent Christians will understand our position and limit these activities. For those who do not, only internal Jewish education will help.

We must create a framework in which we can cooperate as responsible citizens of our planet and of our respective countries while still defending the integrity of our own tradition. Civilized people can work together on what they agree on while expressing their dismay at what offends them.

Jews would not compromise their identity by allowing that, as wisdom literature, the New Testament contains much that is admirable and in no way contravenes a Jewish outlook. We have a problem with the doctrinal aspects of the New Testament, with their pretensions to fulfilling Old Testament prophecy, and with their use in attempts to Christianize Jews. Ecumenism must reflect the ecological model discussed previously in the book, namely a diversity of spiritual approaches to life, not the fiction that we are alike.

The challenge is not to prove (in the name of ecumenism) that the Romans and not the Jews killed Jesus. The challenge is to replace apologetics with honest discourse.

WHAT WE JEWS MUST DO

We must not chastise the Christians for trying to convert us, as long as they do this openly and honestly and not under a Jewish guise. They do this with everyone, even other Christians. The pope has called for a Catholic counterattack against evangelical Christian inroads into traditional Catholic communities.

It is the Jewish responsibility to make Judaism stronger and more attractive by clarifying its basic principles. We must be proactive in publicizing differences between Christianity and Judaism. In a Constitutional democracy, the success of Christian missionary activity amongst the Jews depends on Jewish ignorance. We are now paying the price for years of shallow and kitschy *Fiddler on the Roof* Judaism, and the cultivation of colorful ethnicity. This must be replaced by uncompromising lucidity.

We might create a Jewish organization to address in a coherent and sustained way the above issues. We might create a series of lectures, seminars, and workshops to discuss differences between Judaism and Christianity using the books of Trude Weiss-Rosmarin, Abba Hillel Silver, and Rudolf Augstein. This would teach Jews about their own Judaism as well as specifically clarify ideological differences between various Jewish trends. It also would be more productive for instilling Jewish ambitions than distributing "modern" graphically attractive but intellectually dishonest translations of *siddurim* or sustaining the *bar mitzvah* factory of afternoon Hebrew schools.

An advanced series of lectures, seminars, and workshops might deal with Talmudic thinking versus New Testament thinking. Here, we would be wise to depend largely on non-Jewish sources such as Augstein's book. We might invite Christian thinkers to cosponsor seminars with this subject as its title.

Other activities would include books, booklets, mailings, and Web sites that relate specifically to issues mentioned in this chapter, as well as others. We could also cultivate university debates, and television and radio talk show appearances. We could have a response team of professionals and lay people that would insist that print and electronic media clarify their meaning when using phrases such as "Talmudic thinking" or "driving out the moneychangers" in a pejorative way. We might develop a series of cartoons, videos, and children's books on these and other subjects. University students should have special projects that supply them with material and talking points when confronted with the subliminal anti-Jewish prejudices of Western culture.

All of this can be carried out in a spirit of cooperation, good manners, and good feelings with the Christian community. It must be accompanied by the fashioning of action-oriented projects that reflect our *truly* shared values as well as the long-term vital interests of both communities.

CHAPTER 11

The Future of Jewish Identity

Why is it important that Jews remain Jewish? Who cares? The Jews are perhaps the only people whose members would consciously or even subconsciously ask such a question. This in itself indicates the uniqueness of the Jewish condition.

The question of identity is not, however, unique to the Jews. It is part of every people's national or cultural confrontation with the challenges of modernization and globalization. These challenges present a paradox. The human race has created a secular world of capitalism, technology, mass communications, trade, and individual rights. In our everyday lives, this reality has primacy over group identity. Democracy, commercial law, international trade agreements, and regional trading groups affect us as individuals.

Yet, secularism's triumph as the practical framework of human civilization appears to have created an immense cultural and spiritual malaise. Worldwide, growing numbers of individuals and groups are embarking on spiritual/cultural quests, seeking to correlate spiritual needs with the obvious benefits of living in our technological world. Despite the call of some radical environmentalists to return to the "purity" of preindustrial society, most people would prefer to retain modern technology while finding ways to ameliorate its more negative aspects. It would be foolish to construct a future vision of society on the assumption that vast numbers of people will forgo their consumer lifestyle and give up soap and hot water.

The challenge facing every cultural group in the twenty-first century is to assimilate into the modern world without being assimilated into it. In an increasingly secular world, identity is more a matter of individual choice than of historical inheritance. Modern individuals pick and choose multiple identities of value *for them*. ("It really helped me when I was into Buddhism or Kab-balah.")

Great traditions are no longer sold as being inherently valuable. Their value is argued in utilitarian terms. If you spend a day or two watching the numerous televangelists you will be struck by the fact that almost their entire message deals with how belief in Jesus helps *us* to overcome *our* problems. Their sermons often resemble self-improvement seminars (like EST) clothed in theological garb. This is a radical departure from earlier fire-and-brimstone, fear-of-hell sermons.

It is becoming increasingly clear that the surviving cultures and spiritual traditions will provide spiritual benefit for a critical mass of individuals *over historical periods of time*. New Age spiritual fads that have the lifespan of an MTV promo clip will eventually cease to be attractive.

THE ADVENT OF MULTIFACETED IDENTITY

Identity today is empirical and not transcendental. The mores and prohibitions of the traditional inherited community no longer decide identity, the modern individual does. Identity can be multifaceted. A Jew may decide that he can identify with the Jewish community and yet practice some Buddhist disciplines. These Jewish Buddhists (JuBus) already exist. We may soon see the advent of synagogue-ashrams. And why not? This multifaceted identity is not in itself negative in regards to Jewish survival. The Jewish tradition is flexible, based as it is on personal behavior rather than doctrinal belief. It is capable of accommodating numerous cultural accretions, as long as these do not contain beliefs, practices, or dogmas in direct contravention to the Jewish tradition but rather add another dimension to the Jewish individual's spiritual life.

Judaism can afford to be tolerant of the phenomenon. Imitation is not only the sincerest form of flattery it is also a test of a culture or a civilization's vigor. This is true for both the culture being imitated and the culture doing the imitating. A vigorous culture possessed of self-esteem and self-confidence will take freely from other cultures without fears of cultural pollution and by doing this, add to its own cultural vigor. A closed, ghettoized culture, fearful of the other, will accomplish the cultural equivalent of genetic inbreeding and create cultural dullards.

This tolerance cannot stretch to include the Jews for Jesus. Nor are Jewish communities ever likely to accommodate the Jews for Jesus phenomenon, the manipulative appeal to Jewish open-mindedness notwithstanding. Open-mindedness may be a virtue, but not if one is so open that one's essential identity falls out!

A comparable ideological conflict would exist with Islam. The fact that Mohammed is beyond criticism and that even implied criticism might earn one a death sentence is antithetical to Judaism. Judaism depicts its great biblical heroes in all their human frailties. The Bible depicts Abraham misrepresenting the status of Sarah to gain advantage in a real estate deal. Jacob cheats Esau out of his inheritance by lying to his father, Isaac. Jacob's sons sell their brother Joseph into slavery out of sibling rivalry and jealousy. Moses is depicted in the sources and in popular Jewish culture as having a severe speech defect. (This has generated many Jewish jokes about how this caused grave misunderstandings between Moses and God.) David sends his best friend off to die in battle so that he can sleep with his wife. Solomon had a thousand wives and concubines. Jewish heroes are not wispy, ethereal, "spiritual" beings; they are flesh-and-blood human beings with openly documented flaws. This distinguishes Judaism from other religious traditions.

HUMAN-CENTERED IDENTITY

Judaism is radically democratic; it encourages radical criticism—not passive acceptance. It stresses the centrality of human behavior. This is the source of the Talmudic dictum that man must be a partner with God in the (ongoing) act of creation. It is also the source of the humanistic Jewish concept of *tikkun olam* (repairing the world/Earth). It might also be why, according to Professor Hugo Bergman, Rabbi Abraham Isaac Kook (1865–1935), the first Ashkenazi chief rabbi of Mandated Palestine, saw Darwin's evolutionary theory as closest to the Jewish spirit. In the profoundest Jewish sense, God is evolving into itself with the active participation of humanity.

As we have already pointed out, the primacy of individual moral autonomy appears early in the Bible. Abraham argues with God over the fate of Sodom and Gomorrah. He interrupts a "conversation" with God to go and offer hospitality to three strangers. The Jews say, *"Derech eretz kodem leTorah"*: "Proper behavior takes precedence over the Torah." In other words, your responsibility toward your fellow human beings takes precedence over your obedience to God. This is the true significance of the "Sacrifice of Isaac" story—not Abraham's obedience to God but the end of human sacrifice as a means of placating God, thereby affirming the centrality of human life.

The story related in chapter 10, about the sages who reject the very voice of God as having weight in an argument, highlights the principle of human moral and intellectual autonomy. This story demonstrates both the principle of majority rule/minority rights and human intellectual autonomy and sovereignty, even in regards to God.

IDENTITY AS AN EVOLUTIONARY PROCESS

Although individual identity is empirical, and group identity is to a degree the sum total of individual identities, most individuals composing an ethnic group are still concerned with preserving ethnic integrity against the homogenizing influences of the world market and the world culture. This is so even as they integrate into that world culture and world market.

Identity is an evolutionary process. To be English today is quite different from being English in Queen Victoria's time, Elizabeth the Great's time, and certainly in Alfred the Great's time. Just so, being Jewish today is different from being Jewish a hundred years ago, five hundred years ago, or two thousand years ago.

Identity as an evolutionary process is especially applicable to the Jews. A normative, historically determined and finite definition of what it means to be Jewish is impossible. The Jews are an ideologically and culturally pluralistic people. Ideologically, Jewish identity can include Haredim, Modern Orthodox, Conservative, Reform, Reconstructionist, and Humanist Judaism. It would also include atheistic secularists and secular agnostics. These last definitions would include some of the greatest Jews of the twentieth century: Einstein, Freud, Ben Gurion, Jabotinsky, and others. Culturally, Jewish identity can include German, Yemenite, Russian, Iraqi, and American Jews. The only ideological or cultural norms of Jewish identity are the prohibition against idolatry and the requirement of causal ethics and absolute individual responsibility. The test is empirical. If a form of Judaism survives, it is because, by definition, it has contributed something of value to the Jew's essential human being. It is the spiritual equivalent of the survival of the fittest. What survives does so because it answers a need and gives value to real living human beings, and what does not is of no consequence except for historians and New Age advocates of radical nostalgia as a substitute for human progress.

Culture is not preserved, it is created, and it evolves as a consequence of its dynamic interaction with other cultures and other cultural environments. What does not interact does not evolve; what does not evolve dies.

Orthodox attempts to impose an ideologically normative inherited definition of Jewish identity in order to preserve "authentic Judaism" are completely wrongheaded. So were the attempts of early Zionist pioneers to create an "authentic" Israeli folk culture. No approach could more oppose the attempt to create a future framework of creative and compelling Jewish identity geared to satisfying the spiritual needs of the enlightened twenty-first-century Jew.

According to Orthodox Jewish scholar Professor Joseph Levinson, this ideological approach of politicized Orthodoxy is not *real* Torah or *Halacha*. He posits that a Torah-true *halachic* approach *disallows* such ideological impositions. He opposes the concept of a sectarian Jewry and claims that at root *all* Jewish expressions are temporal, geographical, or cultural *localizations* of the same basic worldview. His emphasis is not upon the worldview per se, but upon nonpoliticized and nonpolemic *halachic* analysis, wherein the Jewish norm *disallows* such ideological impositions.

This is similar to the point I made in the previous chapter when I noted that Judaism is an act- or commandment-oriented approach to life. The *way* you behave (*derech eretz*) is important, not your ideologically motivated belief system, or the political rationalizations of that ideological belief system. The hijacking of Jewish tradition by a politicized religious establishment presenting itself as "authentic" Judaism has alienated many Israelis and Diaspora Jews from Jewish tradition itself.

JEWISH CITIZENSHIP

In the past, a common belief system, common ethnic characteristics, or combination of both may have determined identity. In the future, however, Jewish identity must be pluralistic, based upon common norms of communal behavior and communal obligation—what I would call Jewish citizenship. The very concept of citizenship encompasses behavior, not belief, and is, therefore, secular. According to Professor Levinson, a secular Jewish framework is perfectly capable of being accommodated within a Torah-true *halachic* framework.

In the twenty-first century, Jewish identity must be formulated within a secular pluralistic framework. The component parts of this Jewish identity might be religious or secular. Religious identities can flourish within a secular framework, whereas secular identities have not, as usually constituted, been able to exist within religious frameworks. Compare the United States to Iran: ideologically, the United States is the most secular country on the planet with complete separation of church and state. Sociologically, the United States is one of the most religiously observant countries in the world. Iran, on the other hand, cannot tolerate anything secular and can only barely tolerate different religions in a decidedly inferior position.

A secular Jewish framework based on Jewish citizenship has become a survival necessity at the most prosaic level. In the modern Diaspora, more than 50 percent of young Jews marry non-Jews. Both the Jewish and non-Jewish partner are usually nonreligious and often have trouble with the concept of a transcendent all-knowing, all-judging God. "Religious" conversion is at present the only method available for the non-Jewish partner to "join" the Jewish People. This creates an absurd situation in which the agonistic non-Jewish partner is expected to be more observant than the agnostic Jewish partner. An agreed-upon falsehood becomes the basis for membership in the tribe. Is it any wonder that both Jewish and non-Jewish partners increasingly refuse to partake of this spiritual mendacity? Intermarriage is not causing assimilation, but the lack of a nonreligious means by which people might join the tribe. Developing a concept of Jewish citizenship might ameliorate this conundrum, thus reversing the demographic erosion threatening the very existence of the Jewish People.

PLURALISTIC HETERODOXY VERSUS HOMOGENEOUS ORTHODOXY

The Orthodox demand for a clarified, homogeneous, "authentic" Jewish identity is antithetical to Jewish survival. Pluralistic heterodoxy, not homogeneous orthodoxy, will come to represent the Jewish community as well as the individuals within it.

For example, an individual Jew may be secular (not believe in a supernatural God) yet belong to a conservative synagogue. He would belong because he receives more aesthetic pleasure from the more traditional conservative liturgy and cantorial singing than from a Reform synagogue, and he rejects the separate seating for men and women of the Orthodox synagogue. He might also attend concerts of Hassidic music while feeling distaste for the rabbi worship of some of the Hassidic sects.

The inability of the Jewish People to recognize pluralistic heterodoxy as the de facto norm of Jewish life has created new idolatries. Israel and Holocaust idolatry have replaced God as centerpieces for Jewish communal "worship." Israel is a state, and a state is an instrument, not a holy icon to be worshipped. The Holocaust is a terrible historical event, not a philosophical basis for a new theology.

We should remember that fascism is a perverted secularization of the religious instinct that makes the nation and the state an object of worship. There is a delicate line between patriotism as a healthy love for the scenery, odors, food, and customs of one's own country and one's own people, and a chauvinism that manifests egoistic contempt for other peoples or other countries. The latter is an inevitable consequence of state and nation worship. The Jews in general and the Zionists in particular must be wary not to fall into this trap.

Making religious sacraments out of horrible historical events can cause further atrocities, justified in the name of that historical event. Witness the behavior of the Serbs after the breakup of Yugoslavia, responding to their persecution by the Croatians and the Moslems during World War II. It is often forgotten that the Nazis and their Croat and Moslem accomplices exterminated more than a million Serbs during World War II. Unfortunately, many Serbs rationalized this terrible crime against their people into a new chauvinist ideology that justified "ethnic cleansing" and other atrocities against the descendents of Croat and Moslem war criminals. They thus became war criminals themselves.

When we make the Holocaust the central component of Jewish identity, we can destroy any innate ambitions to remain Jewish of young people looking for something of value for their own futures and not an obsessive preoccupation with terrible past events. Respectful remembrance is historically necessary, politically wise, and spiritually healthy. Feeding young Jews a constant diet of the Holocaust as the defining event of modern Jewish identity, however, is dangerous if our primary aim is to cultivate a healthy identification with both Jewish tradition and a collective Jewish future.

When we speak about a heterodox pluralism, we are not referring to the nostalgia industry that peddles its ethnic kitsch to all comers (Madonna studying Kabbalah for example). Nostalgia might be viewed as a major disease of our time. It reflects a general decadence of cultural creativity into one-dimensional international pop culture or ethnic kitsch.

In the Jewish context, this nostalgia industry expresses itself in making Jewish identity a kind of Jewish Disneyland, wherein we create kitsch versions of various aspects of Jewish culture and history: "Hassidland," "Sephardiland," "Litvakland," "Kabbalahland," "Yeminiteland," "Musarland," and so on.

The worldwide wave of nostalgia and publicly funded national folk projects designed to "save our cultural heritage" does not signify a rebirth of ethnic vigor, only ethnic desperation and cultural barrenness. The periodic celebration of ethnicity is not an organic reflection of ethnic roots in one's everyday life, it is rather a vacuous reflection of a chronic sense of emptiness.

The heterodox Jew may at various times and for various reasons utilize particular elements of past ethnic traditions, but this cannot be the backbone of a future-oriented Jewish identity. It is depressingly sunk in the past. Thirty years ago, Arthur Lewis, a black intellectual, when refuting the ethnic kitsch of black cultural nationalism, wrote: "...only decadent peoples on the way down feel an urgent need to mythologize and live in their past. A vigorous people, on the way up, are more concerned with visions of its *future*."

The fact is that Jewish identity can rest upon neither a doctrinaire interpretation of Jewish religiosity, as the Orthodox would have it, nor upon a Jewish version of earthy Zorba the Greek, as the early Zionist pioneers would have had it. Since the Dispersion, the Jews have developed into a multiplicity of ethnicities. And since the Enlightenment, they have been the quintessential avant-garde of cosmopolitan culture.

Every Jew is at once the possessor of five cultural traditions and identities: (1) the totality of Jewish history, (2) a personal Jewish ethnic tradition (Ashkenazi, Sephardi, or such), (3) all other Jewish ethnic traditions, (4) the culture of the country they live in, and (5) the cultures of all humanity. In this, the modern Jewish world citizen is no different from any other modern world citizen.

Responsible, self-confident Jewish world citizens must balance or collate these five identities into an integrated whole. This integrated whole will be idiosyncratic to each individual Jew. In other words, every Jewish individual will possess his or her integrated whole of Jewish/human identity, and a generally agreed upon system of Jewish citizenship will unify them. This might be the key to the future of communal Jewish identity.

Jewish identity still contains some elements of a tribal identity. Indeed we often refer to ourselves as "the tribe." But the Jews are a unique tribe. We are the only tribe whose fundamental ethos is a universal vision for all humankind. To be a member of the tribe, one must celebrate this universal vision. In its ideal form, the tribal is subordinate to the universal. We justify our own existence and historical role in terms of all humanity and not only in terms of ourselves. Our central national myth has to do with the universal redemption of all humankind. If we turn our backs on humanity, we turn our backs on ourselves, on our own tribe.

Rabbi Kook believed that the world is continually evolving toward universalism, yet because so many of our actions reflect individual nations, the universal ideal must be realized by way of enlightened nationalism. In this, he was an unknowing student of the great liberal Italian nationalist Mazzini. Kook saw Zionism as an essential step in the divine scheme of evolution toward universalism. He considered it the Jewish People's mission to devote themselves to the divine goal of human perfection and universalism. According to Kook, God imposed this task upon the Jews by choosing them, and it is up to the Jews to accept this task and fulfill this divine mission. Here, the Jewish tradition of *tikkun olam* and the Western tradition of Utopianism meet.

Even our folk expressions are cosmopolitan, deriving from cultures in Islam and Christendom. Ironically, the anti-Semites were correct. There is no such thing as Jewish culture in the folkways or aesthetic sense. All Zionist attempts in this direction have also been derivative. So-called Israeli folk music is 90 percent Russian and 10 percent Yemenite. Jewish culture, therefore, fits no easy definitions.

Until the modern era, the Jews survived because of a unified belief and behavior system, not because of unified customs. The State of Israel and the ingathering of the exiles, more than any other event, destroyed the notion of a specific Jewish ethnicity, even as this means of identity gathered force in America's eroding religious observance. "Bubba and Zaida Judaism" or "bagels and lox Judaism" (Judaism based on chicken soup and Yiddish humor) has concluded its brief existence. We now require a unified system of Jewish citizenship (replacing belief and ethnicity) as the basis for a Jewish identity suited to space age realities. This must be a liberal citizenship that relies on neither culturally coercing Jewish individuals nor rejecting the rich variety of modern Jewish identities.

THE TRANSITION GENERATION

We survive today only through the inertia of the forms that grew out of a unifying belief system and the behaviors that grew out of a common ethnicity. We are, however, the transition generation, the cultural equivalent of the "desert generation." How will our children and grandchildren be served by our continued dependence on these outmoded forms? As Rabbi Phillip Sigal wrote in the spring 1970 *Judaism* magazine:

The Jew in America is a pragmatist. He wants to know, even if he finds it difficult to articulate, what he has to do to express his Judaism.... He wants a guide.... He remains cold, however, to the code of law that delighted his grandfather but is meaningless to him ... he wants to know how (to remain Jewish). Instead he is offered fund-raising, anti-Semitism, panic on intermarriage and the Middle Eastern problem.... By staying away from worship the average Jew indicates eloquently the tedium he no longer desires to endure....He cannot pray for rain in October, and he is unable to get excited over medieval poems containing mystical allusions that are religiously unavailable to modern men even when they are translated with clarity and grace...syllogisms, appeals to history, and dogmatic references to tradition will not foster the continuity of our heritage. What is needed is a massive attempt to understand, in Holmes' words "the prevalent moral and political theories" and how they are related to Judaism and how Judaism can, in a relevant manner, be brought to bear on them.

This is the most cogent summation of the modern Jewish dilemma I have ever read. To think that this was written more than 30 years ago is a mind-boggling example of prescient thought. How much more relevant are these sentiments to the Jewish generations that have matured since then? Sigal could have referred to the Jew in Israel, Europe, or Australia in the opening sentence and been just as accurate. His concluding sentence, quoting Holmes, is an anticipation of the concept of Jewish citizenship that we are trying to place on the table of Jewish debate in this chapter. The implication of this sentence is even more profound. It implies that we should not swallow our historical inheritance whole but rather mine this inheritance for the golden nuggets significant for a human being living in the twenty-first century and reject the rest as irrelevant slag.

Our generation still has an inarticulate feeling that Jewish identity is important, even though we cannot say why. This derives to a degree from the more general human need for some kind of particular identity that will function as an intellectual, cultural, and spiritual anchor in an age of alienation. We sense that we have inherited something rich and wonderful, yet in a form that is of little spiritual use to us. We can use this instinctual feeling as a foundation upon which to build a new concept of Jewish identity.

We must, however, pick and choose from Jewish sources according to our modern humanistic standards. We must bravely and openly reject and discard the proto-racist aspects of our tradition as a tribal vestige morally and practically unsuitable for modern life. We must also give up the undignified project of mistranslating, rationalizing, and explaining them away in order to salve our modern liberal consciences. We must reinterpret our tradition in the light of modern needs, following Maimonides's assertion that in every generation we must reinterpret the Torah. We must accept our tradition but decide which parts of it to apply to our modern lives. We would be wise to follow the advice of Sumner Redstone, CEO of Viacom/CBS/Paramount, who, in a television interview, said, "History affects the future, but it should never get in the way of the future." We require a radical reevaluation of our tradition as we review it through the prism of our modern reality. Some possible examples of such a project might be as follows:

Reevaluate the serpent in light of our modern standards of what it means to be a human being; that is, as a knowledge-seeking volitional being who does not obey arbitrary and illogical prohibitions, no matter how "authoritative" the source. A being whose ability for rational inquiry and analysis is its primary instrument for survival and who will not accept limitations on this instrument, a being who is morally autonomous and sovereign and takes responsibility for its own actions, a citizen of a constitutional democracy. If we truly celebrate our human *being*, we must thank the serpent for seducing Eve into eating from the tree of knowledge. The curiosity and ability to know is, after all, what makes us truly human. On a deeper level, we might reasonably assume that God *wanted* man to eat from the tree of knowledge, but *not* by God's command. In other words, God *wanted* Adam and Eve to eat of their *own* volition and not be seduced by the blandishments of another. For this, the serpent and Adam and Eve were punished, the serpent for corrupting the autonomy of Eve, and Eve for allowing her autonomy to be corrupted.

Investigate deeper into God's covenant with Noah that set limits to God's power, thus asserting basic human rights and affirming the principle of "limitations of power," *even in regards to God*. Such limitations appeared in the story in which the sages rejected the very voice of God interfering in their deliberations.

Examine in greater detail Abraham's argument with God over these limits at Sodom and Gomorrah, which is the first recorded case of human rebellion against authority and an affirmation of basic human rights.

Penetrate deeper into the implications of Moses's confrontation with God over who "he" is—"I am that I am" or "I will be what I will be" –that is, God as an incomplete and continuing process, God as a verb, and the Jews as partners in this act of God's ongoing historical "self" creation.

Radical reevaluation does not preclude radical reinterpretation and certainly does not require rejecting the valuable nuggets of our traditional culture because they are often imbedded in slag. In this context, the original intent of the sources is less important than a creative reinterpretation of them. What would be the fate of constitutional law if original intent were applied as an absolute? Would we reject the American Constitution because the founding fathers allowed slavery? Would we reject the American Declaration of Independence because it contains a racist slur against the American Indians? Do we reject the Magna Carta principle that men have property over themselves because its original intent was only for the nobility? Human beings possessed of cultural self-assurance everywhere strive to mine cultural nuggets out of cultural slag without fearing that they are somehow traitors to their people and their tradition. Human beings with healthy self-esteem know that a tradition that does not evolve and develop becomes obsolete and eventually extinct.

FROM RIGHT TO EXIST TO REASON TO EXIST: MEANINGFUL JEWISH EXISTENCE

It is not enough to say that the Jews have a right to exist. Of course we do. The question is why nonreligious Jews should feel the need or perceive the value in continuing to exist as Jews. From a purely rational viewpoint, this question has no answer. From a purely rational viewpoint, assimilation is a perfectly legitimate alternative. This is why those of us most concerned with sustaining Jewish survival into the future must strive to make Jewishness meaningful to the modern Jewish individual. In its present form, the question of sustaining a Jewish identity is meaningless for many young modern Jewish individuals. How do we make it meaningful?

Religious Jews "believe in God." They have an inherent sense of the unique collective mission of the Jewish people in God's service. But many Jews today do not believe in God, and most do not practice the ritual *mitzvot*. Rather they sense a uniqueness about themselves as products of a unique historical and spiritual enterprise. They sense a kind of historically affirmed sacredness about their continued Jewish existence and identity. As Asher Ginsburg (Ahad Ha'Am), the father of spiritual Zionism, who was often called the secular rabbi, wrote in 1910:

A Jew may be a liberal of liberals without forgetting that Judaism was born in a corner and has always lived in a corner, aloof from the great world, which has never understood it and therefore hates it. So it was before the rise of Christianity, and so it has remained ever since. History has not yet satisfactorily explained how it came about that a tiny nation in a corner of Asia produced a unique religious and ethical outlook, which, though it has had so profound an influence on the rest of the world, has yet remained so foreign to the rest of the world, and to this day has been unable to master it or to be mastered by it. This is a historical phenomenon to which, despite many attempted answers, we must still attach a note of interrogation. But every true Jew, be he orthodox or liberal, feels in the depths of his being that there is something in the spirit of our people—though we do not know what it is—which has prevented us from following the rest of the world along the beaten path, has led to our producing this Judaism of ours, and has kept us and our Judaism "in a corner" to this day, because we cannot abandon the distinctive outlook on which this Judaism is based. Let those who still have this feeling remain in the fold: let those who have lost it go elsewhere. There is no room here for compromise.

Ahad Ha'Am was a truly cosmopolitan Jew yet still recognized the distinctiveness of Jewish identity and its unique contribution to civilization as well as to the Jews who persist in their identity. The challenge today is to convey the sense that sustaining one's Jewish identity gives one spiritual and cultural value. Ahad Ha'Am wrote in 1910, when presumably most Jews felt as he did. This is no longer the case.

How can we stimulate Jewish ambitions in the young, university-educated, twenty-first century Jew? This is not only a question of education or propaganda. It requires a substantive redefinition of the contents and forms of Jewish identification. Without an agreed upon arrangement capable of accommodating a pluralistic heterodox Jewish citizenship, we may not achieve a meaningful Jewish identity.

HISTORICAL CONTEXT

The key to the dilemma is to look at the objective social, cultural, and scientific conditions that frame our existence and prompt our search for identity. Individual identity is rooted in the objective conditions that mold our cultural environment.

Judaism flourished in pre-Enlightenment agricultural societies but has never really successfully come to terms with the post-Enlightenment industrial reality that created modern Jewry. In short, a radical disconnect exists between classical Judaism and modern Jewry. Jewish life and survival in the past two centuries have depended, to a great extent, on the inertia of those no longer adequate medieval forms described by Rabbi Sigal, exacerbated by the horrors of modern anti-Semitism, a product of perverse nineteenth-century romantic nationalism.

Jean Paul Sartre was once bitterly condemned by the Jews for claiming that the Jew was the product of anti-Semitism, and not the reverse (implying that the Jews would disappear once anti-Semitism disappeared). This was, of course, just the vulgar Marxist interpretation of history that some French intellectuals have been prone to make. It is certainly an inadequate and impoverished explanation for the whole of Jewish history. Yet, if we were completely honest with ourselves, we would be forced to admit that for much of the twentieth century, what we call Jewish identity has been the product of or reaction to modern romantic nationalist anti-Semitism. Certainly, Zionism and American Jewish organizational life are impossible to understand or explain except in this context.

Indisputably, modern Jewish life is almost entirely a reaction to the internal developments of nineteenth- and twentieth-century European civilization. Zionism, and also the Reform, Conservative, neo-Orthodox, Yiddishist, and Bundist movements were reactions to reactions of European nations to vast social, political, and economic changes. In this regard, the Jews are no different from the Arabs, Chinese, Indians, or Africans. The modern history of *all* non-European peoples is but a reaction to nineteenth- and twentieth-century Europe. The Jews are unique because the primordial stages of their reaction took place on European soil. Some nations have reacted more successfully than others. The Japanese, Chinese, and Koreans have all accommodated the West without sacrificing their uniqueness. The Iranians and other vast segments of the Moslem world have rebelled against Westernization and modernization. Other segments of the Moslem world, Turkey, and Malaysia, for example, have been at least as successful as the Koreans in adapting and most of Africa has not yet found the formula.

The Jews still have three options: the Japanese model, the Iranian model, or the assimilationist model. At its outset, Zionism seemed to anticipate the Japanese model, but today Israeli culture seems a battle between the Iranian and assimilationist (post-Zionist) models. This historical turn of events has grave consequences for the future of Diaspora Jewry also.

Jewish culture, like all non-European cultures, never really underwent a Renaissance or an Enlightenment. Rather, it created frameworks in reaction to the European Enlightenment and Renaissance as well as to the Protestant Reformation. Mendelssohn's reform movement, for example, was self consciously molded on Martin Luther's Reformation.

SPIRITUAL PIONEERS

When the Jews were spiritual pioneers and creators, they were a powerful force in history, imitated by others. Jewish identity, therefore, was inherently compelling. The creation of ethical monotheism and the variegated expressions of its message have sustained the Jews and made them a force in human history for more than 3,000 years. The various Jewish responses to the eighteenth-century European Enlightenment have sustained us for the past two centuries.

Today, however, most Jews do not believe in a supernatural, judgmental God and the secular frameworks of the Enlightenment seem to be increasingly inadequate to meet the spiritual needs of the human race. The growing perception that secular Enlightenment frameworks do not satisfy a basic human need for something "beyond" might be one of the major causes for the worldwide return to fundamentalist religiosity.

These historical and sociological developments have negatively affected the spiritual life of Jewish society and of the individuals who compose it. The particular surviving Jewish responses to the Enlightenment (Reform, Conservative, and Zionism) appear increasingly inadequate to the task of sustaining Jewish identity as a unique historical entity. For the first time in Zionist history, Orthodox Judaism is in the ascendant and secular Zionism is on the defensive. This is not a consequence of the political advantage gained by the various Orthodox trends in Israel. Rather, their political advantage is a consequence of their spiritual ascendance, garnered as a result of their satisfying the spiritual emptiness of more and more secular Jews.

The Orthodox view this situation as a kind of general Jewish validation of their belief system and proof of their eventual triumph within the Jewish world. They can now supply empirical evidence that the only real barricade against Jewish assimilation is belief, and therefore a general Jewish strategy of survival must center on belief. Few Jews can make themselves believe in what they don't believe in, even if it is "good for the Jews." The Orthodox say we must believe in order to survive, but one cannot believe in belief; one cannot believe because it is nice or psychologically healthy to believe in something, or because belief helps preserve our ethnic identity. Most of us must believe in something believable, something real and rooted in the natural world.

Today, we require new Jewish expressions for the postmodern period. The Jews must consciously strive to become spiritual pioneers of the new world civilization necessary if the human race is to survive. The Jews have no models to copy, as they did following the Enlightenment. It is now incumbent upon them to create the model that others will copy. Just as, in an analogous situation, the Jews were spiritual pioneers for all humanity in ancient times when they created monotheism, so must they become spiritual pioneers today. This is the only real, meaningful guarantee for survival as Jews.

It must become a central tenet of Jewish life that Jewish discourse must become directed to the cultivation of ambitions to create "space age" versions of Judaism. The space age is the new *all-human* environment. Either Judaism will have something to say to the spiritual needs of this environment or not. If it does not, it will not survive.

It is certain that various thinkers are making efforts in this direction. One such effort is the brainchild of the late Mordechai Nessyahu, to whom this book is dedicated. Called *Cosmotheism* (see appendix), it is by far the most comprehensive and far-reaching space age worldview I am aware of. It is an example of the depth and breadth of thinking that I believe humanity in general and the Jews in particular must cultivate if we are to survive.

CHAPTER 12

The Cyber World We Live In

Science fiction writer William Gibson first coined the term *cyberspace*. While wandering around video arcades in Vancouver Canada in the early 1980s, he was fascinated by the way players hunched over the glowing screens. He wrote: "I could see in the physical intensity of their postures how rapt the kids were.... The kids clearly believed in the space the games projected."

Gibson was haunted by that image. He knew little about video games or computers, but he knew people who knew more and, as near as he could tell, everyone who worked or played with the video games began to accept the reality of these imaginary spaces. They perceived some kind of actual space behind the screen. Gibson called that imaginary/real space cyberspace and used it as the setting in early novels and short stories, including his breakthrough novel *Neuromancer* (1984). Gibson's cyberspace is a computer-generated landscape that characters enter by "jacking-in," sometimes into a machine and sometimes by plugging electrodes directly into sockets implanted in the brain. What they see is a three-dimensional representation of stored information, a *virtual* reality.

The term *cyber* was borrowed from the word *cybernetics*, coined by renowned MIT mathematician Norbert Weiner in 1948, which he had taken from the Greek *kybernetes*, meaning the steersman of a boat. Cybernetics is the discipline that collates electronic control mechanisms with the human nervous system.

Other names have been given to that shadowy space where computer data resides, but Gibson's term has caught on. By the early 1990s, it had been adopted by the online community to describe today's increasingly interconnected computer systems.

THE SIGNIFICANCE OF CYBERSPACE

Cyberspace describes more than a medium for faster, better ways to do what we have always done. Cyberspace is a completely new and different kind of intellectual and spiritual human environment, analogous in its implications to the invention of alphabets and writing. It signifies an entirely new medium of humanity's *cultural evolution*. The change from pen and pencil to typewriter and to word processor represents humanity's *technical development*, certainly with cultural ramifications, but in no way comparable to the qualitative spiritual, and intellectual potential of cyberspace.

Cyberspace is more an emerging virtual ecosystem than an extended machine. Cyberspace is a universal bioelectronic environment, one that exists everywhere telephone wires, coaxial cables, fiber-optic lines, or electromagnetic waves exist—everywhere and anywhere on the planet and beyond. This environment contains numerous and varied forms of data, information, and knowledge that enable human beings to create and innovate in completely new ways.

This environment is composed of anything that can be digitized (put into a computer code): word text, music, still images and pictures, video, animation, and the emerging world of virtual reality. Unfortunately, because nearly everything can be digitized we have no definite way of knowing if specific information is valid, correct, fair, or true. This determination is the user's responsibility. This makes the old-fashioned classical skills of analytical and critical thinking developed by the ancient Greeks even more relevant as we expand our cyber environment.

CHANGE IN THE RATE OF CHANGE

The cyber environment is expanding at an exponential rate. Faster computers, cheaper means of electronic storage, improved software, and more capable communication channels are all adding to the scope and scale of our cyber environment. The most explosive power of this new cyber reality stems from the integrative multicombinations of all these systems. The buzzword is *interoperability*, which means that everything can connect with everything else, at any time and from any place.

The ongoing creation of this cyber environment has so changed the historical rate of change that we might justifiably say that we now live in the era of real-time change. Historical times of generational changes have become passé. Our human environment no longer changes over traditional periods of time, it changes incessantly in real time. In the time it has taken me to write this sentence, change with potential impact on my life has taken place somewhere in the world. That makes it difficult to write about or discuss this subject. By the time this book is read, part of it will already appear out of date or quaint. We are dealing with a bioelectronic frontier whose rate of expansion will always exceed our ability to explore it.

Not the technical fact of cyberspace, but rather our explorations of its ever-expanding scope have become our human environment. It is no longer human activity in a given environment, but rather human activity itself becoming our environment. This social reality mirrors the new scientific view of reality as an on-going process impossible to pin down or objectify to a precise degree.

JEWS IN CYBERSPACE

The exploration of cyberspace presents individuals and global communities such as the Jews with some of the greatest opportunities and most difficult challenges in human history. Cyberspace could be a path of knowledge leading to wisdom, as is the Jewish ideal. The technological opportunity exists to empower every individual to pursue his or her chosen vocation from anywhere and anytime.

This Jewish ideal is affirmed by a communication on the Internet by Rabbi Jonathan Sacks, chief rabbi of the United Hebrew Congregations of the British Commonwealth:

The Internet is one of the most wondrous developments of all time. The sages said that when the Torah was given on Mount Sinai, the voice of God traveled throughout the world, there was instantaneous communication. That miracle has become our reality.

The Jewish implications could not be more significant. From its earliest days...(until) the West caught up with the idea, Judaism was predicated on universal education and the democratic access to knowledge. Knowledge, said Francis Bacon, is power. That is why, through most of history, it has been jealously guarded by elites.

Judaism is not a religion of elites, least of all in the arena of knowledge...the Torah is the heritage of every Jew. We all have a share. We are all expected to learn. We each have a right to know.

Today, because of the Internet, the vast treasury of Jewish knowledge is open to everyone...what the Web allows us to do is to share the thoughts of teachers throughout the world and sense the fact that we are a truly global people, linked by the shared act of learning.

HIGHWAY OR CYBERSPACE

This newly emerging power requires the radical transformation of the centralistic institutions and organizations that have developed over the past several centuries since the Industrial Revolution. We must develop a new method of human and Jewish organization and governance. The least helpful and most confusing metaphor, but one that has gained a great deal of currency is the so-called information superhighway. Can you imagine a phrase less descriptive of the very nature of cyberspace or more misleading in its cultural implications?

Let us list a set of polarities between the concept of a highway and the true reality of cyberspace in order to better understand just how misleading the information superhighway metaphor is.

Characteristics of a Highway

Limited Matter in Limited Space: Only so many vehicles can travel efficiently and safely on a given area of paved road. Past that number, we have traffic jams and accidents. The entire system is composed of material products that are mined, processed, manufactured, and maintained.

Centralized Government Ownership: Governments, through their agencies, design, build, maintain, and own the highway. The government must use its police powers to extract taxes from us in order to perform these tasks, no matter how frequently or infrequently we use a particular highway.

A Dictated Grid: The government decides for us where we can get on and off, whether it will be a free way or a toll road, and if the latter how much we pay to travel on it. A centralized governmental agency keeps us locked into this grid pattern and thus locked into particular consumption patterns: gas stations, shopping centers, and so on. This limits our options as a citizens and consumers.

Bureaucracy: Keeping the highway system working requires a vast army of officialdom. This reinforces government power and control over citizens, consumes tax money, and invites corruption through the contracting and subcontracting system required to build and maintain the system.

Unions and Contractors: Highways are constructed by the Second Wave industrial system of corporate energy and hired labor. Both unions and companies constitute special interests that can corrupt the political system as large political campaign contributors. Politicians become beholden to interests other than, and often directly opposed to, voters' interests and wishes, as well as the true needs of an efficient transportation system.

Efficient but Unsafe: The highway system works with great efficiency but is also one of the most dangerous places in modern civilization. Fourteen years of the Vietnam War claimed 50,000 American lives. This is the body count on U.S. highways in one year.

Withstand Natural Elements: The highway system is limited by the exigencies of nature and must be built to withstand the problems and limitations of snow, rain, sun, and natural wear and tear.

Liberation from the First Wave and Culmination of the Second Wave: The highway grid enabled humanity to move from a limited, local farming economy into a regional, continental, and global industrial economy. The social and cultural consequences were enormous. An urban civilization emerged, employment options exploded and released entrepreneurial and creative energy, women were liberated, in an urban society the entire concept of privacy and anonymity became more available, and a sexual revolution followed. The automobile and the highway system, have proven the most revolutionary technology in the history of the human race. Still, it has been a material and a mass culture, and today we are fast approaching the limitations of mass material culture, environmentally, psychologically, culturally, and economically.

The above shows how the very use of the highway metaphor limits our imagination and creativity and prevents us from fully exploiting the inherent, as yet little-explored potentiality of cyberspace. We wish to acknowledge Anthony Judge of Brussels for some of the insights in this subsection.

Characteristics of Cyberspace

Unlimited Knowledge: Cyberspace has no limits to the amount of knowledge it can generate and send to anyone, anytime, anywhere. Cyberspace represents the liberation of humankind from the limitations of matter. Humanity no longer deals exclusively with matter but also with elements of our collective human minds electronically encoded. Because the human mind is "the infinite resource" (according to Professor William Hallal in his book of the same name), humanity for the first time has unlimited resources and options to realize its human being.

Decentralized: Even though the Internet was originally a Pentagon initiative, it is not regulated by the government. It is organized by private voluntary organizations that want to keep it open for everyone. Some people believe that the Internet is inherently incapable of being regulated, that the technology and software present the Internet libertarian with constantly increasing opportunities to outflank any attempts to restrict his or her freedom. No one really owns any aspect of cyberspace in the same sense that they own land or building space. Cyberspace is a modern version of the commons. We all "own" it when we use it.

Empowerment and Freedom of Access: No regulation means no bureaucracy to limit parameters of use. The highway grid is replaced by an open system in which we "get on" or "get off" wherever and whenever we please, a system in which we move information in any way necessary to send messages to their destination.

Hospitable when Customized: Computer technology and software present us with a curious and happy paradox. The technology and software are uniform (truly products of Second Wave production methods), but everyone can use them individually to answer his or her specific cyberneeds. This technology liberates us from the Second Wave of massification and enables us to explore the Third Wave of individualization.

THE DEMASSIFICATION OF CIVILIZATION

The Second Wave gave us "the Masses": the mass man, the mass consumer, mass production, mass culture (best-sellers, gold disks), mass knowledge, and mass politics (parties, movements, organizations). Perhaps rapidly increasing apathy toward voting and other duties of mass politics reflects not the demise of good citizenship but rather the growing realization that Second Wave political structures have less and less to do with the real lives of individuals living in the Third Wave.

The advent of the Third Wave and its most palpable characteristic—cyberspace—has fundamentally altered the very nature of knowledge. In the Second Wave we perceived knowledge as mass produced and mass consumed. The truly profound significance of Third Wave/cyberspace civilization is not the technical shift per se (from printed books to electronic storage and retrieval) but rather the shift from a mass production, mass media, and mass culture civilization to a demassified culture, customized for each and every individual.

This has special consequences for the organization and terminology of Jewish institutional life in general and Zionism in particular; the latter is accustomed to speaking in abstractions and generalizations such as the "People of Israel" or the "Jewish People." We must learn to speak of the Jewish person or the Israeli person if we wish to develop a Third Wave Zionism.

Knowledge in the Third Wave is characteristically transient, perishable, and customized: the right information, the right way, to the right person at the right time. The very nature of a mass-produced book is to pass on mass knowledge, the defining characteristic of the Second Wave. This "public goods" knowledge is useful to most people simply because most people's information needs have been pretty much standardized. Third Wave knowledge is "private goods" knowledge. Even the book trade has been greatly influenced by this. New technology has allowed us to customize mass-produced books for smaller niche markets. The book you are reading is a good example of this.

We are the last generation of an old civilization and the first generation of an emergent culture. Much of our personal and collective confusion and social disorientation can be traced to the internal conflicts we experience when our inherited cultural models run head on into a conflicting reality. The cultural models and metaphors that worked so well in the past are becoming less appropriate as we thunder into a new and radically different future.

Second Wave ideologues routinely lament the breakup of society, but we are witnessing only the breakup of mass society. Rather than seeing the rich diversity made available by cybercivilization as an opportunity for human development, it is usually attacked as fragmentation and a frightening loss of social solidarity. We must jettison the frightening but false assumption that more diversity automatically brings with it more tension and more conflict in society. Given appropriate social models, diversity can make for a more secure and stable civilization just as biodiversity makes for a more secure and stable ecosystem.

THIRD WAVE CRITERIA

Let us modify the phrase from *cyberspace* to *cyberspaces*. The plural form is both more accurate and more likely to open minds to the civilizing potential of Third Wave reality. Rather than a centrifugal force threatening to tear society apart, cyberspaces can represent a social glue that holds together the increasingly free and diverse culture it is helping to bring about. The very modalities and etiquette of cyberspace function as a kind of meta-ideology that obligates all users.

Whether we like it or not, or even whether we are aware of what we are doing, all social organizations, including Jewish ones, must remake themselves and redefine their relationships to society at large and to particular constituencies. No single set of criteria will suffice to create future friendly organizations. However we can apply some yardsticks to any future policy proposal:

Are the policy proposals based on the industrial model of standardization, routine, and mass production? Third Wave proposals encourage and empower individual uniqueness.

Do the policy proposals centralize control and power in bureaucratic institutions? Third Wave proposals strive to spread power; to empower those closest to the actual problem or decision.

Do the proposals encourage geographic and physical concentration? Third Wave proposals enable people to live and work wherever they choose.

Are the proposals based on the idea of mass culture, of everyone watching the same television sitcoms, or do they permit and encourage cultural diversity within a broad framework of shared values?

Conflict between Second Wave and Third Wave communities is the central organizational tension cutting through our society today. The more fundamental organizational question is not who controls the last days of industrial society, but who shapes the new civilization rapidly rising to replace it. In other words, who will shape the nature of cyberspace and its impact on our lives and institutions?

Living on the edge of the Third Wave, we are witnessing a battle not so much over the nature of the future, but over the nature of the transition to whatever future will arrive. On one side of this battle are partisans of societal institutions based upon the industrial past. On the other side are the growing millions who recognize that the most pressing and urgent problems can no longer be resolved within the massified frameworks we have inherited.

CHARACTERISTICS OF THE NET GENERATION

Don Tapscott, in his landmark book *Growing Up Digital: The Rise of the Net Generation*, refers to the current generation of children who have grown up with the digital world as their primary information system. Tapscott's book presents a comprehensive and focused analysis of the transformations likely to affect this generation. His analysis and conclusions are especially relevant in regards to the Jewish Net Generation trying to understand what Judaism is all about and how they might see themselves in a relevant Jewish society.

In addressing the needs of this group, we must first define the various generational groups that compose the Jewish community and how their values and habits of thought might affect attempts to address Net Generation needs.

Veterans: The group that established Jewish communal life as we know it today. They are between 60 and 80 years old and most often sit on the decision-making boards of directors of Jewish organizations. They determine budget allocations in general and educational budgets in particular. They are community financial gatekeepers and grandparents of the Net Generation, so it is important to win them over to an understanding of the major shifts taking place in generational consciousness and especially how this might relate to education.

Baby Boomers: Members of the community born between 1943 and 1960. They are the parents of our target generation, and they predominate as communal and educational administrators, principals, and teachers. Although often in direct contact with the Net Generation, they are also often suspicious of its generational consciousness and inflexible in dealing with them.

Generation Xers: Members of the community born between 1960 and 1980. They constitute the dominant generation amongst Jewish professionals as well as teachers and educational administrators. They frequently are in organizational conflict with the baby boomers and veterans. So, even though they may empathize with and understand the Net Generation, they might have trouble advancing programs and projects most suited to their needs. The increased empowerment of Jewish Generation Xers is a necessary precondition to developing relevant Net Generation policy.

Net Generation: Those born after 1980. They are the first generation bathed in digital bits. In America, for example, an estimated 80 percent of all children were computer literate and Internet users by the year 2000. The percentage for American Jewish children is even higher, close to the upper 90th percentiles (reflecting the middle- and upper-middle-class social status of American Jewry). In other words, the vast majority of American Jewish children are online, and that is the dominant social pattern that connects them with one another.

It also makes them comparable to their counterparts in Israel. Despite a digital divide between the world's haves and have-nots, this is not the case in the Jewish world. The percentage of Jewish children in Israel who have Internet access is fast approaching American levels and will increase with time. American Jewish and Israeli children now share a significant common communications system that might develop into a significant bridge between them. This has the potential to revolutionize the very nature of Israel-Diaspora as well as intra-Diaspora relations.

The Net Generation is exceptionally curious, self-reliant, contrarian, smart, focused, adaptable, high in self-esteem, and globally oriented. Values of autonomy and individualism prevail; they want to conduct their intellectual and spiritual search on their own terms and in their own ways. They are concerned more with looking into the future than with dwelling on the past. This last point must be of particular concern to the Jewish community. Although we should expect and teach respect for our history, we must carefully avoid either the appearance or the reality of being stuck in it. The Net Generation might be expected to respect their Jewish history, but they will not be controlled by it. They will grant the past a voice but will not tolerate a veto.

Rabbi Rami Shapiro, a Jewish commentator, writes about the Jewish aspects of the Tapscott model. The following combines his observations and my interpretations thereof, regarding the characteristics of the Net Generation: They like and want options; their world is defined by almost limitless choices. They expect customization, they want their personal preferences honored and their individual needs met. They like to change their minds. Ideologies, like brands, have little staying power. Therefore, they have little respect or patience for dogma or dogmatic people. They like to experiment and to try before they buy. They are hard to impress with glitz and externalities. They are loyal to whatever serves their needs as long as it proves itself.

Rabbi Shapiro also suggests that Net-Geners are polymorphic thinkers. Having been reared on multilayered Internet texts and media, they are not constrained by linear thinking. They proactively look for hyperlinks to other ideas that often spin off into new and unexpected directions. Free association as much as deductive reasoning keeps them focused. This is analogous to the model of Talmudic thinking and hints at the strategy we might pursue in order to develop Jewish ambitions in Jewish Net-Geners.

CHAPTER 13

The Future of Jewish Spirituality

This chapter deals with potential Jewish spiritual renewal amidst current fears of massive Jewish assimilation in the Diaspora and growing Jewish fundamentalism in Israel and the Diaspora.

We will posit a third alternative: a heterodox Jewish spiritual renewal made possible by a new, spiritual ecology developing within cyberspace. This spiritual ecology's potential Jewish component might contribute particular added value for young, university-trained Jews in both Israel and the Diaspora.

This investigation will be informed with the spiritual approach of Rabbi Abraham Isaac Kook, who invited the Jews to "renew the old and sacralize the new." In accordance with Kook's admonition, we will explore the implications cyberspace presents for renewing the old and sacralizing the new as a way to make Judaism more relevant to young Jews. Rabbi Kook was a rare twentieth-century phenomenon—a religious mystic who took an active interest in practical human affairs.

Most non-Jewish mystical systems require people to divest themselves of the restraints of material and physical existence to unite their souls with the ineffable, to achieve *unio mystica*. Kook, however, strove to combine the communicable with the ineffable, to infuse individual physical life with religious purpose. Self-abnegation was not part of his system. Like another Jewish thinker, Abraham Heschel, Kook saw endless inherent spiritual possibilities in our mundane physical existence. Both thinkers considered religious discipline a means to reconcile the spiritual with the physical by investing the physical with spiritual meaning and acknowledging spiritual merit only as it is manifested within the physical world.

JUDAISM AS A VALUE-TROPIC SYSTEM

Torah, as it is meant to embody all of Jewish tradition, is not only a vast realm of information, it is also an inherently value-tropic system. This system constantly tends toward values and does not merely pass on information.

Human beings are cultural and symbolic as well as economic creatures; they cannot live without values. We have already discussed the moral and spiritual desert created by an intellectual culture of valuelessness and the implications of the subsequent moral and spiritual vacuum. The growing realization that this state of affairs cannot continue has become dramatically self-evident. A renewed search for value-laden, or at least value-tropic, systems has become manifest in recent years.

Value-oriented social thinkers are seeking to mine intellectual raw materials out of older traditions such as Utopianism. Utopianism, like Judaism, is essentially value-tropic. This chapter makes an axiomatic assumption that the Jewish spiritual tradition, an ancient value-tropic system, might contain spiritual raw material of value to the modern university-trained Jew, as well as to the world at large. Both the values and the metaphors of Judaism might have a unique and special role to play in the emerging, multidimensional, spiritual ecology implicit in the very nature of cyberspace.

AND LET THERE BE LIGHT

The spiritual implications of the light metaphor are apt for our discussion, especially as information technology is increasingly based on light by way of emerging photonics technologies. The first thing that God "says" in the Bible deals with light. The Jewish tradition is replete with references that connect mind and consciousness with various aspects of light. Light is a powerful and consistent metaphor in Judaism as well as other cultures. The Hebrew term *hitbonenut* is usually translated as "meditation." In the Kabbalah, it refers to protracted concentration of thought on the supernal lights of divine worlds. The Jewish concept of God we call the *Shekhinah*—"Divine Presence"—implies a numinous immanence of the presence of God in the world.

Rabbi Kook's writings in particular contain much about the spiritual dimensions of light and imply that the very medium of light has its own inherent spiritual characteristics. This could be considered a Jewish anticipation of Marshall McLuhan's famous dictum that the medium is the message. This traditional Jewish view, that light carries its own inherent spiritual and intellectual potential, finds its parallel in European intellectual history, as reflected in the historical designation *Enlightenment.*

Although dubbed the patron saint of the media age, McLuhan was a deeply religious person. Born a Protestant, he converted to Catholicism and received a rigorous Jesuit education. He began every day by reading a chapter of the Bible in English, Latin, Classical Greek, and Hebrew. One can only speculate why he would read the same chapter in four different languages. I would like to think that it was in order to see the text from four different linguistic perspectives and thus gain deeper insight into the endless ways that we might understand something. I see this echoed in the Jewish tradition of *pilpul* and Kook's metaphor of lights and feel deep brotherhood with McLuhan's spiritual discipline.

The word *lights* was Kook's governing metaphor. His works had names such as *Orot HaKodesh* (The Lights of Holiness), *Orot HaTorah* (The Lights of Torah), and *Orot HaEmunah* (The Lights of Faith). A Web site of his writings is www.orot.com. His consistent use of the plural *lights* probably reflects the same kind of spiritual intuition that motivated McLuhan to read the Bible in different languages. Different lights shed different perspectives in the same way that different languages do. When we speak about shedding light on something (to "see" it), doesn't what we see depend on the light we use? And shouldn't we try to see it from as many different perspectives as possible in order to approach understanding?

The metaphor of light informs a worldview that celebrates the constant search for truth, for enlightenment. This is suggested in the Jewish injunction to be partners with God in the ongoing act (*mitzvah*) of creation. Light discloses reality and facilitates enlightenment. This enables us to widen our range of activity and our ability to create. Kook writes: "The more we increase knowledge, increasing spiritual illumination and a healthy physicality, so will this wondrous light shine in us, a lamp on the path of our life" (*Orot HaEmunah*, p. 80).

Kook refused to see a sharp dichotomy between the sacred and the profane, maintaining that all that was essential to human life was potentially sacred. All the advances in science were part of the intellectual growth of humankind, and if these advances appeared to undermine religion, there was no reason to suspect their intrinsic value. In his view, the fault lay not in scientific progress, but in failure to keep the intellectual level of religious thinking proceeding at an equal rate.

The physical concerns of human beings are inseparable from their spiritual aspirations. His view was that "the sacred and the profane together influence the spirit of man and he becomes enriched through absorbing from each whatever is suitable." In other words, to achieve holiness, the sacred and the profane must be synthesized. He saw the Torah of God—the written Torah and the Torah of Man—the Oral Torah—converging "and the two lights make a complete world, in which heaven and earth kiss" (*Orot HaTorah*, ch. 1).

SCIENTIFIC FOUNDATIONS

Kook's spiritual intuitions regarding light have been affirmed by modern science. The two great paradigm shifts of modern physics—relativity and quantum mechanics—derived from the exploration of anomalies in the behavior of light and both led to radical new understanding of the nature of light. Light seems to occupy a special place in the cosmic order. In some ways, light is more fundamental than time, space, or matter. This may also be true of the inner light of consciousness.

Modern physics teaches us that light is a fundamental characteristic of the universe. We know from quantum physics and Planck's constant that light, rather than matter, energy, or time is at the core of our cosmos. Planck's equation holds that quanta of light are also quanta of action.

Philosopher and scientist Peter Russell posits that physics, like Genesis, suggests that in the beginning there was light, or rather, in the beginning there is light, for light underlies every process in the present moment. Any exchange of energy between any two atoms in the universe involves the exchange of photons. Every interaction in the material world is mediated by light. In this way, light penetrates and interconnects the entire cosmos. An oft-quoted phrase comes to mind: God is Light. God is said to be absolute, and in physics so is light.

Consciousness is often spoken of as the inner light. Light seems in some way fundamental to the universe. Its values are absolute, universal constants. The light of consciousness is likewise fundamental; without it there would be no experience. Do physical reality and mental reality share the same common ground and does this commonality depend on our understanding of light?

The Jewish tradition in the Kabbalah anticipated this association between the inner and outer worlds, but until now all of this was considered to be within the realm of the esoteric—wisdom for the initiated few. Now, these traditional teachings as well as their correlations with modern developments in physics, the life sciences, and psychology are accessible to everyone in cyberspace. Scientific research in the twenty-first century might be able to actualize the Kabbalic ambition to develop a science of the *Neshama*, a science of the human spirit. This will almost surely derive from a deeper understanding of the pervasive role of light lying behind every material and psychic activity in the universe.

In other words, not only can the Jewish tradition contribute to the more general spiritual ecology now evolving in cyberspace, it can also use the spiritual potential of cyberspace to give its own tradition new meanings and new dimensions. Indeed, cyberspace might be the very vehicle the Jewish spiritual heritage needs to realize its own potential. It could certainly offer greater opportunities to explore the spiritual potential of the Kabbalah and the rest of the Jewish spiritual heritage—especially its explorations of the sacred dimensions of being when being has been radically redefined by virtual reality and cyberspace. Where are we when we are located at our e-mail address, and what are we when we travel in cyberspace? Both our location and our travel are being defined by light.

CONCEPTS OF TIME

The Jewish concept of time is different from the Greek/Western concept of time. Western tradition treats time as isomorphic: that is to say, all 60-second minutes are exactly the same. This secular, universal/uniform concept of time was essential to Western intellectual and technological development. Without it, we would not have the clock or the clockwork universe or Newton's concept of absolute time—all of which were necessary prerequisites of the Scientific Revolution, the Enlightenment, and the Industrial Revolution.

Yet, undifferentiated time is spiritually one-dimensional. It has indirectly contributed to the apparent emptiness of modern life, which asks us to kill time, to fill time, and to have free time but does not help us develop a sense of unique or special time, to sanctify time. It does not give us a sense that "the time of our lives" has some special meaning, a sense that the time we spend living is meaningful.

The Jewish tradition, on the other hand, makes anti-isomorphic, qualitative distinctions between different types of time. The Jewish Sabbath is sacred time because it is literally set aside, separated from the rest of the week, from regular time. Its sacredness lies in its aim to put human beings more in touch with their essential human being by separating them from distracting daily routines. Sabbath's primary purpose is not to achieve mystical communion with God but to enable meaningful communion with one's own human self.

Consequently, a 60-second minute on the Sabbath is essentially different from "profane" or normal time. During sacred time, the human spirit has the potential for different and special spiritual experiences. What potential significance might this anti-isomorphic concept of time have in a cyberworld ruled by nanoseconds? Such a question offers Jewish thinkers rich opportunities to renew the old and sacralize the new. Unfortunately, most modern Jewish thinkers are past oriented, not future oriented.

A notable exception would be Rabbi Joseph Soloveitchik, who claimed an essential difference between the Jewish perspective of history and the secular perspective of history. The secular world generally sees history as an unfolding out of the past, as if the past is pushing history forward, but Judaism believes that the future is activating history. History is being pulled not pushed toward the future. This is a much more amenable view of history to the futurist or neo-utopian thinker. Judaism is essentially futuristic—that is, positing a future vision and working toward that vision instead of deterministically being pulled along by inchoate events.

MATERIAL AND NONMATERIAL

Jewish civilization has been unique in human history in that, while preoccupied with the physical life of its adherents, its particular characteristics are essentially nonmaterial. Buildings do not characterize Judaism but rather ideas. Since the fall of the Temple, Judaism has been an information/wisdom civilization, a civilization indifferent to the external package and preoccupied with the content and meaning of our physical existence and constantly searching for its spiritual potentialities. It celebrates the human mind and abstract thought as they pertain to life. The medium of its messages is nonmaterial—

writing and talking—and not material buildings or works of art. This might explain why archeology has had such a difficult time in chronicling the Jewish presence in the Land of Israel.

Cyberspace is essentially a nonmaterial medium. We use *nonmaterial* in its popular sense and not in the philosophical or physics sense. Cyberspace is, after all, the product of an objective, physical, material universe. It is not a Platonic idealistic construct. In the popular sense, it is, however, definitely nonmaterial and indicative of a revolutionary change in human civilization.

The central event of the 20th century is the overthrow of matter. In technology, economics and the politics of nations, wealth—in the form of physical resources—has been losing value and significance. The powers of MIND are everywhere ascendant over the brute force of things.

In the First Wave economy, land and farm labor are the main "factors of production." In the Second Wave economy, the land remains valuable while "labor" becomes massified around machines and larger industries. In a Third Wave economy, the central resource—a single word broadly encompassing data, information, images, symbols, culture, ideology and values—is ACTIONABLE KNOWLEDGE. ("Cyberspace and the American Dream: A Magna Carta for the Knowledge Age," www.townhall.com, August 1994)

Once, a few thinking human minds molded, moved, and manipulated great masses of matter and masses of other human beings. Agriculture and industry are, after all, products of the human mind. Today, an infinitesimal amount of matter (the chip) serves great masses of individual human minds in molding, moving, and manipulating great masses of information and ideas.

LIVING IN CYBERIA

"Immaterial" media have traditionally been the domains of religious and spiritual traditions. We ask, therefore, what is spiritually unique about cyberspace and what is unique about the Jewish tradition by which we might Jewishly use this new spiritual ecology of cyberspace? How does the Jewish concept of spirit relate to a nonmaterial spiritual life in Cyberia?

Cyberia is a double play on the words *Siberia* and *suburbia* that has gained currency in cyberculture. It signifies an actual space where millions of people live, work, play, and envision their futures. Cyberspace is a theoretical representation of digitized space. Cyberia is the reality of that representation.

Author Douglas Rushkoff has written two books on Cyberia: *Cyberia: Life in the Trenches of Hyperspace* (1994) and *Cyberia: Life in the Trenches of Cyberspace* (2002). He claims that the technological strides of postmodern culture, coupled with the rebirth of ancient spiritual values, have convinced a growing number of people that Cyberia is the dimensional plane in which humanity will develop. Search "Cyberia" on the Internet, and you will find more than 100,000 sites listed.

THE NATURE OF JEWISH SPIRITUALITY

Now let us explore the interrelationship between technology and spirituality through a Jewish prism and its implications for humanity's spiritual quest. This will be a departure from conventional thinking about computer mediated communications. Many people might even doubt the propriety of discussing spirituality in regards to cyberspace. Such a perspective views cyberspace and the online world as a function of wires, silicon, software, electronic circuits, and algorithms. This produces a limited view of human spirituality, seeing as all technical developments are products of the human spirit in the broader (and certainly Jewish) sense of that term.

The Jews have never dichotomized the concepts of body and spirit—in contradistinction to the Western tradition that has its roots in Plato, Christianity (Augustine especially), Descartes, and others. The Hebrew word *nefesh*, which is usually mistranslated as "soul," refers to the entire person: body and mind as one. This reflects modern concepts of intelligence as being a consequence of the interactions between body and brain. A particularly cogent presentation of this view is to be found in Edward O. Wilson's *Consilience: The Unity of Knowledge*.

As mentioned, both Kook and Heschel held this view. Both would almost certainly intuit that the new technological functions of material society present us with new spiritual opportunities. They would have held that technological innovation is not counter to spirituality but reflects the inherent greatness of the human spirit and the means by which we might expand humanity's spiritual potential.

Developments in the general culture reflect this approach. The dominant cultural symbol of the late twentieth century and early twenty-first century is the picture of the blue marble of Earth hanging in the inky blackness of space. It has become a spiritual icon of our age and is a consequence of the greatest technological achievement of our age.

If one were to examine the writings of the late Enlightenment thinkers, one would conclude that they viewed the Industrial Revolution as a significant spiritual event. They believed it would provide infinitely greater opportunities for the creative human spirit to express itself as well as provide the means to liberate the human spirit from its preoccupation with gathering the most basic necessities to sustain a bare physical existence. Before industrialism, human beings were one step above the animals, spending their entire existence obtaining the means to subsist. Postindustrialism, technology, and especially cyberspace present us with the means to climb several steps up the spiritual ladder, to move closer to the godly.

The entire Kabbalistic system, cleansed of its accretions of mystical superstition, might, therefore be the most suitable metaphor for the cyber age. Could it be that Jewish tradition has anticipated the human spirit's potential and that Jewish tradition has had to wait on humanity's innovations to reach its spiritual maturity?

In this connection, we claim that the significance of cyberspace goes far beyond its technology. Its historical significance (like space exploration) is essentially spiritual. We do not make the claim that cyberspace itself is spiritual, or that the search for spirituality will be limited to cyberspace, or that cyberspace will usher in the messianic age. We have outgrown the naiveté of modernism that viewed technological progress and moral progress as a unicum.

More and more people will be "living" more and more of their lives in cyberspace. This requires us to explore the spiritual potential of cyberspace both generally and Jewishly. We believe cyberspace might be particularly suited to the Jewish spiritual tradition.

DETERMINISM AND VOLITION

The Jewish tradition has a beautiful saying: *HaKol Tsafui vey HaRashoot Netuna*. A literal translation would be "All is foreseeable (determined) but the decisions are up to us (volitional)." In its original formulation, it is meant to correlate the apparent contradiction between an all-powerful, all-seeing God (who already knows everything that will happen) and the ethical obligations of sovereign individuals that by definition requires free will. In other words, God has determined everything already but free will (volitional good or evil activity) is still the preserve of every individual human being.

I would like to secularize this particular Jewish tradition and posit that this could be the slogan of a value-laden social science or of a neo-Utopianism. Notwithstanding the wishful thinking of romantic primitivists, no force on earth can prevent the technological revolution from progressing at a breathtaking pace—that is determined (*HaKol Tsafui*). Indeed, even today we could say the change in the rate of change forces us to be part of a world to which we must adapt in real time. What we do with this self-evident reality is completely up to us, that is, it is volitional (*HaRashoot Netuna*).

Every language of the human race is blessed with two sacred words: *yes* and *no*. Human decision making revolves around to what we shall say yes and to what we shall, can, and should say no. We cannot say no to technology and human innovation per se. In the moral realm, this would be to deny the very thing that makes us human: our creativity. Indeed, the human ability to create (tools, art, music, organization, technology, science, mathematics) is what makes us Godlike and is what is meant when the Bible says we were created in the image of God. God creates, and man creates, and no other creature on the face of the earth creates.

The Jewish tradition says that man is a partner with God in the *ongoing* act of creation. This is a Jewish anticipation of the evolutionary attitude, one that implies that human creativity is a necessary part of God's creativity—that God's creation could not exist without human beings. Such a view invests daily mundane tasks with great spiritual potential. It more efficiently addresses the spiritual needs of modern men and women than the view that human beings must deny, subsume, or escape their physical and material existence in order to achieve spirituality.

In the practical realm, it is impossible to say no to technology. Human beings cannot forget nor can they deny what humanity has created. Radical primitivists who view technology as satanic and whose ambition is to negate the Industrial Revolution and to return to a standard of living of pre-Carolingian Europe are missing the mark. Not only is the call to give up soap and hot water and live in teepees unlikely to generate much resonance among the vast majority of the human race, it is spiritually bankrupt. What would be the level of the human spirit in a society in which people die before the age of 35, are illiterate, and live their entire lives in physical pain and abysmal superstition and ignorance—the prevailing preindustrial reality?

Ever-increasing technological innovation is a deterministic given that reflects the very nature of the inquiring human spirit (*HaKol Tsafui*); it cannot and should not be stopped, unless one's hatred of humanity is equivalent to Hitler's hatred of the Jews.

If continued technological innovation is a deterministic given (*HaKol Tsafui*), what we do with it is a moral, volitional decision (*HaRashoot Netuna*). If human society is to be a *human* society it must be value-laden; these values must be chosen/volitional values, adopted by free, sovereign, autonomous human beings (*HaRashoot Netuna*). Cyberspace is humanity online, and wherever humanity goes, so too goes the contemplation of what it means to be human, and that must include humanity's spiritual quest. The questions for Jews are whether or not the Jewish tradition has a special contribution to make to this all-human quest and whether or not Jewish individuals can derive unique added value out of this Jewish tradition that encourages them to explore and delve into it further.

DEFINING OUR TERMS: WHAT DO WE MEAN BY RELIGION AND SPIRITUALITY?

We define religion (small r) as that heritage of religious wisdom, ritual, tradition, and communal and collective practice that all Jews have come to see as being uniquely Jewish over the past 3,000 years. We define Religion (big R) as the current Religious establishment. For some Jews, r = R, for others they are two separate rubrics in which R acts to the detriment of r and disabuses many young Jews from even trying to develop Jewish ambitions.

Religion (big R) is essentially institutional; religion (small r) is essentially communal; and spirituality is essentially individual. Religion coerces us, religion communally obligates us, and spirituality requires that we examine our own selves and endeavor to gain insight into or connect with a divine source on an individual basis without the necessary mediation of either institution or communal tradition. There is no prohibition on using institutional or communal traditions to facilitate one's personal spiritual quest, but spirituality is, by definition, subjective and individual. The personal attempt to cultivate a sense of connectivity to something beyond our daily preoccupations is not dependent on doctrine, institution, or tradition but only on the individual's personal free will (*HaRashoot Netuna*). What do we mean by divine? The *Random House College Edition Dictionary* (1968) offers several definitions:

1. Of, pertaining to, or preceding from a god, esp. the Supreme Being
2. Godlike; characteristic of or befitting a deity
3. The spiritual aspect of man; the group of attributes and qualities of mankind regarded as godly or godlike

If we choose to use the third definition, connecting with a divine source means nothing more than connecting with one's own spiritual potential as a human being and aspiring to live according to the second definition (*imitato dio*). In other words, even Jews who do not believe in a transcendent, supernatural God, as per the first definition, can aspire to a rich spiritual life within the Jewish tradition.

We would further claim, in keeping with the researches of Professor Joseph Levinson, that the metaphysical concepts of a transcendent supreme being are Hellenistic accretions not necessary to the Jewish system. Indeed, he goes so far as to say that Judaism is not even a religion, in the Western sense, but rather a life system for human beings. He acknowledges, however, that both these concepts are practically necessary for most Jews even if they are not conceptually necessary for a Jewish worldview. He posits that as the Jews evolve to ever-higher levels of understanding we might even shed these concepts and arrive at the core of the Jewish insight about existence.

This jibes, somewhat, with Dr. Arthur Green's definition of Jewish spirituality, that it is distinct from most non-Jewish concepts of spirituality, which are "inevitably opposed in some degree to corporeality or worldliness (all apologetics notwithstanding)" (Cohen and Mendes-Flohr, pp. 903, 904). In this view, Green would be a disciple of Kook and Heschel.

Authentic Jewish tradition sees spirituality as the consequence of living and working in this world. *Ruhaniyut*, the Hebrew equivalent of spirituality, is a medieval Hellenist accretion found neither in the Bible nor in the early rabbinical sources (ibid.).

The above definitions of *divine* and *spirituality* are important if we want to cultivate the spiritual ambitions of Jews (perhaps the majority today) who do not and cannot believe in a transcendent supreme being and require a Judaism that reflects this.

THE EVOLUTION OF JEWISH SPIRITUALITY

During the biblical period, the Jews had cultivated concepts of holiness connected with sacred space (the Temple) and sacred time (sabbath and holidays). Following the fall of the Temple and the almost total dispersion of the Jewish People, sacred time and the sanctification of daily activity became dominant. Jewish spirituality, therefore, is neither a doctrine nor an attempt to transcend or escape the limits of one's earthly existence. It strives to be a celebration of self and the wonder of existence; it is both a self-exploration and a self-realization. It is in no way a denial of self and in no way a call for selflessness. As we have discussed in previous chapters, Judaism is a system of behavior that places absolute responsibility for actions on the individual.

In the Jewish spiritual tradition, the desire for selflessness would be synonymous with the desire to abrogate one's individual ethical responsibilities. For if one is selfless, that is, without a self, how can one be moral or ethical? Furthermore, how could one be a communal being with communal responsibilities if one lacks a sense of one's self?

Here, the Jewish spiritual tradition offers rich resources with which to bridge the modern chasm of radical individualism and undifferentiated social responsibility. The latter requires one to subsume one's own individuality into the "general will" (to use Rousseau's chilling phrase) and the greater good (that unspecified and unlimited Utilitarian concept). This question has begun to preoccupy social thinkers over the past several decades. How can we repair the damage to our social fabric caused by the adolescent self-indulgence of radical individualism without falling into the totalitarian trap of Rousseau's general will and the undifferentiated majoritarian democracy that was its consequence?

Ruach Ha-Kodesh (the holy spirit), in the Jewish tradition, is nothing more than a human state achieved as culmination of moral, virtuous, and responsible deeds in one's worldly existence. It is not an ethereal otherworldly concept; it is an earned product of living in this world in a virtuous manner. It is an earned (that is, causal) state of affairs and not something given freely by the grace of God. It is not deterministic (*HaKol Tsafui*); it is volitional (*HaRashoot Netuna*). It is not the product of a free gift of God; it is the product of individual responsible effort. It is man striving to realize his very being as being in the image of God by acting in a godly way, which means by creating. In this context, any denial of technology would be a denial of the very ability to be spiritual, to realize oneself in the image of God.

We would reiterate that the life of holiness, of achieving the Holy Spirit, can only be achieved by the requirements of a this-world sustenance. For the Jew, the entire world is potentially holy space, and we can only realize holy time *within* this space, not by separating ourselves out from it. Indeed, given the Einsteinian concept of space/time as a unicum, this Jewish intuition might have anticipated the inherent spirituality of cyberspace (which is also cybertime). Indeed, cyberspace could easily be renamed cyberspace/time.

THE SEARCH FOR SPIRITUALITY IN CYBERSPACE

Many observers are beginning to see cyberspace/time as the harbinger of a major transformation of the very concept of human consciousness. They would view cyberspace/time as an integral part of developing new frontiers in the concept of mind. Such developments transcend anything we humans have been dealing with in the past few centuries. How might the Jewish heritage contribute to this growing world of consciousness in cyberspace?

Peter Russell, cited above, has described the development of a universal cyber consciousness in his book *The Global Brain*. He bases much of his thinking on the concept of the "noosphere," developed by Jesuit philosopher and scientist Teilhard De Chardin. This evolutionary concept of the human spirit envisages a developing global consciousness that will envelope and define the entire planet. The Israeli thinker Mordechai Nessyahu, completely ignorant of the work of de Chardin and Russell, expanded this vision to include the entire cosmos in his life work entitled *Cosmotheism*. Nessyahu envisioned the evolution of consciousness through the prism of Jewish tradition and saw the entire cosmos as eventually becoming a conscious entity.

Ken Wilber has defined spirituality as "the basic desire to find ultimate meaning and purpose in one's life and to live an integrated life." This basic desire drives the arts and sciences. This search for meaning, purpose, wholeness, and integration is a lifelong process—a never-ending process and task. A mature person recognizes this as a process and realizes that he or she will never arrive at a definitive answer but also realizes that a life without this search is an impoverished, one-dimensional life. For a mature person, spirituality does not merely provide peace and contentment, it also profoundly unsettles and acts as a spur to constantly improve the human condition in each of us, personally, and in general for the entire human race. *Tikkun olam* (repairing the world) is, therefore, an essential part of the mature person's spiritual project.

A childish person, on the other hand, demands immediate, simple, clear answers and is thus easy fodder for cults, religious charlatans, and political fanatics. An empty-minded person fails even to recognize the need to ask questions about meaning and might be described as spiritually deprived—someone who believes that God created the universe as a place to put shopping centers. An evil person would try to manipulate this search for his or her own narrow ends. Indeed, fascism and Stalinism both can be called perverted manipulations of twentieth-century man's search for meaning.

SPIRITUALITY IN REAL LIFE

The search for meaning has become a ubiquitous phenomenon in our society. Many people see the quest for spiritual fulfillment in their work as appropriate, even though these same people would see religion in the workplace as inappropriate. Managers, organizational consultants, and employees are beginning to view spirituality as one of the most important determinants of organizational performance. Individuals with a highly developed spirituality appear to achieve better results in almost any organizational framework. This is an interesting development from the Jewish point of view and might be considered an affirmation of the Jewish approach to life.

The word for craftsman in Hebrew is *ooman* (and for artist, *oman*), which comes from the same word root as *faith, belief, amen*. It implies that even one's daily occupation must be endowed with a sense of sanctity; that creativity of any sort, no matter how mundane, has cosmic value (apropos the butterfly effect of chaos theory); and that this exemplifies being created in the image of God. Just as all that God creates is sacred, so too must we strive to make sacred all that humanity creates.

The Jewish tradition could contribute to the modern concept of work with its affirmation that work should not be laborious routine that dulls the soul but a creative celebration of the spirit. The Third Wave and cyberspace in contradistinction to the First and Second Waves, replaces laborious soul-dulling work with a creative celebration of the spirit. The Jewish tradition and cyberspace meet.

SPIRITUALITY VERSUS RELIGION, NOT SECULARITY VERSUS RELIGION

A unique characteristic of cyberculture is its detachment of the spiritual quest from traditional Religion. This is not to suggest that organized religion lacks spiritual dimensions or that spiritual persons cannot be religious, but the centuries-long linkage between spirituality and religion is no longer self-evident. Since the Enlightenment, the basic dichotomy has been religious versus secular; today, increasingly, the dichotomy is becoming spiritual versus religious.

In Israel, this new dichotomy has become palpable. Israel seems to be experiencing a two-pronged sociological phenomenon. On the one hand are (1) the continued politicization of religion into Religion and (2) the creation of growing walls of separation, mistrust, and even hatred between secular and religious people that stems from religious politics. On the other hand is a growing spiritual quest that lies increasingly outside the Orthodox religious establishment with no apparent need of proposed Reform, Conservative, or Reconstructionist alternatives. Where once Jews saw the synagogue and organized Jewish community as having the monopoly on spirituality, today organized Religion projects a decidedly antispiritual image that has alienated and apparently will continue to alienate many young Israelis from seeking religious sustenance within the Jewish tradition. This may be why so many young Israelis, belatedly aping the American '60s generation, who also rebelled against traditional institutional forces, are seeking spiritual sustenance not in the Judaism as it is practiced in Israel but in the Far East: India, Japan, and elsewhere.

Here, we see a repeat of the paradox that we discussed in a previous chapter. Just as the self-proclaimed authentic Zionists of Gush Emunim have turned so many young Israelis into post-Zionists or even anti-Zionists in the name of Zionism, so has Israel's religious establishment, representing so-called authentic Judaism, turned so many young Israelis into post- or anti-Judaism Jews in the name of Judaism. Considering the centrality of Israel for world Jewry, this situation is creating a general Jewish spiritual crisis. Jewish spiritual ecology in Israel and the Diaspora is increasingly impoverished because of the Orthodox monopoly in Israel.

As with natural ecologies, monoculturalism leaves a system prone to disease and collapse. Rich variety provides us with natural and cultural and spiritual resilience. Israel's spiritual monoculturalism greatly weakens Jewish spiritual strength and the ability for Jewish survival. Israel, created to strengthen and preserve the Jewish People, is weakening the spiritual immune system of all Jews by sanctioning an Orthodox monopoly on interpretation of Judaism while delegitimizing all other interpretations of Judaism. What an irony, given the historical ambitions of the Zionist founding fathers.

RELIGIOUS AND SPIRITUAL REVIVAL: THE SPIRITUAL PARADOX

The last several decades of the twentieth century were witness to a massive worldwide religious revival. This was in total contradiction to the prognostications of social scientists that religious observance was on the wane and that religions in general would have less impact on society. The hypothesis that civilization was about to become totally secular has not realized itself. The human situation is much more complex and paradoxical.

Globalization is a secular phenomenon because it is based on trade, production, finance, and communications, which are all secular activities. Secular globalization, however, provides no meaning, and as it expands, need for spiritual exploration and spiritual development expands, too.

The paradox is that the global increase of secular activity and secularity appears to be creating a growing need and space for spiritual initiatives. Cyberspace is the most dramatic example of how technology (a human creation for human use, and thus secular) is providing the space/time for new kinds of spiritual endeavor.

Futurologists who use historical analogy as their primary methodology might have predicted this. The last great religious revival in the United States, for example, occurred when the American economy shifted from an agricultural to an industrial society. When people are buffeted by powerful cultural changes, which they neither control nor often even understand, the need for some kind of spiritual sustenance grows in direct proportion to the radical nature of the change.

Fritjof Capra analyzed this in his highly original, now classic, book *The Turning Point*. People who live through turning points, who find themselves in those historical creases between two eras, when old values appear to be eroding and new values are not yet self-evident, often experience great anxiety, feel themselves adrift, and search for answers outside their own mundane material existence.

The most common and often easiest answer is to be found in traditional religion, especially the most fundamentalist religions. These project such absolute surety in their answers that they make their adherents feel safe within the tremendous storms of change. Religions that are more ambiguous and heterodox, that celebrate the question more than the answer, do not do as well in such periods and indeed appear to lose ground. People in these historical creases do not go to church to hear more ambivalence, they want to hear answers. They want to hear people who really know.

These traditional religious systems may appeal to certain kinds of spiritual laziness. I may not, in such an instance, know or have the ability to know, but I do know who knows: the priest, rabbi, kadi, or minister. I know this because the members of his or her congregation or community all tell me so. Because a great deal of the alienated individual's spiritual search has to do with finding a community and being part of something, the communal affirmation and identity just adds to the surety.

We must not ignore the sociological and psychological aspects of this modern spiritual search. A group that demonstrates concern and embraces lonely, alienated people can be irresistibly attractive. This is the tactic of cults as well as the more established proselytizing religions: identify lonely, confused people; tell them they are even more lonely and confused than they think they are, and tell them that your group has the answer. At this point, they are introduced to members of the group who relate how confused and lonely they were and how the group has now answered their needs—empirical proof.

In addition, traditional religions have been around for centuries, and this longevity gives them authority. Who are we, after all, to question the accumulated wisdom of generations? And even if I as an individual do not know, I can assume that God at least does know, and the historical staying power of traditional religious frameworks indicates to me that God is speaking to humanity through the prism of these religions.

A second path would be more inner directed; it would seek out spiritual traditions that seem to appeal to our own intuitive senses. These traditions are often less authoritarian and more dependent on the individual's own interpretation. These traditions may have more relevance for the individual that takes responsibility for his or her own life than the more outer-directed religious traditions. In the Jewish community, especially, we seem to be witnessing a collective "no" to organized religion and a collective "yes" to spirituality. This has become so pronounced that many Diaspora synagogues are attempting to combine traditional practices with innovative spiritual initiatives within the walls of the synagogue. This may explain why some of the more mystical sects of Hassidism (those that combine spirituality and traditional rituals) have been doing so well while other expressions of Judaism appear to be in decline.

In the Jewish and Israeli context, the paradox might be described in the following way: the number and percentage of young Jews and Israelis being turned off by organizational Judaism is directly proportional to the number and percentage of young Jews and Israelis engaging in some kind of fashionable spiritual quest—New Age, far Eastern, or Jewish mystical.

Naisbitt, in his book *Megatrends*, wrote that the world is undergoing a revival in religious belief and spiritual quest. This revival is not occurring in mainline churches and synagogues, which have been in decline for decades. The new trend is in multiple-option, individuated, networked processes, outside of mainline institutions. The most exciting breakthroughs of the twenty-first century will not occur because of technology but because of our expanding concepts of what human possibilities are, facilitated by technology. What could the Jewish contribution be to this endeavor?

TALMUD AND HYPERTEXT

Historical analogy is useful in exploring the spiritual potential of any new medium. For example, as Professor David Porush has pointed out, it is undeniable that the organization of the Talmud page greatly influenced the intellectual and hence spiritual development of the Jewish People. Its multilevel, associative layout had an inherent ability to stimulate creative thinking and the essential limitlessness of alternative solutions to problems or dilemmas.

Studying the Talmud combines the precision of deductive logic with the creativity of associative thinking. This combination of intellectual precision and creativity molded the Jewish mind for centuries. This may be one reason why the Jewish People have produced so many intellectual pioneers as Western civilization underwent its secularization process over the past several centuries. It is certainly not because the Jews are inherently more intelligent than non-Jews.

It is interesting to note the congruence between the medium and the message, as developed in the printed Talmud page, and its potential ramifications for the Internet and Web site design.

The Talmud is proto-hypertext in nature; it is always self-referential: Talmudic discourse is the constant interpretation and reinterpretation of what the Talmud itself means. Talmudic discussions about what the Talmudic text means always refer to each other over the entire wide range of Talmudic literature. The printed Talmudic page (as distinct from scribed Talmudic scrolls) made the self-referential, proto-hypertext nature of the Talmud even more profound.

Let us explore the congruence between the self-referential nature of the Talmud and the self-referential nature of cyberspace. Can Jews use cyberspace to develop new methods of imparting their tradition in the same way that they used the new medium of print after Gutenberg? Moreover, can they modify the very use of the medium to better reflect its inherent Jewish potential in the same way that the Talmudic page modifies the linear print format?

Most Web sites that deal with Jewish materials, like most Web sites in general, usually encode linear text (like the printed book) but in electronic format. Even when images, music, and video are added they are still for the most part organized in linear format. When virtual reality realizes its potential, however, we are likely to see a much richer set of options. How can we use these new media tools in an authentically Jewish manner whereby the cyber-medium becomes congruent with the cybermessage?

Such adaptability has become a Jewish cultural characteristic. Invention of the printing press enabled the Jews to use books to disseminate information and knowledge to the Jewish community. In addition to conventional linear print, the Jews developed unique ways to organize and use print.

Apropos admonitions against the "Nation that Dwells Alone" syndrome, the inventor of the Talmudic page as we know it was a non-Jew, Daniel Bomberg. In other words, two non-Jews (Gutenberg and Bomberg) indirectly laid the foundations of Jewish culture as it has been practiced for the past 400 years.

Because Church authorities forbade printing of the Talmud by Jews, Bomberg, a sixteenth-century Venetian printer, perceived a potential market for his services and printed several editions of the Talmud. Faced with a problem of organization inherent to the Talmud he was forced to invent the Talmud page, as we know it. When the Talmud consisted of series of scrolls of various commentaries, the problem of organization did not exist—a student moved from scroll to scroll. Printing the Talmud as an all-inclusive entity, however, presented a different challenge. How was one to organize the commentaries on commentaries on commentaries?

Bomberg liberated the typography of the printed page from its linear form. He achieved a work of art in which the medium is indeed the message. Looking at any printed book, regardless of language or content (including the book you are now reading), we see an orderly procession of words representing ideas lined up in a lockstep form like soldiers in a line. This forces the reader to see and read in a linear lockstep model.

The Talmud, on the other hand, has an open format that invites the reader into what is in effect a symposium, much like the ancient Greek symposia. The Talmud organizes its knowledge base as an ongoing multilogue, more extensive than a dialogue between only two persons, across time and space. This is similar to the Internet, which is also a multilogue discourse across space and time. The Talmud page has the oldest and most authoritative texts in the center of the page with succeeding margins of commentaries unfolding around it.

The fundamental concept of the Talmud and hypertext might be analogous. In the Talmud page, the little notations on the side of the page are like hot buttons, the different commentaries are like frames, a common HTML implementation process. Different sections of the text are read as accompaniments to each other at different times and speeds.

Beyond these physical similarities, hypertext and the Talmud imply a *way* of knowing that differs from the linear book format and design. The Talmud medium captures the noise of the symposium, a hot and multivoiced discussion. Sometimes we know the names of the speakers and sometimes we do not—much like Internet chat rooms, bulletin boards, and e-mail postings. Talmudic debate and discussion extends over vast stretches of space and time. The central texts, from about 1,500 years ago, are based upon biblical references of 3,000 years ago.

Digital technology has the capability of adding entire new dimensions to the Talmudic tradition. Both Talmud and hypertext are texts—words, but we soon will be dealing with hypermedia, not only words, but images, sounds, music, and perhaps even touch and smell when virtual reality realizes its potential. What the digital world could accommodate and make available to the human spirit boggles the imagination.

KABBALAH IN CYBERSPACE

It is not a coincidence that the increased study of Kabbalah parallels cyberspace development and a growing popular understanding of light's role as the essential quality of existence. It reflects a search for alternative ways to connect to reality in a spiritually enhancing way.

The metaphors of Kabbalah are particularly apt. One, the Tree of Life, models the universe as various aspects of the divine. Its graphic depiction is composed of the 10 *sefirot* and 22 connecting lines representing each letter of the Hebrew alphabet. The energy that progresses through the *sefirot* is light, the foundation of quantum mechanics and cyberspace.

We will not attempt a detailed analysis of the vast world of the Kabbalah and the study of the *sefirot*. Many are intrigued with the potential correlation between these various subjects and perceived synergies between Kabbalic insights and models and the essence of quantum mechanics and cyberspace.

The Kabbalah sees God, the cosmos, human spirit, and knowledge as composed of one unified and unifying essence—light. Other spiritual traditions also correlate light with human energy centers. The Hindu concept of *chakras*—wheels of light as described in the Vedas—is one example.

The 10 dimensions of the Kabbalistic universe, as represented by the 10 *sefirot*, could also be utilized as a metaphor for the 10-dimensional superstring theories of contemporary physics as well as for the inherent complexity of the human mind. The Kabbalah sees every aspect of the world—spiritual, psychical, or material—as being composed of varying degrees and combinations of these 10 dimensions. These include the human qualities of will, wisdom, love, and compassion.

The 10 dimensions of the Kabbalist universe constitute a sophisticated guide to the divine inner nature and the psychological development of the human personality. They form a set of archetypes through which spirit is structured both in the cosmos and in the human mind.

One of the *sefirot, Tiferet,* might be the most appropriate to our attempt to spiritualize cyberspace. It is the most central and interconnected part of the Kabbalistic network of energy movement. It is the one through which individuals might channel their own internal divine human energies through their own psyches, and in the process transform themselves and the world at large—*tikkun olam.*

FROM INFORMATION TO ACTION, FROM TORAH TO *MITZVOT*

In this chapter we have already made three axiomatic claims:

1. Judaism does not separate body from spirit; it is in the corporal and material world that we fulfill our spiritual potential and not outside of it.
2. Torah—the totality of Jewish tradition—is value-tropic.
3. *HaKol Tsafui vey HaRashoot Netuna*—that is, "We can foresee every trend, but what we do with it is up to us."

In other words, Jewish spirituality must be renewed within the real technological world we live in; it must strive to exploit the spiritual potential of this new technology as well as provide cogent answers to the spiritually searching individual in the twenty-first century. Putting medieval Talmudic debates on the Internet or databasing the entire Jewish tradition may be a valuable effort, but it is just information and has nothing to do with the spiritual and religious renewal we are talking about in this chapter. Having information is one thing, knowing how to use it is quite another. Knowing Torah is not the entire story, indeed, those in the Jewish world who worship Torah knowledge itself might even be accused of *Avoda Zara* (idolatry).

Once you *know,* you are admonished and obligated to *do,* and such commitments and obligations the Jews call *mitzvot,* actionable commandments to act in this world. In other words, the covenant of Israel is not only information based, it is *mitzvah* based and by definition must be directed toward the purpose of *tikkun olam*—repairing the world—this world.

CHAPTER 14

The Future of Jewish Learning

This chapter deals with Jewish learning and modern information technology. I believe that modern information technology offers significant opportunities for new modes of Jewish learning. I also believe that traditional methods of Jewish learning anticipated the educational potential of modern technology and are better suited to exploit it than other educational traditions—particularly the European and American industrial model.

The industrial model is fundamentally inadequate to Jewish educational aims, and the Jewish educational establishment's attempts to accommodate Jewish school systems to it have been nothing short of pathetic. These attempts have become *doubly* pathetic in recent years as more non-Jewish school systems have realized the industrial model's inadequacies and have begun to experiment with methodologies partly analogous to traditional Jewish learning.

In pursuing this thesis, I will refer to distance learning, home learning, and teacher evolution from the Sage on the Stage to the Guide by the Side. I will show how these developments might apply to Jewish learning strategies and describe how Jewish educators may become adept at "edutainment"—the integration of education and entertainment in the cyberworld.

I will explore the possibility of developing authentic models of Jewish learning using these new information technologies. I believe that traditional methods of Jewish learning are intriguingly similar to hypertext: that on-screen windows resemble the Talmudic page. As a consequence, cyberlearning techniques could be more efficient at teaching Jewish subjects than the linear industrial teaching model we have copied from the West.

LEARNING, NOT EDUCATION

Education describes what we have been doing for the past 150 years. Education is designed to train, condition, and discipline children in order to make them useful members of industrial society. It is a nineteenth-century response to a nineteenth-century need. In the last three decades of the twentieth century, the inadequacies of this model had become painfully apparent. The for-profit business sector first perceived this inadequacy and began critiquing it. This is ironic because modern educational systems were created to serve the human resource needs of industrial capitalism, and now postindustrial capitalism is telling us the system is a failure.

The industrial educational model has contributed to the creation of modern industrial civilization, but it *no longer works*. In historical perspective, industrialized educational systems have been great successes, but in the postindustrial Information Age, they have become dysfunctional.

Modern Jewish education has been woefully inadequate from the outset. The operative word in most commentaries on Jewish education is *failure*. David Schoem, assistant dean for undergraduate education at the University of Michigan has written that the Jewish afternoon and Sunday Hebrew school is a categorical failure in every area pertinent to creating an educated identified Jew. Children leave this system knowing virtually no Hebrew, Jewish history or Bible. As Schoem says, because "the great majority of American Jews receive their Jewish education in the Jewish supplementary school," this is an insufferable circumstance.

Innovative educators, recognizing they were part of a failing system, developed interim strategies that changed some educational procedures and tried to make conventional schooling more palatable. These were mere Band-Aids and aspirin for a seriously ill system. Schoem denigrated these minor attempts at reform and called for "dramatically increased support for bold structural changes in supplementary schools at all levels" (pp. 163–68).

Modern information technologies provide us with new educational opportunities, universally accessible for adults as well as children, which might enable us to implement these bold structural reforms. These technologies enable us to entertain the possibility of a paradigm shift of monumental significance: a shift from nineteenth-century industrial models of education to twenty-first-century *strategies for learning*. We may now be capable of transforming the very nature of learning—from schooling to self-learning to learning how to think.

This will not be an easy transformation, but future Jews will see it as self-evidently right. As John Stuart Mill once wrote, "It often happens that the universal belief of one age, a belief from which no one could be free without extraordinary effort of genius or courage, becomes to a subsequent one so palpable an absurdity that the only difficulty is, to imagine how such an idea could ever have appeared credible." It is my contention that the universal belief in *compulsory* (and coercive) education, conducted in factory-like environments that stifle the creative imagination, will come to be seen as one of these palpable absurdities.

In order to reconceptualize learning we must define our terms precisely and differentiate between data, information, knowledge, understanding, and wisdom. Tapscott, in *Growing up Digital* (p. 32), dealt with four of these, and we have added a fifth (understanding) and have expanded on his definitions.

Data. Raw data are brute disorganized, empirical facts, meaningless in and of themselves. They are senseless and amoral.

Information. Raw data organized into a coherent and intelligible fashion, usable by the volitional human mind. They are now sensible but still amoral. We are at the level of hard-news journalism.

Knowledge. Information interpreted and organized into a larger system, with applied utilitarian value. Knowledge is sensible and based on the moral value of objective interpretation and application of information. We are at the level of journalistic commentary, as well as engineering, social criticism, and management.

Understanding. The ability to abstract knowledge into first principles in order to perceive underlying reality and truth and thus greatly expand the field of human inquiry. We are at the level of science, mathematics, and philosophy, which are based upon the moral value of objective methods of interpretation and application of knowledge.

Wisdom. Knowledge and understanding that carries profound, trans-historical insights. It reflects the ability to apply understanding and knowledge in our societies and cultures in a moral way. In the Jewish tradition, wisdom cannot arise without information and knowledge, but neither of these can guarantee wisdom (something the postmodernist critique of Modernism perceived). Moreover, wisdom without action is inert and useless. Judaism tells us to act in this world, that action is a condition for wisdom, that without action in this world (*mitzvot*), wisdom cannot be attained and is but a meaningless abstraction.

The new information technologies enable us to move up the wisdom food chain in a more efficient way than the linear industrial model, and they are better suited to value-tropic Jewish educational ambitions. Jewish education should be both purposeful and value-tropic, and its aim should be to achieve wisdom.

THE "CYBER OR" PROJECT

The word *or* is the Hebrew term for light. Light is a fundamental spiritual metaphor in Jewish tradition. It is a common figure of speech for God-Torah-Israel. "God is my light and my salvation" (Psalms 27:1); "The commandment is a lamp, Torah is light" (Proverbs 6:23); "A light unto the nations" (Isaiah 42:6). Hence, our term *Cyber Or*, a powerful metaphor by which we might relate to cyberspace in a creatively Jewish way as we proceed to reinvent Jewish learning.

External developments may have anticipated this objective. Steven Spielberg, being interviewed on *Actors Studio*, was asked about his pervasive use of light in his films. He answered that, for him, light symbolizes life. This is a Jewish view. Technological developments also present us with Jewish educational opportunities. The most recent information technologies are based on powerful systems that manipulate photons, which are packets of light. Creative Jewish educators could use this technological fact as an educational hook for Jewish Net-Geners.

Assuming that Marshall McLuhan was right, that the medium is the message, the question arises: is there a unique Jewish medium? We answer, yes. The Jews have organized information and knowledge in special ways, congruent and consistent with content.

The goal of the Cyber Or project would be to develop Jewish knowledge-organizing systems appropriate for Jewish learning in cyberspace. These would build on the foundations of traditional Jewish knowledge-organizing systems, but could also use the raw materials provided by popular culture, such as Spielberg's movies and their use of light.

TECHNOLOGY AND THE JEWS

The introduction of new technologies always results in significant cultural transformations. All human culture is affected by technology, including the Jews. The Bible tells us how technology affected the way ancient Israel governed itself.

When the Israelites conquered Canaan, Israelites and Canaanites used Bronze Age technologies. A few centuries later, an invading sea people, the Philistines, brought with them the new technology of iron. All local populations were subject to the power and control of this new technology. "No iron smith was to be found in all the land of Israel, for the Philistines were afraid that the Hebrews would make swords and spears" (I Samuel 13:19).

The divided Israeli tribes could not cope with this challenge and insisted that they needed a single unifying leader—a king. This was foreign to the Israelite way of governance, but Realpolitik took precedence. Samuel was the last of the biblical judges, and he anointed the first king in Israel. Samuel warned the people about the negative aspects of a monarchy and only relented under pressure.

The shift in technology, from bronze to iron, transformed the Israelite community. In the same way, the Industrial Revolution transformed Jewish life in the nineteenth century. And in the same way, cyberspace will transform Jewish life in the twenty-first century.

An analogous cultural adaptation occurred about 2,500 years ago. The Jews in Israel were exiled to Babylon in the year 586 B.C.E. About 70 years later, they returned to establish the Second Commonwealth and to begin to rebuild the Second Temple. Within these 70 years, just three generations, the Jewish community forgot how to read the original Hebrew script of the Bible. This is related in the books of Ezra and Nehemiah.

Ezra, the scribe and high priest, ordered the Bible rewritten into Assyrian-Aramaic script, so the people could read it. He left the old Hebrew characters to the Samaritans (Sanhedrin 21b). Assyrian-Aramaic was the common language of the time. Ezra was aware of the current communication and hence education needs, and had the authority and wisdom to adapt to them. If he had not instituted this radical change, Jewish tradition itself would have been lost.

His achievement was so great that in the Talmudic tradition it was said of him, "If Moses had not preceded him, Ezra would have received the Torah (Tosephta, Sanhedrin, 4:7). He restored and reestablished the Torah that had been almost completely forgotten (B.T. Sukkah 20a). Continuing to take cognizance of the general environment, he also ordained that the public readings of the Torah should take place not only on the Sabbaths, but also on Mondays and Thursdays, (Megillah 31b), the market days when the farmers would come from the fields to buy and sell their produce. He established schools everywhere to fill the existing needs for teaching Torah.

Ezra did not build walls around Jewish tradition, he adapted Jewish tradition to his environment and used that environment to change, enrich, and spread Jewish tradition. His adaptation to his environment made Ezra great. If he had turned his back on his environment, the Jewish tradition would not have survived. Let us emulate Ezra as we strive to accommodate Jewish education in the twenty-first-century environment. Universal technological and social changes have always changed the way Jews think and do things. More than 2,000 years ago, the Jews responded to their new environment and in doing so changed the way they behaved. Even then, we were never a nation that dwells alone.

Disruptive technologies have emerged throughout the history of human adaptation to changing environments. These technologies changed how people lived. In our century, electricity, railroads, automobiles, plastics, radio, and television were technologies that disrupted previous habits of life.

In our generation, microelectronics and the Internet are the disruptive technologies. The Internet might be the single most important development of the late twentieth century. It will certainly shape twenty-first century development in ways that we cannot yet imagine. The Internet and cyberspace are changing all of the rules of human interaction and behavior but could have their greatest impact on education.

TECHNOLOGY AND EDUCATION

No social institution has been *less* affected by technological advances than education. Since 1850, farmers, bankers, factory workers, doctors, business owners, and others have been radically affected by many technology-driven changes in their work and professional environment. By contrast, teachers from 1850 visiting a modern classroom would see little difference from what they did and how they did it. For thousands of years, most Western education has centered on two basic types of knowledge sources: the lecturing teacher and books as an extension of the knowledge of dead or otherwise unavailable teachers and scholars.

In coming decades, advances in information technology will transform learning systems as they have transformed other human activities. We need this to prepare our future citizens to perform these activities in an efficient way. We cannot continue to use industrial methodologies to *manufacture* citizens of a nonindustrial society.

Information technology has the potential to transform classrooms into *reality amplifiers*, in which learners can synthesize all kinds of knowledge from a rich mixture of real and simulated experiences. This process has already begun in many Western countries, as well as Israel, but is lagging in most Diaspora Jewish educational frameworks.

We must determine whether traditional educational systems will be able to accept and use these vast ranges of powerful information technologies. Can they be a driving force in creating innovative learning modalities? Or will traditional educational systems use information technology as fashionable ornaments to the conventional classroom, in order to show how up to date they are? If the former, they will become a transformational force within the emerging cybercivilization. If the latter, they will become a major inhibitor in the development of cybercivilization.

THE PEOPLE OF THE BOOK SYNDROME

We know that Judaism is book centered. Are not our most precious possessions our books—Bible, Talmud, and Siddur? Are we not the People of the Book who brought the Book to the world?

The appellation People of the Book derived from the early history of Islam. In Islam's first century, Moslem leaders divided the world into two camps, *Dar Al Islam*, the community of Islam, and *Dar Al Harb*, the world of the sword, those who were not yet Moslem but would soon be or would be put to the sword. It soon became clear to Moslem rulers that converting *everybody* to Islam was not an option, and killing all those whom would not convert proved a decided practical disadvantage.

Islam saw itself as the third and final covenant between God and a religious community. The Koran validates God's first covenant to the Jews in the Torah and the second covenant to the Christians in the New Testament. Islam was adamant that after Allah gave the Koran to Mohammed, these two earlier covenants were no longer valid, and the only valid covenant was now the Koran and Islam.

For numerous historic reasons, however, the two religious communities that had a covenanted text with God, Jews, and Christians, received a special legal status. In the classic Muslim state, this *Dhimmi*, protected minority, status was given to Jews and Christians who possessed the first two sacred covenants, *Ahl Al-Kitab*, people of the sacred text. This was translated into Hebrew as *Am Hasefer*. Later, translated into English, it became the well-known People of the Book, an appellation that refers to Christians as well as Jews. The word *Kitab* is a cognate word for that which is written, a text. The Hebrew term *sefer* only recently came to mean a book, that is, a codex of pages between two covers—a much more convenient medium than stone tablets or parchment scrolls.

People of the Book refers not to any book, or codex, but to *the* Book, with a capital *B*, namely the Bible. The word *bible* derives from *byblos*, or "book." When we refer to the Bible as *Sefer Torah*, we do not mean what we call a book, which is the familiar codex design of Roman origin.

When we refer to the *Sefer Torah*, we mean the scroll. The original Hebrew and Arabic meant a text of words, not *how* they were encoded—what was written, and not in what format it was written. The words were first encoded on stone tablets and later a parchment scroll, which are still used today in synagogues.

Books, as we know them, are a product of Europe in the past few centuries. The printed book became the primary vehicle of the Renaissance, Enlightenment, and Industrial Revolution. It created modern civilization. This development has had a revolutionary impact on the Jews. It enabled the creation of the great Eastern European *yeshiva* culture, as well as every other form of Jewish cultural expression in modern times. As mentioned previously, the codex book form was introduced to Judaism by two non-Jews: the first, Johannes Gutenberg, indirectly, by the invention of the printing press, and the second, Daniel Bomberg, by being the first to print the Talmud in codex form.

Jewish education must not remain based on the book because it was always so. The Torah's words were always so, not the method of encoding them. Jews have always used various ways to encode their sacred texts.

We can now encode sacred texts electronically, in addition to other ways. Each medium creates specific ways of learning and teaching. From stone tablets of the biblical period, to parchment of the rabbinical period, to paper of the Industrial Revolution, to silicon electron-based electronics, and now silicon *light*-based electronics—photon technology. These various media are replete with innovative ways to deal with the sacred covenant in both its oral and written forms. To limit this to what we know as books is simply absurd.

We do not claim that computers and videos will replace books, but we can use this powerful new medium in Jewish learning environments, which might be more suited and less restricting for the presentation of traditional Jewish values to Jewish Net-Geners.

FROM PEOPLE OF THE BOOK TO PEOPLE OF THE STORY

The Jews are primarily the People of the Story—*Am Ha-Sippur,* a never-ending story. Like Ezra, we need to learn how to tell our story in the medium and the idiom appropriate to the times.

In addition to the teacher, the Jewish tradition also has high regard for the religious storyteller. The *Maggid* (teller of stories) would go from community to community, relating a vast range of Jewish stories. Some historians have suggested substantial parts of the social and religious transformations that influenced Jewry during the seventeenth and eighteenth centuries in Europe relied on these itinerant *Maggidim* who functioned as a sort of nonestablishment intelligentsia. They provided social criticism and social guidance.

We will still use books in the future, but we will use them differently. Hypertext models teach us how to deal with interactive pages in books and on line rather than static materials on a printed page. Both the page and the site will likely change as learning skills and habits evolve. The core message may not change, but the way we deal with it surely will. Learners will develop new versions of the commentary layout form akin to the Talmud page.

Learners might split the screen between other peer learners, regardless of where they may be. I will be able to see what I write and I will see what you write. I can change or edit my ideas or your ideas, and the changes and comments will be displayed. The Talmud relates to the Oral Torah, which is constantly changing. The sage, rabbi, or teacher will act like a chat group moderator, who deals with quality control. In our age, it is our need and indeed our obligation to develop a cyber Oral Torah of ongoing Jewish commentary and discourse.

FROM BROADCAST EDUCATION TO INTERACTIVE LEARNING

Growing up is about learning, and children today are learning and growing up in an environment radically different from the generations that went before them. Their destinations are different, and the routes they take are different, therefore the learning methods must be different. Historically, education has focused on instruction. Tapscott calls this *broadcast learning*. The very word *teacher* implies an expert in exclusive possession of information that he or she transmits or broadcasts to the students. The products of this exercise are predefined, precise outcomes and behaviors that can be measured by way of some kind of testing procedure.

Lectures, textbooks, homework assignments, and schools in general are all analogs of the broadcast learning method. They are one way and centralized. They emphasize predefined, off-the-shelf, structures designed for a mass audience that must be educated. This is an authoritarian top-down, teacher-centered model that goes back centuries. It is also the primary model for most present-day Jewish education across the world, yet is the antithesis of traditional Jewish learning.

Even most computer-based instruction packages and programs remain based on this broadcast method of learning. They transmit information by way of experts who, it is assumed, know the best materials and information to transmit and in what sequence. They still reflect a one-size-fits-all design based on grade levels and on all learners doing the same thing in the same sequence most of the time.

I am not simply extolling the power of technology but rather its inherent potential for learning, its potential to move beyond the broadcast model to the interactive learning model. Tapscott cites a high school cyberarts teacher, Kathy Yamashita, who thinks it is "essential that ... students have access to technology," but "believes strongly" that what she teaches "has nothing to do with technology." She wants them to learn now to think, plan, and become adept at problem solving. She wants them to learn how to "create dreams and ways to attain those dreams" (p. 147). If we do not use this new technology to serve her vision of learning, we have completely missed the point.

The following is derived from the models that Tapscott proposes. I have attempted to relate them to Hebrew supplementary schooling. Tapscott posits eight profound shifts that reflect the transformation from classical broadcast education to the new interactive digital learning.

From Linear to Hypermedia Learning

Traditional approaches to learning are linear. The book is usually read from beginning to end as a learning tool. Stories, novels, and most narratives are linear. Most textbooks are designed to be read from beginning to end. Television shows and instructional videos are designed to be watched from beginning to end. But Net-Gener access to information and knowledge is more interactive and either nonsequential or multisequential.

The Talmud page format is suited to this type of hypertext learning. Its organization is nonlinear, and learning is associative. The learner bounces back and forth from one section to another. The learners teach one another in dyadic groups or clusters of peers, and the teacher moves from one to the other offering assistance when and if needed. Both the page and the method liberate the typography and the format from its linear, mechanical form.

How has this medium-is-the-message style organized Jewish learning? In the *yeshiva*, students are not sitting in rows as in an industrial-age factory or standard school setting. The very design of the learning room is different. Students are clustered in *hevruta* (groups of learning friends). This peer-to-peer learning allows learners to teach other learners. Instead of a teacher, a rabbi/scholar moves from one learning cluster to another to deal with problems, perhaps to offer some guidance to the learners.

Beyond the physical layout of the knowledge systems, both the Talmud and hypertext imply a way of knowing strongly different from the linear book. They contain hotly debated multivoiced discussions of important and often ambiguous questions. Many questions are left unresolved.

We have many nonlinear ways to deal with organizing and designing models of knowledge. Moreover, if we are trying to design Jewish learning systems, let us use those models in a modern media context that reflects authentic Jewish learning systems.

From Instruction to Construction and Discovery

The shift is away from pedagogy—the art, science, and profession of teaching—to the creation of learning partnerships and learning cultures. In some locales, schools are becoming places to learn rather than a place to teach. Pedagogy deals with optimizing predigested information. Net Generation children do not want optimized, predigested information. They want to learn by doing, whereby they synthesize their own understanding, most often based on trying things out by themselves and in clusters of learners. Learning becomes experiential. Late nineteenth- and early twentieth-century philosopher and educator John Dewey's vision is made real by way of information technology. As Professor Seymour Papert relates on the Internet:

It is almost 100 years since John Dewey...probably the...deepest critic of the structure of the school began to formulate his criticism...and to put in...place his concept of learning through experience, the concept of learning by engaging in activities that mean something to you, that you care about or identify with, in which you will collaborate with other learners....During these past 100 years, what we know as progressive education, open education, child-centered learning have generated a lot of writing and talk. They have generated very little change in the educational system. There are two reasons for this. The first is that Dewey came to this problem with a philosophical argument and no philosophical system, no matter how valid can change...a social institution as deeply rooted in its own traditions as schools. The second reason is that there was no technological infrastructure to actually do it. Now there is and it is the digital world of learning. (Seymour Papert, *Child Power: Keys to the New Learning of the Digital Century*, www.papert.org/articles/childpower.html)

We should, of course, continue to design and develop curricula and learning environments. They will be more effective, however, if they are designed in collaboration with the learners, or even by them, and constantly modified in real time as the learning process continues.

Educators describe this learning approach as the constructivist model. Rather than assimilating information or knowledge broadcast by the teacher, the learners construct their knowledge anew. Constructivism suggests that people learn best by doing rather than simply being told. Seymour Papert says, "The scandal of education is that every time you teach something, you deprive a child of the pleasure and benefit of discovery." The Jewish learning tradition has always known this.

From Teacher-Centered to Learner-Centered Education

Information technology enables the learning experience to shift from the transmitter—the teacher—to the individual learning with his peers. This improves the motivation to learn, and is more interesting and more demanding. Learning and entertainment converge into edutainment, a combination of learning and entertainment.

This is not to suggest that the teacher will play a less significant role in the life of the child. Teachers are still critical to the learning process. They are essential in creating and structuring the necessary digital learning environments. This role is also more interesting for the teacher who is now part of the learning environment, but in an entirely different way. Training and retraining our teachers is a vital component of this shift.

This proposed shift will be difficult to deal with in the usual Hebrew school. It requires significant rethinking of what students, teachers, and parents mean by "going to Hebrew school." Indeed, significant rethinking for all Jewish-learning stakeholders.

From Absorbing Material to Learning How to Navigate and How to Learn

Information technology helps students acquire analytical skills and synthesize vast amounts of information. It helps them construct higher-level knowledge systems. We can no longer say to students "here is your curriculum. I will broadcast it to you, and you will somehow absorb it then move on and be prepared for your Jewish adult life. We need to address the concept of learning how to learn. Learning how to learn is the classical *yeshiva* learning environment. Jews must relearn their *own* learning tradition if they are to make proper use of new technology. The ability to Jewishly navigate the Internet must also become a skill learned in Hebrew school.

From School to Lifelong Learning

Baby boomer lives have been divided into two periods: *learning* and *doing*. You went to school to *learn* what you were going to *do* when you entered adult life. The classic Jewish learning model is a lifelong enterprise. One never stops learning. The vast majority of Jewish children today cease their Jewish education after *bar* or *bat mitzvah* training. This leaves them with a child's range of Jewish knowledge, which is minimal and is supposed to sustain them Jewishly for the rest of their lives. This is simply absurd.

We are sending our children into the world with the equivalent of a first-grade Jewish education. A child attends public school for about 180 days a year, about 6 hours a day. This comes to about 1,080 educational hours per year. The same child would attend 5 years of afternoon Hebrew school for about 1,000 hours. This amounts to less than a first-grade public school education.

From One Size Fits All to Customized Learning

Mass education is the product of the industrial economy. It came along with mass production, mass marketing, and mass media. The digital media now afford us the possibility of developing an educational market of *one*. In other words, we can develop learning environments that fit each individual learner, while modifying them on a weekly or even daily basis to fit solitary or group learning environments.

Howard Gardner, of the Harvard Graduate School of Education, suggests that customary schooling is a mass-production idea. We teach the same thing to all of the students in the same way and assess them all in the same way. The digital media, on the other hand, allow each student to be treated as an individual, with learning packages based on their own particular background, individual talents, age level, cognitive styles, interpersonal preferences, and so on. Each learner can discover his or her personal paths to learning; here each student is special.

We know that children and adults learn differently. We acknowledge this, then promptly forget it and continue to do what we have been doing for decades. Professor Gardner has developed a coherent theory of what he calls "multiple intelligence." He suggests at least eight such intelligences: verbal-linguistic, logical-mathematical, kinesthetic, visual-spatial, musical, interpersonal, intrapersonal, and naturalist. For detailed information about Gardner's theory, an Internet search will produce a great deal of material.

Most schools (Hebrew schools included) deal with only one or two of these intelligences and simply ignore the others. Yet, digital media and their attendant technologies can provide learning options suitable for all of Gardner's eight intelligences, even in regular classrooms with off-the-shelf hardware and software.

How to develop Jewish teaching and learning strategies to accommodate these eight intelligences in a Jewish context will be one of Jewish education's greatest challenges in the coming decades. The one-size-fits-all model no longer works and is no longer desirable. The Net Generation will demand, and we will have to deliver, far more options and variations for their learning. Up until now, we could do little about this. Now the Internet and cyberspace provide us with the technical ability to do so.

From Learning as Torture to Learning as Fun

Torture, as Tapscott himself suggests, may be an exaggerated expression, but school is not exactly the highlight of the day for most children. This is doubly true for children in Hebrew schools.

We tend to relate learning to the no-pain-no-gain model of thinking. We tend to say that if learning is fun it cannot be challenging. Why? The definitions of to entertain in *Webster's Ninth College Dictionary* include "to keep, hold, or maintain in the mind," and "to receive and take into consideration." Using digital media, teachers can become entertainers and can create learning environments based on enjoyment, motivation, and responsibility for learning.

The Net Generation will come to school accustomed to enjoying the process of gathering information, and they will accept nothing less in schools. Edutainment is not new. It was described in the Talmud, nearly 2,000 years ago. "Before starting to teach, Rabbah joked and the pupils laughed, afterwards he started seriously teaching *Halacha*" (Babylonian Talmud, Shabbat 30b).

In Psalm 119, the term *Lesha'ashea* with Torah is used seven times. This term is most often interpreted as playing with the Torah. I suggest that we are now developing new ways to play with the Torah. We want our children to acquire deep and practical knowledge by which they can live as Jews and responsible global citizens of the cyberworld. If we design edutainment models dedicated to this aim, we will recreate the same play model suggested in Psalm 119.

From the Teacher as Transmitter to the Teacher as Facilitator

We have used the phrase *from the sage on the stage to the guide by the side*. We require teachers who can deal with this reality. They will need to learn new skills, new approaches, and new tools. The tools are already available. Resistance to change, low teacher morale, lack of time in classes, and limited budgets will hold up the reform process, but it must be done.

We are at the beginning of the twenty-first century. The Internet and Web sites are still relatively primitive. Imagine what will be available in the next decade or so. In the world of cyberspace, something 10 years old is prehistoric. These technologies will become faster, cheaper, and more powerful. Every year, revolutionary new systems are available. There is no way to stop it, and there is no reason to stop it. We as Jews are a learning people, and anything that can enhance knowledge building we should welcome and embrace.

HOME LEARNING

Although education takes place in schools, learning can take place anywhere, in any space. Today, more learning might be taking place in the home than at schools. The media systems many middle-class children possess at home are more powerful than those in most schools. Inferior school technology increases the child's contempt for the system. Modern information technology brings the locus of learning back to where it belongs—to the home. How can we develop Jewish learning experiences that are sufficiently exciting that children will explore them at home as homework?

It is wrong to think that no alternative exists to the synagogue-based afternoon Hebrew school. Across the United States, hundreds of thousands of parents are turning to the Web for help in educating their children at home. Online resources are growing to meet this demand. Home learning has become legal in most of the 50 states and in countries around the world. The current estimate of U.S. children being home-schooled is approximately two million and growing by about 10 percent each year.

Home learning is also common in Europe and is growing faster there than in the United States. While home schooling is not as yet legal in Israel, pressure is growing to make it a legitimate alternative to school schooling. In the United States, the charter school phenomenon is another expression of dissatisfaction. This has its parallel in Israel in various kinds of "democratic schools." Dissatisfied parents all over the Western world are deciding against existing school systems.

Some claim that although this might be a trend in general education, it will not be so in Jewish education. They do not give any logical reasons for their views, and experience indicates the opposite. If the children and parents do not find what they want in congregational Hebrew schools, they will turn to other solutions. Now that they have options, what will happen to synagogues when the Hebrew school no longer brings in parents and children? Will they sustain membership levels?

A vast amount of learning materials dealing with Judaism is currently available on the Internet. In the future these cyber age materials will only increase in scope and sophistication, and they are suitable for home learners of all ages, not only children.

THE JEWISH EXPLORATORIUM

In the cyber age, learning takes place wherever the learners are. The museum is one example. New types of museums, called Exploratoriums, invite hands-on discovery and idea exploration and use varied forms of information technologies.

Many large cities have Exploratoriums, where visitors are invited to learn about their physical world experientially through the use of light, sound, motion, the environment, and more. Urban-dwelling Jews have easy access to these museums.

We could develop learning experiences and programs in cooperation with these institutions, where Jewish children would learn about natural phenomena and relate them to Jewish living. This radical shift in learning about Judaism would not require specific Jewish exhibits. We could use existing exhibits and relate them to Jewish subjects.

Learning about Judaism through natural phenomena is consistent with Judaism's concept of nature and material existence as divine. For example, we might accompany a lesson about lighting Shabbat candles with a learning trip to the local Exploratorium to learn about light. Thus, we would accommodate the multiple intelligences of each individual learner, child, and adult alike. An Internet search of the San Francisco Exploratorium Web site turned up 30 different exhibits dealing with light in different ways. Additions from popular culture, such as Spielberg's films, could make the learning experience even richer.

Another example suitable for such a learning strategy would be the *Havdalah* ceremony that separates sacred time from normal time at the end of the Jewish Sabbath and traditionally calls on all of the five senses: candle-light; incense-smell; prayer-hearing; wine-taste; holding-touch. Imagine a series of learning experiences using a child's multiple intelligences in such a learning environment. These would be easily integrated with the themes of high-tech and high-touch to which our Net Generation children have grown accustomed. Many Exploratoriums also have simple "cookbook" experiments that can be done in any school or home setting.

The various stakeholders within Jewish educational establishments must be convinced of the efficacy of such learning strategies. We can anticipate at least three types of responses: Conservative—accepts digital learning as complementing the normal and prevailing school pedagogic strategies; Moderate—accepts digital learning as replacing prevailing pedagogic strategies or at the least transforming them; Radical—accepts digital learning as replacing the prevailing systems, transforming didactic teaching, and at the same time changing other fundamental aspects of the school.

Generating significant changes in the public school system is a major process involving many competing groups and is often a matter of politics rather than education. The synagogue Hebrew school could be an easier institution to effect change in because each school is basically an independent entity.

A fascinating seminar, attended by 30 high-powered Jewish educators from Israel and North America, took place in March 2001 in Bet Yatziv, Be'er Sheva, Israel. We have incorporated some of the ideas presented here. Interestingly, none of those present had read Tapscott's *Growing up Digital*, yet all of them were aware of school uses of information technology, and most were long-time computer users.

Many said that this was the first time a group of Jewish educators had taken the issue of cyberspace seriously. All had attended conferences on information technology use in schools, but these dealt with information technology as supplementary classroom tools. They simply were not aware of the potential radical transformations these digital technologies could effect in a Jewish Cyberia.

They set up a task force to generate a set of vision statements on Jewish education over the next five years, with full consideration of the global revolution in information technology and its potential for Jewish learning environments. The process is happening, and the Jewish educational community is beginning to explore the potential of information technology for Net Generation Jewish learners.

CONCLUSION

The primary function of all educators is to create citizens capable of functioning in the future. What resources might we use to create a Jewish futurist curriculum that would cultivate futurist thinking skills in our Jewish children?

Futurist literature itself credits the Jewish People with inventing the very idea of the future. We also have many Jewish resources at hand, including the prophets, various Talmudic sources (such as the sage Rabbi Simon), the entire body of Zionist literature from Herzl to Ben Gurion and beyond, as well as modern Jewish thinkers such as Soloveitchik. How might we use historical analogy to create futurist-thinking models?

Another challenge for the Jewish educator is how to educate toward a democratic Jewish citizenship. Here, we would use much that was mentioned in chapter 4, "The Special Case of American Jewry," as well as other references. The particular Jewish challenge of futurist thinking, democracy, and citizenship must become a preoccupation of serious Jewish educators.

CHAPTER 15

The Jewish Community in Cyberspace

Who is a Jew and what is Judaism have been and probably will continue to be the perennial Jewish questions, with no real answer. Jews have been arguing over this since the European Enlightenment and will probably continue to do so for generations to come.

Less controversial and with greater consensus is the perspective that being a Jew means to feel oneself a part of a community or a member of a tribe. Jewish identity and Jewish community are for all intents synonymous. Indeed, significance of community is a fundamental value of Judaism. Alienation from the community is a central cause of assimilation, *not* one's lack of ritual observance or religious agreement.

Being Jewish is a sense of belonging and an active ambition on the part of the Jewish individual to attach himself or herself to some aspect of Jewish communal life no matter what his or her level of religious observance. Although it is impossible to call someone an agnostic or atheist Christian or Moslem, the phrases "he is an agnostic Jew" or "she is a Jewish atheist" are perfectly logical in a Jewish context. Judaism might be a religion, but Jewishness is an ethnicity, an almost tribal identity. Indeed, Jews will often refer to themselves as "the tribe" as in "is he a member of the tribe?" Modernity has been eroding this sense of community for the past several centuries, and globalization has presented even greater challenges to its continuity.

This chapter will discuss ways and means by which we might turn alienated globalization into cybercommunalism. How can we use the cyberrevolution to transform Jewishness, as the historic identity of a particular people, into a future-oriented identity that resonates with modern young individuals searching for communal identity without having to sacrifice their individual growth and aspirations?

THIRD WAVE JUDAISM

Alvin Toffler, in his now classic book *The Third Wave*, posited three waves of civilization. The First Wave was the agricultural era, the Second Wave was the industrial era, and the Third Wave is the present information era. Judaism, as every other religious and spiritual tradition, was born in the agricultural era and made heroic attempts to adapt to and evolve in the Enlightenment/industrial era. The Jewish year cycle and most Jewish holidays reflect the phases of agricultural society. Succoth and Shavuot represent harvest and planting times. Hanukkah occurs at the winter solstice, and Tu Bishvat celebrates the beginning of the spring planting season. Reform, Conservative, and Modern Orthodox Judaism as well as Zionism have all been attempts to adapt Jewish tradition to the postindustrial reality, but they remain mostly rooted in an agricultural perspective, and this presents a problem. Agricultural models are inherently inadequate to the communal needs of the most urbanized people in the world.

We usually think of community as some geographically bounded space where a specific group of people lives. Can we develop a virtual community without geographic boundaries but linked by a shared consciousness? Can awareness of belonging to a global Jewry exist independent of geographical space? For the past several centuries, most Jews have been urban dwellers and part of urban civilization. They have determined community by living in predominately Jewish neighborhoods or at least in areas with large Jewish concentrations, which has helped preserve a sense of Jewish identity, a sense of Jewish belonging.

Rates of assimilation increase in correlation to dilution of Jewish community. In the United States, for example, rates of assimilation increase as you move westward, away from the traditional ethnic communities of the East Coast.

People no longer live *only* in identifiable communities. Modern life is diffuse and multilayered, a consequence of information technology and globalization. More and more people are connected in virtual "communities," separated in geographical space by thousands of miles but united in cyberspace by common commercial, scientific, and cultural activity. Increasing numbers of individuals, organizations, scientists, executives, and artists are functioning outside of traditional concepts of space, ignoring the national and natural boundaries that separate them.

How might world Jewry exploit cyberspace possibilities to reinvent Jewish communal identification? How might the development of Jewish cybercommunities ameliorate the connection between Israeli Jews and Diaspora Jews? How might it help create what Gad Yaacobi, former Israeli cabinet member and ambassador to the United Nations, has called a "new partnership" between Israelis and world Jewry?

FROM CONTINUITY TO DISCONTINUITY

In previous chapters, we have discussed the impact of the increasing rate of change. First Wave Judaism succeeded primarily because it had time to adapt itself to change. Second Wave Jewish social and cultural patterns have been less successful because change has been so abrupt. As soon as we formulated a response to a challenge, it had died a natural death or had so evolved that any attempt to find an ultimate solution was inadequate at the outset.

Third Wave Judaism faces an even more radical rate of change, one that requires us to radically rethink our mindsets. A recent Jewish buzzword has been "continuity," an attempt to preserve First and Second Wave Judaism's creations. Much of the organized Jewish community is engaged in a giant, inherently past-oriented conservation project that says what was should continue to be and that our ambition should be to guarantee its continuity. Continuity means more of the same, looking at our yesterdays and the achievements of our yesterdays in order to make our unpredictable tomorrows more palatable and bearable.

This, at a time when most social science (especially futurist) literature indicates that this is both impossible and undesirable. We are living in an age of discontinuity. Those who cannot adapt to this new reality and invest it with meaning and significance will increasingly find themselves alienated from their environment and find their ability to persevere diminishing.

It is self-evidently impossible and undesirable to attempt a clean break with the past and begin from scratch. The world and the Jewish world both derive from the past and are by definition a continuum, but change has become demanding and immediate. We require cultivation of purposeful and directed change, evolutionary creativity, and not fossilized continuity. Many American Jewish organizations have already recognized this and are moving past the slogan of continuity to a new slogan: "Renaissance and Renewal."

TOWARD A FOURTH WAVE JUDAISM

Judaism has been historically adaptive and so the Jews have survived. From the patriarchs through the judges and kings to the prophets, through the entire 2,000-year, constantly changing history of rabbinical Judaism, the Jews have proven creatively malleable to the necessities of historical pressure. For the past 2,000 years, mostly negative external forces forced this adaptability upon them. The Jews now have the opportunity to exploit their adaptive gifts as a positive agent for their own creative growth rather than as a response to negative externals. Through this opportunity, the Jewish People may become pioneers in the development of a Fourth Wave model of human existence: the age of wisdom.

An age of wisdom would celebrate diversity. Globalization has created its own antithesis, the desire of "small" peoples to maintain their cultural uniqueness. This desire is welcome and healthy, if we apply the ecological model to human culture. As mentioned earlier, species diversification characterizes a healthy ecology. As with nature, so with human culture. Cultural homogenization is reactionary, from the evolutionary point of view. By creating a Jewish cybercommunity out of self-interest, we might create a model that other cultures would imitate. In this way, the Jews would use the *light* of photonics to truly become a light unto the nations.

The Talmudic sage Rabbi Simon asks, "Who is wise?" and responds *"Ha Roeh Ha Nolad"*: he who perceives what is about to occur. Wisdom is not the state of knowing, it is the state of sensing what is about to occur. It is the highest level of the intelligence food chain. Rabbi Simon might be defined as having been a proto-futurist; he understood that wisdom consists of being midwives to the future.

CYBER-ZIONISM

We have discussed various aspects of Zionism in previous chapters. In this section, we will correlate Zionism with an emerging cyberreality that the founders of Zionism could not have predicted. This cyberreality should engender a new variety of Zionism suitable to global developments.

Classical Zionism saw the Land of Israel as the only place where Jews could prosper and maintain their heritage. Today, however, globalization and the affirmation of cultural pluralism is enabling various ethnic diasporas to maintain and even enrich their cultural heritages in countries far away from their homelands. The Indian and Pakistani communities of Bradford, England, for example, boldly claim that Bradford has become the world center for Indian and Pakistani cuisine, better than in their respective homelands.

The question of sustaining a diaspora identity is no longer an exclusively Jewish issue. The existence and success of other diaspora global tribes is well documented in Joel Kotkin's book *Tribes*. The universal Jewish Diaspora must cease to be viewed as a disease that the Jews must be cured of (the view of classical Zionism). Let us see it, instead, as a Jewish and Zionist resource that would have to be invented if it did not already exist.

Cyberspace, joined to the hard fact of Israel's existence as the largest Jewish community in the world, changes the very concept of *aliya*. We may now posit the plausibility of "intellectual *aliya*." A Jew might live in London, New York, or Los Angeles and transmit his or her intellectual product to Israel, to an Israeli company or organization operating outside of Israel, or to other Diaspora communities.

Zionism in the twenty-first century might increasingly come to resemble the vision of Ahad Ha'Am rather than that of Herzl. Herzl envisioned one central site for the Jews, whereas Ahad Ha'Am envisioned a national cultural center serving a universal Diaspora. If we go one step further than Ahad Ha'Am, we may develop a reality characterized not by one cultural center but by numerous cultural nodes existing on a global Jewish cultural network and reflecting the rich cultural pluralism that characterizes *every* Jewish community in the world today.

In other words, the future may hold 50 Israeli cultural nodes, 20 North American Jewish cultural nodes, and 15 European Jewish cultural nodes. Rather than one Israeli-Diaspora relationship, we might have a multitude of Israeli-Diaspora relationships, as well as Diaspora-Diaspora relationships. Innumerable such relationships already exist because Jewry constitutes a sophisticated world community of metanetworks, networks, and subnetworks.

SYNTROPY AND THE JEWISH QUESTION

Syntropy, a term coined by the two-time Nobel Prize winner, Hungarian scientist Albert Szent-Gyorgyi, is the antipode to entropy. Entropy is the fundamental natural process described by the second law of thermodynamics and refers to the pervasive tendency of inorganic matter or nonliving systems to gradually decay into ever-lower levels of organization. Organic matter and life systems, on the other hand, tend to evolve toward increased levels of organization and complexity. Syntropy is the antipodal force driving living systems to achieve higher and higher levels of organization, systemic order, and harmony. It deals with higher states of complexity and new forms of organization in living systems. It is the tendency that propels matter, mind, and consciousness toward new forms of organic and *cultural* organization, wholeness, and unity in living systems.

Teilhard de Chardin called this process complexification. He perceived human cultural evolution reaching a state wherein the entire planet would be engulfed in a layer of human consciousness, which he called the "noosphere." Peter Russell picked up on this intuition and perceived the communications revolution as the means by which this would occur. He called this the global brain. Mordechai Nessyahu went much farther in *Cosmotheism*. He perceived the *statistically inevitable*, culturally driven, organic evolution of innumerable humanoid life systems throughout the cosmos into a pervasive, unified, and universal consciousness able to survive when entropy eventually transformed the cosmos into uniformly distributed, undifferentiated particles.

Such a development, in his view would be a cosmic given (*HaKol Tsafui*), in keeping with the laws of statistical probability and the immeasurable numbers of humanoid life systems that have inevitably arisen throughout the cosmos. The choice (*HaRashoot Netuna*) of each humanoid life system is to first discern this cosmic process and second to choose to act in such a way as to become an integral part of it. The alternative is to become one of the cosmos's failed evolutionary experiments and become extinct.

On the more mundane level, the Jews also face a cultural and communal choice, either to strive for cultural syntropy between Jewish culture and global culture or to perish. Historical records reveal examples of cultural synthesis and cultural synergies that have created new cultural patterns. On rare occasions, we have witnessed cultural syntropy, which has advanced both cultures to a higher stage of creativity. The development from synthesis to synergy to syntropy has been a key element in Jewish history. It must become our cultural Grand Strategy to cultivate value-tropic syntropy between global and Jewish cultures.

Jews have lived in Babylon, Egypt, Canaan, Greece, Rome, Medieval Christendom, Islam, Modern Europe, and North America. Many of these experiences were syntropic. These cultures contributed to and transformed the Jews, and the Jews in turn made tremendous contributions to and transformed them. The quintessential example of this syntropy is the American Jewish experience.

By adopting a cultural Grand Strategy of syntropy, we must disabuse ourselves of the notion that the history of the Jews is one of only suffering and persecution. We do not ascribe to the lachrymose theory of Jewish history that issues a carton of tissues with every chapter. Many peoples have suffered terribly in human history, the Jews included, but neither human history nor Jewish history is simply the story of Jewish suffering. It was much safer, for example, to be a Jew than a woman during the witch-hunting Renaissance.

The recognition that Jewish history has not been one long tear-wrenching soap opera is not to discount the uniqueness of the Nazi Holocaust, but the Czarist Pale of Settlement has its parallel in apartheid South Africa. The Jews' limitation to certain trades has its parallels in the Eta of Japan and the Untouchables of India. And pogroms, massacres, and lynchings are a universal and not a uniquely Jewish phenomenon. The twentieth-century histories of the Armenians, Tutsis, and American Blacks confirm this.

The lachrymose historical theory and cultural practice of the Jews is a major threat to their existence. It is so inherently unattractive that it has begun to alienate increasing numbers of young Jews, neutralizing whatever incipient Jewish ambitions they might have possessed. What mentally healthy person wants to be part of a culture that is dedicated to never-ending mourning, let alone devote his or her life to that culture?

We need a positive vision of a creative Jewish future based upon the *positive* aspects of our history. The Jews have contributed parts of every civilization they have ever lived in, shaped by and shaping them. This must continue to be the case as we contribute to the creation of cybercivilization and are molded and changed by our own creation.

The second stage of the Jewish liberation movement called Zionism must be a new kind of "auto-emancipation" from our own self-pity. The Jews need a fundamental, soul-searing change that appreciates our past, honors our heritage, and pays tribute to the grand achievements of previous generations but looks forward into the future, to living and contributing to the cyberworld of the twenty-first century.

INDIVIDUALISM AND COMMUNITY

Assimilation has increased in the years 1950–2003, as Jews moved out of traditional Jewish neighborhoods into mixed communities. This has been particularly evident in the university communities and presents a paradox. On the one hand, every good Jewish mother and father want their child to go to university (and well over 90 percent do so). On the other hand, the university community constitutes a liberal, multiethnic, open environment at the time that people are becoming most romantically and sexually active—the perfect breeding ground for assimilationist conditioning. But must dispersion continue to be inimical to fostering a sense of community, or does cyberspace present us with new kinds of opportunities?

We must disabuse ourselves of the notion that the rise of individualism necessitates a breakdown of community. We must change our mode of thinking from breakdown to transformation. Communal patterns must transform themselves from the industrial, mass model into new communal patterns that reflect and foster the individual search for meaning. This would be a new kind of social contract, whereby the individual's responsibility to the community depends on the community providing space for individual actualization.

Cyberspace offers us a new environment for the individual search for meaning. Jewish thinking must become attuned to this new reality and new opportunity. Virtual communities are just like any other community—groups of people with common cause and some reason to care about one another. Can we create Jewish virtual communities?

Only by recognizing and even celebrating individualism can we begin to establish new kinds of communities. Individualism has become a necessity to societal enrichment and survival; cultures that subjugate the individual cannot prosper or even survive in a world characterized by rapid rates of change. Jewish communal planning must recognize this new reality rather than condemn radical Jewish individualism. Moralistic preachments about social responsibility and negatives about self-concern will only alienate young Jews even more and will only prove to them that Jewish communal involvement is not relevant to their lives.

In *Megatrends 2000* John Naisbitt and Patricia Aburdene devote an entire chapter to "The Triumph of the Individual." The unifying theme of the nineteenth and twentieth centuries was the "mass." The unifying theme of the twenty-first century is the significance of the individual. This is as much a doctrine of individual responsibility as of individual self-realization. We are not speaking about the self-indulgent individualism of the "me" generation. We are speaking about a new ethical concept that elevates individual responsibility to a global level and recognizes that individual efforts matter and are central to social morality.

This is reflected in classical Jewish sources. Hillel begins with the individual: "If I am not for myself, who will be for me?" He recognizes, however, that without society individual existence is essentially meaningless when he continues: "If I am only for myself, what am I?" This view is reflected in the story of Robinson Crusoe. Did Crusoe's life have any meaning until he met Friday? Isn't this view also reflected in Dunn's famous phrase, "No man is an island"? Hillel goes on to recognize the significance of time in the individual/society equation when he queries, "If not now, when?" Can any quotation in the history of culture have anticipated the needs of cybercivilization so succinctly? Hillel addresses the centrality of the individual, the necessity of society, and the exigencies of time. When individuals act "in time" for themselves and society, they sanctify time. In the true sense of Jewish anti-isomorphic time, the Jews can now sanctify the mundane by actualizing themselves, each component—individual, society, and time—acting in the service of the other.

Another Jewish source says *"Bishvili Nivrah Haolam,"* "For my sake the world was created." This means that "I" am the aim and the purpose of creation, and my existence is its own justification. It also means that I am responsible for this world, else I will not exist.

Information technology has extended the power of individuals. Jewish institutions must become attuned to this new individualist reality. New human interactions require new frameworks. The family is no longer a reliable framework for transmitting Jewish values. Traditional communal substitutes for the family, such as Hebrew schools, camps, youth groups, community centers, and others have been less than successful. We suggest that digital networking might offer one alternative solution. We must provide Jewish Net-Geners with Jewish edutainment to help them network Jewishly.

CUSTOMIZATION AND COMMUNITY

The Jewish experience must be customized to the needs of the Jewish individual. The individual Jew must become the center of our concerns. Platonic abstractions such as the "Jewish People" will be meaningless unless they are directed to the real needs of real Jewish persons. What type of Jewish community will help the Jewish individual realize his or her Jewish individuality?

We require a flexible dynamic, malleable, communal framework dedicated to serving a Jewish market of "one." Second Wave institutions such as summer camps, Hebrew schools, youth groups, and such will prosper in the twenty-first century only if they transform themselves into Third Wave institutions responding to Third Wave needs.

The Jewish community is selling old mass-appeal "public goods." The Holocaust and Israel will continue to have declining appeal for Jewish Net-Geners unless we can demonstrate how Jewish identity benefits their own lives, making their own particular lives more creative, meaningful, and value rich. If Israel is incapable of adapting itself to the age of individualism, what happened to the kibbutz on a microlevel will happen to the country on a macrolevel.

The reverse Darwinian process occurred on the kibbutz because the kibbutz was incapable of seeing the individual kibbutznik as his or her own justification and that the aim and purpose of the kibbutz was to optimize the range of self-actualization. Thus, many of the best and the brightest kibbutzniks left the kibbutz. Unless Israel customizes itself to the individual Jewish person's desire for self-actualization through excellence, a mass emigration of the best and brightest individuals will occur. The loss of these individuals will threaten the very existence of the Israeli community.

GLOBAL PARADOX AND ZIONIST VISIONS

Renewed Zionist visions must take into account the political, cultural, and social changes and opportunities that will characterize the twenty-first century and the global village. Political Zionism, as a nineteenth-century development, relied on the sovereign nation-state as the fundamental model of national organization that would guarantee Jewish well-being. Well-being here refers to individual Jews realizing their individual human potential as well as to Jews as a cultural/ethnic collective realizing their collective human potential. Collective well-being depends on the ability to optimize the individual well-being of increasing numbers of Jewish individuals. The call for Jewish individuals to sacrifice their own individual interests in the name of collective well-being is an existential contradiction in terms.

The concept of Zionism as centered on some absolutist concept of national sovereignty has become anachronistic and increasingly out of touch with the reality of how the Jews really live their lives as Jewish individuals, as Jewish communities, and *as a Jewish country*. We are all, whether we like it or not, part of the new reality of global trade and labor markets held together by an integrated global telecommunications system. We must adapt to this new human environment or fossilize and perish. This environment has reduced the significance of the nation-state to the national collective's well-being.

The paradox is that in order to strengthen the nation-state's ability to serve both its citizens and the national collective we must surrender many aspects of state sovereignty and monopoly on power. This also coincides with the fact that as we proceed into the twenty-first century, the nation-state is no longer the dominant, organizing factor of the human race.

Regional frameworks such as the European Union and NAFTA, global economic frameworks such as the WTO, IMF, and World Bank, international political frameworks such as the United Nations, and innumerable bilateral and multilateral economic and political agreements have replaced the nation-state as the dominant organizing factor. All of these entail, as a condition of membership, the foregoing of certain aspects of national sovereignty. In other words, to strengthen national sovereignty, we must forego certain aspects of national sovereignty. John Naisbitt documented this trend in his best-selling *Global Paradox*.

The nation-state has been the dominating organizing factor of human interaction for the past 200 years. It developed as a consequence of European industrial society and was exported to all corners of the globe. The information society and the global markets it has made possible have changed the very nature of the nation-state. National egoism is now cultivating a desire on the part of thinking governments to become members in good standing in as many regional, international, and global organizations as possible.

One of the greatest challenges facing Zionism in the twenty-first century will be how to relate to this novel global circumstance. Perhaps, the traditional concept of the Jews as a global community, a concept anathema to classical Zionism, should be refurbished as a global cybercommunity and serve as the future model of Jewish existence.

PRACTICAL ZIONIST IMPLICATIONS FOR JEWISH-CYBERCOMMUNALISM

The most obvious implication is to relinquish the concept of eliminating the Diaspora as one of the central Zionist tenets. The global Jewish community must celebrate a multitude of options for the Jewish People—those who want to live in Israel, those who want to live outside of Israel and those who want to have one foot in Israel and one foot in the Diaspora (which may one day be the majority of the Jews).

All of these options must become legitimate and acceptable components of the global Jewish commonwealth. World Jewry and Israel should encourage and empower the awareness of this new reality as much as possible. A neo-Zionist ideology must be developed to give intellectual coherence to this developing global Jewish consciousness.

Such a development requires a rethinking of the entire concept of the Israeli émigré or *yored*, as discussed in chapter 7, "Reinventing Israel-Diaspora Relations." We live in a highly mobile world with new "tribes" of "nomadic" skilled professionals moving to greener pastures of professional advancement as a way of life. These moves may be for years or even decades. More skilled Israelis are becoming members of these global professional tribes and are discovering that in order to realize themselves as individuals they must spend years and decades outside of Israel.

On the other hand, Israel's dynamic and interesting economy may offer Diaspora Jewish members of these global professional tribes the opportunity to spend years and decades in Israel. The dispersion of professional Israelis around the world could be cultivated as a cultural asset to local Jewish communities, just as Western Jews in Israel could be cultivated as a civic asset to local Israeli communities. The Israeli Diaspora could become a conduit through which Diaspora professionals connect to Israel, spending parts of their professional lives actually working or cyberworking in Israel.

FROM ALTRUISTIC ZIONISM TO SELF-INTEREST ZIONISM

Spending work time in Israel would not be a contribution or self-sacrifice but rather an integral part of professional and individual development, comparable to the professional Israelis living and working outside of Israel. A neo-Zionist might call this intellectual *aliya*. The vast power of the Internet could enable professional Jews around the world to become an integral part of an Israeli/Jewish knowledge-brokering infrastructure that could import information, transform this into knowledge products, and export it to customers all over the world. Israel could perform the same function in reverse for its global Jewish partners. None of this would be based on altruism; all of it would be based on mutual self-interest. The Quakers used to have a saying, "doing well by doing good." Nonaltruistic neo-Zionism would reverse this into "doing good by doing well."

This does not mean a self-indulgent glorification of one's own desires at the expense of everyone else. It means that each individual is not only a value unto himself or herself but also, at the more utilitarian level, the most necessary component of the new global reality because of the rapid rate of change. Paradoxically, as the human community becomes more unified within the emergent global system, the individual becomes more important and, because of information technology, more powerful. Here is yet another manifestation of the demassification of human life made inevitable by information technology.

This is not a throwback to radical rugged individualism. Cyberspace, by increasing communal options, enables individuals to form communal bonds that help them confront an ever more complex world. Contrary to pessimistic predictions about the growing isolation of the individual in cyberspace, cyberspace actually has the potential to reverse the alienating tendencies of modernity. The modern individual need not face the world alone. We are now building virtual communities of individuals who can freely associate with other individuals on a scale never before possible. Information technologies have changed the very scale of human interaction and have extended the power of the individual to act and interrelate with others.

This does not challenge the State of Israel's importance or its special significance for world Jewry. Simply, the nation-state's significance is being transformed: from a political, economic, and social entity to an entity dedicated to the preservation and development of a particular ethnic culture as well as to the optimal well-being of its citizens as individuals.

Israel is still of central importance, even as the very concept of geographic centrality becomes obsolete within the concept of network. All nodes are not equal. Some are more important than others, depending on situation and historical context. Israel is unique. If you doubt this, conduct the following mental experiment: Try to imagine a Jewish future if Israel were to disappear, then try to imagine a Jewish future if *any* other Jewish community were to disappear. More important, try to envisage a Jewish future if Israel develops into a third-rate, mediocre country.

Tsion, the root of *Tsionut* (that is, Zionism), is in popular terminology a synonym for Jerusalem, but one of its roots is *tsayen*, which means "to point out." From this, we derive the word *lehitstayen*, which means "that which is worthy of being pointed out" or, in other words, the idea of excellence. We would like to suggest that at least one expression of a neo-Zionist vision would be to empower a generation of Jews to fulfill their passion for individual and social excellence by way of the Zionist project no matter where they might live.

This has surprising implications for the very concept of Zionism. If Zionism (*Tsionut*) can be seen as a synonym for excellence, then mediocrity or satisfaction with mediocrity is in its very essence anti-Zionist. Israel, in its present mediocre state, is therefore an anti-Zionist entity. The Jewish paradox is that it has become the task of the Diaspora to assist Israel to "Zionize" itself—to achieve excellence.

THE CYBERSYNAGOGUE

Any discussion of a Jewish communal renewal and Jewish cybercommunities must relate to the synagogue and a possible future cybersynagogue. Some reasons for developing such an institution are obvious. Many people are physically or geographically incapable of attending a regular synagogue: the physically disabled, shut-ins, prison populations, the seriously ill, and individuals or families living in remote areas. They might appreciate a cyberspace alternative to sustain a sense of Jewish community independent of their physical presence at a conventional synagogue.

Attempts to adapt traditional synagogues to special-population needs exist and are welcome, but they address ways to transform existing traditional synagogues. They do not address ways to develop synagogues appropriate for the cyberworld.

Authentic Jewish sacred space has undergone many transformations, from Bezalel's Tabernacle, to the First and Second Temples, to the subsequent development of the synagogue. Synagogues, too, have undergone radical change over the past 2,000 years: from village synagogues, to urban synagogues, to suburban synagogues, to exurban synagogues, and now possible cybersynagogues.

A cybersynagogue must address the three traditional functions of a synagogue: a house of assembly, a house of study, and a house of communal prayer. How might each of these functions be developed, extended, and augmented in cyberspace? *Beit knesset* is the house of assembly and community. This synagogue function can be provided online. *Beit midrash* is a house of study and learning. Jewish learning is already ubiquitous online; thousands of sites offer Jewish learning opportunities of every conceivable type in at least a dozen languages. A cybersynagogue would simply have to correlate these sites.

Beit tefillah means house of prayer. This function presents the biggest challenge to the concept of a cybersynagogue. Private prayer is of course no problem, but *tefillah be tzibbur* (public prayer) that requires a *minyan* (the traditional Jewish prayer quorum of 10 Jewish men) presents major challenges. First of all, at the most prosaic level, many Jews have abandoned the male-only requirement and count women as part of the *minyan*; more traditional Jews are appalled by this development.

More fundamental questions address the very essence of *minyan* as being in physical proximity with fellow Jews, as well as the question of time zones (when you would pray the morning, afternoon, and evening prayers).

The Conservative movement determined in 2001 that "a minyan may not be constituted over the Internet, an audio or video conference, or any other medium of long-distance communication. Only physical proximity, as defined, that is, being in the same room with the *shaliach tzibbur* (prayer leader) allows a quorum to be constituted."

A cybersynagogue can therefore satisfy many traditional functions. The time-related morning, afternoon, and evening prayers could be satisfied longitudinally, when and if the proximity requirement of *minyan* is modified. Study functions could also be satisfied latitudinally.

The latitudinal and proximity limitations of prayer might also be overcome as we proceed ever further into the space age. Some creative future-oriented rabbi might issue a *halachic* ruling altering this limitation. If space travel and global commerce make a uniform "Earth time" necessary, Jews from every corner of the earth who *chose* to live in this unified earth time could form a cyberminyan and perform these prayers as a community.

Rabbinical Judaism has already made radical adjustments in consideration of technological changes. Even today, observant Jews are forced to pray in an artificial time when they travel long distances. Air travelers are not praying during the afternoon of the place they are situated at the particular time they pray, but during the afternoon of the place they left or the place they are going. Consider also the *halachic* ruling pertaining to a fictional Orthodox Jewish astronaut circling the globe every couple of hours. He would not be required to pray morning prayers every time the sun came up or evening prayers every time the sun went down, lest he be spending every minute of his life praying. In any case, we may expect future Jewish trends to come up with pluralistic alternative responses to such challenges.

We might have to relate to the type of training necessary to prepare a rabbi to function in cyberspace, or decide whether a cyberrabbi is even needed. Perhaps cyberspace will reinstate individual Jews as being responsible for their own Jewish life. This might liberate Jews from passive dependence on the sage-on-the-stage rabbi, a passivity that often results in spiritual laziness. This development would be analogous to the move from passive television watching to interactive Internet surfing.

FROM SYNAGOGUES TO *HAVUROT*

For the past 2,000 years, the synagogue has been the place where Jews physically gathered to be together, to study, and to worship. The synagogue site depended on a Jewish community that would support and use it. The synagogue was the center of a community within walking distance, and the size of the community depended on human endurance and convenience. In modern suburban non-Orthodox communities, car travel extended the synagogue's size and range. Parking lots became a necessary addition to the synagogue. Cyberspace is a conceptual space connected by electronics and not a physical space connected by automobiles. Its range would be the entire world.

In the past, when Jews wished to connect with other Jews we had to bring the entire body along, even if we only wanted their minds. To do this, we had to provide buildings with heating, cooling, lighting, seating, maintenance, and insurance. All of this required funding, and addressing this financial need has been one of the most constant activities, major burdens, and human energy drains of all synagogue communities.

These financial needs required an economy of scale. Size became a serious factor in meeting economic viability. Yet size required a constant demand for money. Both the constant demands for money and synagogue size estranged many Jews. Size requires a hierarchic structure whereby the rabbi is the leader who "knows" and the board is analogous to corporate management. The hierarchic model in the private sector has all but been replaced by a network management system. Communal Jewish life has begun to experience a similar development in the *Havurah* movement.

The *Havurah* movement grew because some Jews found the anonymity and financial demands of superlarge synagogues intolerable. *Havurot* introduced a desired closeness at much lower cost. They encouraged active involvement on the part of their members, superseding the passive "entertain me" style of the regular synagogue.

Havurot did not replace synagogues but provided an additional option within the community as well as an added dimension to synagogues that encouraged the development of in-house *havurot*. These developments encouraged women to play an active role, as members of *minyan*, and now even rabbis.

Perhaps we should be discussing *cyberhavurot* rather than cybersynagogues. Like the Internet, the havurot encourage a more intimate, informal, and unmediated interrelationship. They enable individual mobility from one havurah to another or being engaged in several at once. Neither the Internet nor the *havurot* require institutions with large physical plants preoccupied with their own material sustenance. Perhaps in such a milieu, a greater spirituality might develop.

CONCLUSION

Cyberspace represents an evolutionary development of human consciousness into omniconsciousness—a new transpersonal level of human awareness. This requires new concepts of community and human interactivity, enabling us to create a sustainable environment while still seeing as our primary purpose as uplifting humankind.

Cyberspace can be a vital force for personal and planetary transformation. It not only represents a quantum leap in individual options, it can help us to create a truly global community. Individualism no longer stands in antithesis to community and social solidarity. Individualism is as necessary to create a healthy community as community is to create the environment necessary to enable the individual to realize him or herself.

How can we make this enlightened vision of cyberspace a reality? *HaRashoot Netuna.*

Appendix: A Brief Introduction to the Cosmotheistic Hypothesis of Mordechai Nessyahu

One cannot do justice, in a short appendix, to the profound and complex 40-year life work of a deep and original thinker. The subject described here deserves its own book. I would entitle it *Cosmotheism: A Worldview for the Space Age*. Nessyahu viewed his life work as a product of his Jewish identity and his particular interpretation of Jewish history. He assigned a special place for the Jews and the Jewish outlook on life in the realization of his vision. I would be remiss, therefore, if I did not include at least a brief outline of his ideas in a book entitled *Futurizing the Jews*.

The Cosmotheistic hypothesis posits that the evolutionary nature of cosmic development now being revealed by the new physics and new cosmology makes it is statistically certain that huge numbers of conscious life forms (equivalent in self-awareness to human beings) have arisen throughout the cosmos. A very small *percentage* (but large in number) of these conscious civilizations have expanded or eventually will expand throughout their own solar systems and eventually achieve interstellar exploratory capabilities. By doing so, they will of necessity have raised themselves to new levels of consciousness.

The vast majority of conscious civilizations will destroy themselves by failing to meet the challenges of their own nuclear stage of development or by ecological collapse. Many will survive these dual challenges or will have developed by different means.

These surviving conscious civilizations will continue to expand throughout the cosmos. Eventually, a tiny percentage but still substantial number of them will succeed in transcending (by scientific and technical means) the physical limitations of their bodies, thus isolating and enhancing the most essential part of their "humanness," their consciousness. They will in effect become pure consciousness, or if you will, pure spirit. This will be an evolutionary prerequisite to survival as the cosmic environment races towards inevitable "heat death."

The iron laws of entropy dictate that the cosmos will eventually "die," that is, all its complex constructs will eventually dissolve into undifferentiated particles of radiation uniformly distributed throughout the cosmos. Conscious life forms that dedicate themselves to adapting to this inevitable cosmic environment could survive; others will perish. Adaptation, by definition, means liberating "human consciousness" from its physical framework and becoming pure radiation.

The further expansion of conscious life throughout the cosmos will be unfettered by its physical limitations, and eventually conscious life will fill the entire cosmos. It will become coeval with a cosmos that has dissolved into pure radiation as an inevitable consequence of entropy. Thus, the cosmos will become *in its entirety* a conscious being—that is, the cosmos will have become God. Cosmotheism posits God as the consequence of the cosmos, and not as its cause. Not, in the beginning God created the Universe, but, in the end the cosmos will have created God.

The fateful question that every conscious civilization throughout the cosmos must eventually address is will we take part in this cosmic race for survival and strive to survive in the cosmic "end of days," or will we chose to perish along with the rest of cosmic matter? Will we accept the limitations of our physicality, or will we try to transcend them?

Nessyahu did not see his hypothesis as a deterministic teleology but rather as a volitional teleology as it pertained to the human race. His hypothesis was rooted, however, in what one might term a neoteleological interpretation of cosmic evolution. In other words, he claimed that certain cosmic developments were inevitable based on empirical scientific evidence and deductive logic as applied to that empirical scientific evidence. They depended completely, however, on volitional decisions of human beings on this planet, if they wanted to take part in these cosmic developments, thus guaranteeing their "spiritual" survival well past the physical existence of the planet Earth. This would guarantee the cosmic significance of the billions of years of life on this planet. Failure to do so would guarantee the complete cosmic insignificance of life on this planet and would be a tragedy.

The thesis of God as the consequence rather than the cause of the cosmos is not new. Intimations can be found in the philosophy of Aristotle. Twentieth-century British philosopher Samuel Alexander championed this view. Jesuit theologian and philosopher Teilhard de Chardin presented the idiosyncratic view that God was both the cause and the consequence (the alpha and omega) of cosmic existence and evolution. He saw the end of human history as pure consciousness merging with the Alpha God to create the Omega God. Modern German literature and philosophy is rife with human ambition to be godlike.

As Robert Tucker points out in his book *Philosophy and Myth in Karl Marx*, "The movement of thought from Kant to Hegel revolved in a fundamental sense around the idea of man's self-realization as a godlike being, or alternatively as God" (p. 31). Marx was attracted to Hegel and used his philosophy as his own philosophical infrastructure because "he found in Hegel the idea that man is God" (p. 75). History, for Hegel, was God realizing itself through the vehicle of man. This is the underlying intimation of all Enlightenment thought.

Carl Becker, in his classic book *The Heavenly City of the Eighteenth Century Philosophers*, demonstrates how the Enlightenment is but a secularization of the search for the Godhead. Enlightenment thinkers called it "natural law" and wanted to base political organization on it. This was the subtext of all Western political theory from Hobbes onward—how to create political cosmos out of political chaos—that is, to be godlike in terms of our own human society.

Nessyahu must be seen as a continuation of this Enlightenment tradition. His contribution has been to base his thinking on a solid foundation of the most up-to-date cosmological thinking, framed by rigorous deductive logic and related to the present revolution in human means of production. In his perception of a special role for the Jewish People in this all-human project, he harks back to the liberal nationalist tradition of Mazzini that saw an all-human role for every nation. This liberal nationalist tradition found its Jewish echo in Moses Hess's *Rome and Jerusalem*. Hess, an early follower of Marx turned Zionist, agreed with Mazzini and saw a special role in all-human civilization for the renewed cultural dynamism of both the Italians and the Jews.

Nessyahu foresaw a special place for the Jews and the Jewish outlook on life in influencing the rest of humanity to join what he called this "cosmic race for survival and significance." He based this would-be Jewish ambition on the historic role the Jews had played in the development of human civilization.

The Jews for him were an *am olam*—a universal people, or a people of the entire world, or a people whose very peoplehood depended on and reflected its ongoing interaction with and contribution to the other peoples. This concept of the Jewish People as an *am olam* is deeply rooted in the Jewish tradition and must serve as one of the foundation rocks of any Jewish identity in the space age, whether one accepts the Cosmotheistic hypothesis or not.

Nessyahu had a deep-rooted belief that because of their special historical travail, the Jewish People had been particularly endowed with characteristics and capabilities that would enable them to take a pioneering role in establishing the Cosmotheistic project on this planet. He believed that the character and needs of modern Israel and world Jewry made them the most suitable objectively and the most needful subjectively to engage in a heroic project of this type. He agreed with Ben Gurion that unless modern Jewry strove to be a "Light Unto the Nations" in regards to the all-human challenges of the twentieth and twenty-first centuries they would not and could not generate the energy to survive as a people. He was fearful of the Zionism of mediocrity, advocated by the early Zionist thinker Jacob Klatzkin, that would encourage the Jews to be satisfied with the banal attributes of "normalcy." He viewed *Tsionut* (Zionism) and *Hitztaynut* (excellence) as synonyms, and mediocrity as by definition anti-Zionist.

Nessyahu based his views on an historical analogy. He believed that the modern Jewish situation of a national center (Israel) interrelating with a universal Diaspora paralleled that era when a national center (Jerusalem) interacted with a universal Diaspora (primarily Babylon), which created both the Jerusalem and Babylonian Talmud and codified monotheism. This worldview united the far-flung parts of Jewry into a unified culture and changed the course of all of world history. He believed that Cosmotheism (like monotheism in the past) would create a new Jewish cultural energy and once again change the course of all of world history.

Nessyahu rejected the "Nation that Dwells Alone" concept. He knew that both ancient and modern Jewish cultures were built with the raw materials of non-Jewish civilizations and cultures. Monotheism was clearly formulated by the Jews, but it built on the raw materials taken from other peoples, and it came to world cultural predominance by way of other religions (Christianity and Islam).

So it would be with Cosmotheism. The raw materials will have come from other peoples (as well as unrelated disciplines such as cosmology and physics), and its success will depend on other peoples, cultures, and religions adopting its basic principles and adapting them to their own cultural traditions. The Jews can be those people that "chose" themselves to become the progenitors and propagators of this project as well as to be a living example of it. Thus, we would have to invent a new space age interpretation of the "Chosen People" concept and being a light unto the nations.

He believed that just the ambition to implement the Cosmotheistic project would recharge and rejuvenate human civilization and rescue it from the malaise of postmodernism. He certainly believed that it would rejuvenate Jewish identity and provide added value to the young, university-educated, non-Orthodox, and modern Jew.

One can ascribe to the notion that we must cultivate ambitions to create space age versions of Judaism without subscribing to the Cosmotheistic hypothesis. We all, however, must recognize the need to proffer alternative Jewish visions of a depth and a breadth that at least approaches that of the Cosmotheistic hypothesis if we are to generate Jewish ambitions in the twenty-first century.

Glossary

Achdut Avoda
One of the historical components of the Israeli labor movement. Identified with the Kibbutz HaMeuhad movement. Tended to be the most hawkish and territorially maximalist component of the united Israeli Labor Party.

Aliya
Literally, ascent; going up to Israel; immigrating to Israel. This is the same term used by Jews in "going up" to read from the Torah in a synagogue, seeing political immigration as a spiritual/religious act. Used only in relation to immigration to Israel; the ingathering of the Jewish people in its historic homeland. A major ideal of Zionism, it implies personal participation in the rebuilding of the Jewish homeland through self-fulfillment; The coming of Jews to the Land of Israel for permanent settlement.

Am Olam
A synonym for the Jewish People. Literally, the universal nation or alternatively the eternal people. Often used to signify the universal message and duties of the Jewish People.

Baalei Tshuva
Jews who have recently returned to Orthodoxy. Literally, penitents.

Bamidbar Rabbah
A Rabbinic *midrash* (commentary) on the book of Bamidbar (Numbers) of the Torah.

Bar mitzvah
The age at which a Jewish child becomes solely responsible for keeping the religious commandments (13 for boys and 12 for girls). As this was historically accompanied by being given an *aliya* in the synagogue (that is, reading from the Torah in public) it became over the years to be considered a Jewish rite of passage at puberty.

Ben Gurion, David (1886–1973)
Considered the founding father of the State of Israel, its first prime minister.

Ben Yehuda, Eliezer (1858–1922)
Generally considered the father of modern Hebrew and one of the first active Zionist leaders.

Berachot
Literally, blessings; also one of the volumes of the Talmud dealing with the various blessings.

Bnai Akiva
Literally, Children of Akiva—the Rabbinic Sage; refers to the youth movement of the Orthodox Jewish community.

Bnai Brak
City of the ultra-Orthodox community in Israel.

Borochov, Ber (1881–1917)
Socialist Zionist leader and one of its foremost theoreticians; scholar of the history, economic structure, language and culture of the Jewish people.

Bubba
Grandmother.

Bundism
A Socialist Jewish National party emphasizing Yiddish culture, in Russia in the early twentieth century.

Deganyah
The first Jewish communal settlement (kibbutz) founded in 1909, it is considered the "Mother of the Kibbutzim."

Delphi poll
A model of future forecasting methodology through the analysis of expert opinions by suggesting specific events with their probable year of occurrence.

Derech eretz
Literally, the way of the people of the land, refers to good manners, appropriate behavior.

Desert generation
The generation of transition from one major status to another. A metaphor taken from Moses' 40-year wandering in the desert until the slave mentality generation died out and only free men and women were left. In modern time, often refers to the first generation of immigrants to Israel.

Development town
Planned towns built in peripheral areas for the specific purpose of absorbing the mass immigration that came to Israel during the 1950s and 1960s.

Dimona
The second largest (after Beersheva) Jewish city in the Negev Hills in Israel.

Edutainment
Computerized learning systems combining both education and entertainment.

Eretz Yisrael
Literally, the Land of Israel. Refers roughly to the same area covered by mandated Palestine.

Eshkol, Levi (1895–1969)
Labor leader, statesman, third prime minister of Israel.

Future studies
Alternatively known as futurology or futuristics. Refers to systematic informed speculation about future developments in technology, society, economy, and culture and how human society might envision more positive alternative futures based upon these developments.

Galut (gola)
Literally, Exile from the Land of Israel, used both in political and spiritual senses.

Gaon of Vilna (1797)
Helped create Vilna as the "Jerusalem of Lithuania," the most stimulating religious and spiritual center; strongly opposed the new emerging Hassidic communities.

Golden Age of Spain
Refers to the glorious days of the Jews in Spain when there were many interreligious and intercultural connections among the Jewish, Moslem, and Christian communities; during the eleventh to thirteenth centuries.

Gordon, A.D. (1856–1922)
Hebrew writer and spiritual mentor of the Zionist labor movement that emphasized self-realization through settlement on the land in Palestine. An apostle of Tolstoy in that he believed that working the land had inherent spiritual value.

Goy (plural, goyim)
Literally, a people living on its land; since the Jewish exile from the Land of Israel in 70 C.E. Goy refers to non-Jews.

Green line
The territory of Israel before the Six-Day War, refers to the green markers used in designating the boundaries on the armistice maps.

Gush Emunim
Political movement advocating permanent Jewish occupation of the entire Land of Israel.

Ha'Aretz
The Land of Israel.

Hagana
Defense Force of the Histadrut. At its height had more than 60,000 men and women in arms. Became the fundamental building block of the Israeli army after creation of the state.

Hagshama atzmit
Personal fulfillment through settling the land of Palestine, personal participation in the rebuilding of the Jewish homeland.

Halacha
The vast range of Jewish religious law.

Halutz
Literally, vanguard, or pioneer; refers to the pioneers of the Jewish settlement of the land of Palestine.

Haredi
Ultra-Orthodox Jewish community. Traditionally anti-Zionist in ideology. Today most would be considered as non-Zionist rather than anti-Zionism. They view Zionism as human interference in God's plan for the Jews. A small but growing number would consider themselves as Nationalist Haredim (Zionist de facto).

Hasidim
A popular religious movement emerging in Eastern Europe in late eighteenth century; distinguished by ecstasy, mass enthusiasm, close-knit cohesion, and charismatic leadership of the Rebbe.

Haskala
Jewish Enlightenment movement in the nineteenth century, based upon the eighteenth-century European Enlightenment. Gave birth to Yiddishism, Hebraism, Zionism, and Bundism.

Havurah (plural havurot)
Literally, fellowship in Hebrew. The term describes a wide range of alternative and nonestablishment approaches to the spiritual and intellectual life of American Jewry in particular. Typically, they are small groups that gather for study, celebration, and personal association. The first modern one was established in 1968 as Havurat Shalom in Sommerville, Massachusetts, a suburb of Boston.

Hebreism
The movement to reintroduce Hebrew as a living language.

Hegelian
Refers to the German philosopher Hegel.

Herem
The social quarantine Jews place on other Jews when they are seen not to be acting according to accepted social norms. If formalized, it is a kind of excommunication. Spinoza was subjected to this.

Heschel, Abraham Joshua (1907–1972)
One of the leading Jewish philosophers and scholars in the United States.

Hess, Moses (1812–1875)
German socialist, a precursor of modern Zionism and the father of Zionist socialism.

Hirsh, Rabbi (1808–1888)
Founder of neo-Orthodoxy. Tried to combine the *Haskalah* with tradition.

Histadrut
The General Federation of Labor in Israel, founded in 1920.

Hizballah
One of the Palestinian military groups.

Humash
Literally, five; referring to the Five Books of Moses; the Pentateuch.

Hutz L'Aretz
Outside of the Land of Israel; Diaspora.

HTML
HyperText Markup Language. The coded format used to create documents on the World Wide Web.

HTTP
HyperText Transfer Protocol. The computer protocol developed and used by the World Wide Web.

Hyperlink
Links in HTML documents that users click on to go to other Web resources.

Ideological settlements
Settlements established in West Bank as part of the "Greater Israel" movement.

Inverted pyramid
The economic phenomenon of Jews in Eastern Europe where the Jews were fewest in the production of goods and were more numerous in the intellectual fields; a significant aspect of the "Jewish Problem"; considered not normal in economic terms.

Jabotinsky, Zeev (1880–1940)
Leader of antisocialist opposition (the Revisionists) in the World Zionist Organization before the creation of the State of Israel. Arch foe of Ben Gurion and Labor Zionism.

Jewish Agency
The international, nongovernmental body representing the World Zionist Organization (WZO), whose aims are to assist and encourage Jews to help in the development and settlement of pre-state Israel.

Jewish National Fund (JNF)
The land purchase and development fund of the Zionist Organization, founded in 1901.

Jihad
In Islam, the obligation to holy war against the infidel. One of the Palestinian military groups.

Judenrein
Clean of Jews.

Joint
American Joint Distribution Committee, popularly known as the JDC or the "Joint"; founded in 1914 to provide relief for the Jews who were suffering during World War I.

Kabbalah
The traditional and most commonly used term for the esoteric and mystical teachings of Judaism.

Kaftan
An outer garment worn by the ultra-Orthodox Jews.

Katznelson, Berl (1887–1994)
A central figure of the Zionist Labor movement, educator, and writer.

Kibbutz
A voluntary collective community in which there is no private wealth and which is responsible for all of the needs of its members and their families; a unique creation of the Zionist Labor movement and the Jewish national revival movement in Palestine.

Kibbutz HaMeuhad
Proto "Land of Israel" movement.

Kibbutznik
A person living on a kibbutz.

Labor
Referring to the Labor political party of Israel, often associated with the political "left."

Ladino
The language created by the Sephardic Jewish Community (a sort of Sephardi Yiddish).

Law of Return
A fundamental law of the Jewish State that guarantees any Jew, anywhere in the world, the unconditional right to immigrate to Israel and to immediately become an Israeli citizen. The only exception being if the Jewish individual is using this right to escape justice for a criminal act in another country.

Lay tefillin
The Orthodox Jewish act of putting on the prayer phylacteries as part of morning prayers.

Levantine
Middle Eastern (often used in a pejorative manner). Its most accurate definition would be a person of middle-eastern origin who adapts the externals of Western culture but none of its values and therefore becomes alienated from his or her own tradition without really becoming part of Western culture.

Likud
A major political party in Israel, often associated with the political "right."

Maimonides (1135–1204)
Rabbinic authority, codifier of Jewish law, philosopher, and royal physician; considered to be the most illustrious figure in Judaism in the post-Talmudic era. Also called "Rambam" (Rabbi Moses Ben Maimon) by the Jews.

Mapai
The Hebrew Workers Party of the Land of Israel. Fundamental component of modern Israel Labor Party.

Mea-Shearim
A section of Jerusalem, a center of the ultra-Orthodox community in Israel.

Meir, Golda (1898–1978)
Labor leader and Israel prime minister during the Yom Kippur War of 1973; affectionately known as "Golda."

Mendelssohn, Moshe (1729–1786)
Philosopher of the German Enlightenment and spiritual leader of German Jewry during the early *Haskalah* period.

Midrash
Literally, to search, to seek; a genre of rabbinic literature consisting of homilies, commentaries, history, and folklore expounding the Bible.

Mitzpim
Small Jewish hilltop settlements.

Mitzvot
Jewish religious and spiritual commitments and obligations.

Mizrahi
The religious Zionist movement founded by Rabbi Meir Berlin (Bar-Ilan) in 1902, motto: "The land of Israel for the People of Israel according to the Torah of Israel."

Modern Orthodox
Orthodoxy in the tradition of the Enlightened Orthodox, in contrast to the ultra-Orthodox.

Moshav
Cooperative smallholders' villages in Israel, combining some of the features of both cooperative and private farming.

Mukhtarism
Political corruption in the Arab community (after the traditional name of the local village head, Mukhtar).

Musrara
The Jewish North African Jerusalem slum.

Mussar movement
A modern religious movement that placed emphasis on the idea of "imitation of God," the ideal toward which man's ethical behavior should aim.

Myth (mythology)
The fundamental narrative of a people, composed of fact and fiction but representing a basic truth for that people.

New Israel Fund
A small, alternative fundraising organization that raises money for progressive avant-garde social and cultural activities in Israel with which the Federation/UJA would not involve itself.

Olim
Jews who made *aliya*, immigrated to the Land of Israel (see also *aliya*).

Oriental Jews
Usually refers to all those Jews whose origins are in Africa and Asia.

Ost Juden
Jews of Eastern European origin.

Peace Now
Political movements in Israel pushing for peace under nearly any conditions.

People of the Book (*Ahl al-Kitab*)
A term devised by Islam referring to Jews and Christians recognized as the two earlier monotheistic religions; because of this status they were considered a "protected people" within Islam.

Post-Zionism
A collection of widely varying views in Israel that have one thing in common—Zionism is no longer relevant for the citizens of modern Israel.

Project Renewal
A program initiated by Menachem Begin that involves the Diaspora directly with urban renewal in the poorer neighborhoods and towns in Israel.

Ramat Gan
A suburb of Tel Aviv, noted for the successful integration of the Iraqi Jews there.

Rambam
Rabbenu Moshe ben Maimon (see also Maimonides).

Revisionist
A maximalist political Zionist movement founded by Vladimir (Zeev) Jabotinsky in the 1920s suggesting a Jewish State with a Jewish majority on "both sides of the Jordan."

Saadya Gaon (882–942)
The greatest scholar and author of the Geonic period and one of the dominant figures in the development of Judaism and its literature; the head of the Academy of Sura in Babylonia in the tenth century, philosopher engaged in much political struggle within the Jewish community in Palestine and with the Karaites.

Sabra
A local plant that is prickly outside and sweet inside, the popular metaphor for the Israeli.

Sapir, Pinhas (1907–1975)
Israel labor leader, active in Israeli politics especially in the area of government finances.

Second Wave
A phrase coined by Alvin Toffler to describe the industrial era in Europe, 1750s to the 1950s.

Sefer
Literally, scroll, in common Hebrew usage; a book.

Sefer Torah
The Scroll of the Torah, containing the Five books of Moses written by hand on parchment, considered to be the most sacred Jewish object; used mainly for reading during Jewish public worship services.

Sefer Yitserah
The earliest Hebrew text of the Jewish esoteric speculative tradition (circa eleventh century). A basic text of the Kabbalah.

Sefirot
A basic term of the Kabbalah, designating the primordial "numbers" and the stages of the emanation of God's manifestation into the world.

Sephardi Jews
Literally, Jews whose origins are in Spain (*Sepharad* in Hebrew) and who left Spain and settled around the world as a result of the inquisition. Speak their own language (Ladino).

Seven Commandments of Noah (Noachian Laws)
The seven laws considered by the rabbinical tradition as the minimal moral duties enjoined by the Bible on all humanity. They are prohibitions against idolatry, blasphemy, bloodshed, sexual sins, theft, and eating from a living animal, and the requirement to establish a legal system.

Shas
The political party of the Oriental and Sephardic ultra-Orthodox community in Israel.

Shnorrer
Beggar, usually used in a derogatory manner.

Siddur (plural, siddurim)
Literally, order (of prayers); refers to the Jewish prayer book.

Silicon wadi
The Israeli analogue to Silicon Valley in California; The term *wadi* is Arabic for valley.

Syrkin, Nachman (1868–1924)
The first ideologist and leader of Socialist Zionism, developed a complete synthesis of Socialism with Jewish Nationalism as embodied in Zionism.

Talmud
Literally, studying, learning; the most basic set of texts, after the Bible, dealing with Jewish law, lore, and history. The text was edited about 500 C.E., and it is still the core of Jewish scholarship.

Tfuzot
Literally, dispersion; Diaspora.

Third Wave
The phrase coined by Alvin Toffler in his book by the same name that has become part of our jargon, refers to our current information/knowledge age.

Three waves
Alvin Toffler used this metaphor to describe the three basic eras of humanity: First Wave is the agricultural age (10,000 years ago until about 1750), Second Wave is the industrial age (1750s until the 1950s), and the Third Wave (1950s until now) is the information age we are now living through.

Tiferet
Translates as beauty or compassion. One of the *sefirot* of the Kabbalah. The most central and connected *sefira* of the Kabbalic Tree of Life.

Tikkun olam
Literally, healing and repairing the world, one of the most basic Jewish aspirations and commitments.

Tolstoyan-Gordonian Myth
The creation of the noble Jewish peasant worker myth.

Torah
Literally, teaching; refers to the vast range of Jewish religious and spiritual knowledge.

Toynbee, Arnold (1889–1975)
One of the major historians of the modern period, who was not particularly sympathetic to the Jews, calling them a historical fossil.

Tzedaka
Literally, justice, the Jewish term for philanthropy.

Ulpan
A center for intensive study by adults, especially of Hebrew by newcomers to Israel.

Value tropism
The built-in natural tendency toward acting with positive values. In botany, for example, tropism is the tendency for a plant to lean toward the light.

Wahabi
The most fanatic and intolerant Islamic sect. It is to Islam what the Ku Klux Klan is to Christianity.

White man's burden
A phrase coined by Rudyard Kipling to justify the moral basis of colonialism. It indicates that the White race has been "chosen" to bring Enlightenment to the colored peoples of the world.

Williamsburg
A section of Brooklyn, New York, a center of the Hassidic community.

Yad Mordechai
Kibbutz named for Mordechai Anilevich, one of the leaders of the Warsaw ghetto uprising in 1944.

Yeshiva
An advanced Jewish learning academy, institutes of Talmudic learning.

Yiddishism
A movement for the enrichment and promotion of Yiddish culture. Associated with Bundism.

Yiddishkeit
Literally, behaving like a Jew, in the Jewish manner. Jewish cultural characteristics.

Yordim
Those who go down—leave Israel (the opposite of *olim*).

Zaida
Grandfather.

Bibliography

Abramov, Zalman S. *Perpetual Dilemma: Jewish Religion in the Jewish State*. Cranbury, NJ: Associated University Press, 1976.

Adler, Haim, and Michael Inbar. *Ethnic Integration in Israel*. New Brunswick, NJ: Transaction Books, 1977.

Augstein, Rudolf. *Jesus, Son of Man*. New York: Urizen Books, 1977.

Banerjee, Neela. "The High Hidden Cost of Saudi Arabian Oil." *New York Times*, 21 October 2001.

Barnatt, Christopher. *Valueware*. London: Adamantine Press, 1999.

Barrett, William. *Death of the Soul*. Garden City, NY: Doubleday Anchor, 1986.

Barrow, John D., and Frank J. Tipler. *The Anthropic Cosmological Principle*. Oxford: Oxford University Press, 1988.

Becker, Carl L. *The Heavenly City of the Eighteenth-Century Philosophers*. New Haven, Conn.: Yale University Press, 1964.

Becker, Ernest. *The Denial of Death*. New York: The Free Press, 1973.

———. *Escape from Evil*. New York: The Free Press, 1975.

———. *The Structure of Evil*. New York: The Free Press, 1976.

Bell, D., and B. Kennedy. *The Cybercultures Reader*. London: Routledge, 2000.

Bell, Wendell. *The Foundations of Future Studies*, 2 vols. New Brunswick, NJ: Transaction Publishers, 1997.

Benedikt, Michael, ed. *Cyberspace: First Step*. Cambridge, MA: MIT Press, 1995.

Bisk, Tsvi. "Israel Towards the 21st Century" (in Hebrew). *Shdemot Magazine*, Winter 1990.

———. "Judaism." In *Encyclopedia of the Future*, edited by George Kurian and Graham Molitar, 524–26. New York: Simon and Schuster, Macmillan, 1996.

———. "Labor Movement Towards the 21st Century" (in Hebrew). *Shdemot Magazine*, Winter 1990.

———. "Middle East." In *Encyclopedia of the Future*, edited by George Kurian and Graham Molitar, 615–17. New York: Simon and Schuster, Macmillan, 1996.

————. "Towards a Practical Utopianism." *The Futurist* (May/June 2002).

————. "Utopianism Comes of Age: From Postmodernism to Neomodernism." In *Utopian Thinking in Sociology: Creating the Good Society*, edited by Arthur Shostak. Washington, DC: American Sociological Association, 2001.

————. "Zionism in the 21st Century." *Midstream Magazine*, May 1990.

Brown, M., and B. Lightman, ed. *Creating the Jewish Future*. Walnut Creek, CA: Altamira/Sage, 1999.

Bury, J. B. *The Idea of Progress*. Mineola, NY: Dover Publications, 1987.

Calvin, John. *The Institutes*, "Ecclesiastical Ordinances and the Obedience Owed Rulers." In *Sources of the Western Tradition*, 2nd ed., vol. 1., edited by Marvin Perry, Joseph Peden, and Theodore H. Von Laue. Boston: Houghton Mifflin, 1991.

Capra, Fritjof. *The Turning Point*. New York: Bantam Books, 1983.

Coates, J., and J. Jarratt. *What Futurists Believe*. Lomond, MD: World Future Society, 1989.

Cohen, A., and P. Mendes-Flohr. *Contemporary Jewish Religious Thought*. New York: Free Press, 1972.

Cornish, Edward. *The Study of the Future*. Washington, DC: World Future Society, 1977.

Curtis, Michael, and Mordechai S. Chertoff. *Israel: Social Structure and Change*. New Brunswick, NJ: Transaction Press, 1973.

Davies, Paul. *About Time*. New York: Simon and Schuster, 1995.

Dawson, Christopher. *The Making of Europe*. New York: Meridian Books, 1956.

Edwards, Jefferson, Denis Eklof, and Daniel Yergin. "Fueling Asia's Recovery." *Foreign Affairs* 77, no. 2 (Mar/April 1998).

Ellul, Jacques. "The Betrayal of the West: A Reaffirmation of Western Values." In *Sources of the Western Tradition*, vol. 2, edited by Marvin Perry, Joseph Peden, and Theodore H. Von Laue, 364–68. Boston: Houghton Mifflin, 1987.

Encyclopedia Judaica. Jerusalem: Keter Publishing House, 1974

Frankl, Victor E. *Man's Search for Meaning*. New York: Pocket Books, 1977.

————. *The Unheard Cry for Meaning*. New York: Pocket Books, 1985.

Fromm, Erich. *Escape from Freedom*. New York: Avon Books, 1965.

————. *You Shall Be As Gods*. New York: Fawcett World Library, 1969.

Gerstenfeld, Manfred. *Israel's New Future: Interviews*. Jerusalem: Rubin Mass, 1994.

Gibson, William: *Neuromancer*. New York: Ace Books, 1984.

Green, Irving. *Judaism on the Web*. New York: MIS Press/Holt, 1997.

Greenblatt, Mattis. "Prophet of Spiritual Renewal." In *The Jewish Action Reader*, 1998 (www.orot.com/prophet).

Greer, Thomas H. *A Brief History of Western Man*, 2nd ed. New York: Harcourt Brace Jovanovich, 1972.

Halkin, Hillel. *Letters to an American Jewish Friend*. Philadelphia: Jewish Publication Society, 1977.

Halal, William, ed. *Infinite Resource: Creating and Leading the Knowledge Enterprise*. New York: Jossey-Bass, 1998.

Hammerman, Joshua. *The Lordismysheppard: Seeking God in* Cyberspace. Deerfield Beach, FL: Simcha Press, 2000.

Harman, Willis. *Global Mind Change*. Indianapolis, IN: Knowledge Systems, 1988.

Hertzberg, Arthur, ed. *The French Enlightenment and the Jews*. New York: Jewish Publication Society, 1968.
———. *The Zionist Idea*. New York: Atheneum, 1969.
Heschel, Abraham J. *Who Is Man?* Stanford, CA: Stanford University Press, 1965.
Hoffer, Eric. *The True Believer*. New York: Perennial Library, 1966.
Hoffman, Charles. *The Smoke Screen: Israel, Philanthropy and American Jews*. Silver Spring, MD: Eshel Books, 1989.
Israel Pocket Library. *Zionism*. Jerusalem: Keter Books, 1973.
Jaffe, Amy Meyers, and Robert A. Manning. "The Shocks of a World of Cheap Oil." *Foreign Affairs* 79, no. 1 (Jan/Feb 2000).
"The Jewish State: The Next Fifty Years." *AZURE* (Winter 1999).
Kadushin, Charles, Shaul Kelner, and Leonard Saxe. *Being a Jewish Teenager in America: Trying to Make It*. Waltham, MA: Brandeis University, Cohen Center for Modern Jewish Studies, 2002.
Kafih, Joseph. *The Customs of Yemenite Jews* (in Hebrew). Jerusalem: Ben Zvi Institute, 1978.
Kaku, Michio. *Hyperspace*. New York: Doubleday Anchor, 1994.
———. *Visions*. New York: Anchor/Random House, 1997.
Kamenetz, Rodger. *The Jew in the Lotus*. San Francisco: Harper San Francisco, 1995.
Kelman, Stuart, ed. *What We Know about Jewish Education*. Los Angeles: Torah Aura, 1992.
Kennan, George F. *Russian and the West under Lenin and Stalin*. Boston: Little, Brown, 1961.
Kirby, R., and E. Brewer. *The Temples of Tomorrow: World Religions and the Future*. London: Grey Seal Books, 1993.
Kook, Avraham. *Lights of Holiness*. Translated by Yakov Schulman. www.orot.com/lights_holiness, 1998.
———. *Orot*. Translated by Rabbi Bezalel Naor. Northvale, NJ: Jason Aronson, 1993.
Kotkin, Joel. *Tribes*. New York: Random House, 1992.
Kuhn, Thomas S. *The Structure of Scientific Revolutions*, 2nd ed. Chicago: University of Chicago Press, 1970.
Kurian, George, and Graham Molitar. *Encyclopedia of the Future*, 2 vols. New York: Macmillan, 1996.
Kurzweil, Ray. *The Age of Spiritual Machines*. New York: Penguin Books, 1999.
Lee, Susan. "We Can Live without Saudi Oil." *Wall Street Journal*, 14 November 2001.
Lerner, Eric J. *The Big Bang Never Happened*. New York: Vintage Books, 1992.
Lewis, C. S. *The Abolition of Man*. Oxford: Oxford University Press, 1982.
Liddell-Hart, B. H. *Strategy*, 2nd ed. New York: New American Library, 1974.
Levy, Pierre. *Becoming Virtual: Reality in the Digital Age*. Translated by Robert Bononno. New York: Plenum Press, 1998.
Margolis, Jonathan. *A Brief History of Tomorrow*. New York: Bloomsbury, 2000.
Matson, Floyd W. *The Broken Image: Man, Science, and Society*. Garden City, NY: Doubleday Anchor, 1966.
Michener, James A. *Centennial*. London: Transworld Publishers, Corgi, 1975.
Naisbitt, John. *Global Paradox*. New York: Morrow, 1994.
———. *HighTech-HighTouch*. New York: Broadway Books, 1999.

Nessyashu, Mordechai. *Cosmotheism: Israel, Zionism, Judaism and Humanity. Towards the 21st Century* (in Hebrew). Ramat Gan, Israel: Poetika Press, 1997.

———. *Israel As a Challenge* (in Hebrew). Tel Aviv: Am Oved, 1969.

———. *The Scientific Revolution and the Developing World* (in Hebrew). Tel Aviv: Am Oved, 1965.

Nietzsche, Friedrich. *Beyond Good and Evil*. New York: Vintage Books, 1966.

Patai, Raphael. *Israel between East and West*. Philadelphia: Jewish Publication Society, 1953.

Peters, Ralph. "The Saudi Threat." *Wall Street Journal*, January 2002.

Pole, J. R., ed. *The American Constitution: For and Against*. New York: Hill and Wang, 1987.

Popper, Karl R. *The Poverty of Historicism*. New York: Harper Torchbooks, 1964.

Price, Alan. *Israel in the Year 2025*. New York: Vantage Press, 1988.

Prigogine, Ilya, and Isabelle Stengers. *Order out of Chaos*. New York: Bantam Books, 1984.

Putnam, Robert. *Bowling Alone*. New York: Simon and Schuster, 2000.

Randall, John Herman Jr. *The Making of the Modern Mind*. New York: Columbia University Press, 1976.

Rittner, Stephen. *Jewish Ethics for the 21st Century*. Boston: Rittner Publishing, 1977.

Rosen, Jonathan. *The Talmud and the Internet*. New York: Farrar, Straus, and Giroux, 2000.

Rotenstreich, Nathan. "Can There Be a Revival of Zionist Ideology?" *Midstream Magazine*, May 1990.

Rushkoff, Douglas. *Cyberia: Life in the Trenches of Hyperspace*. New York: Harper Collins, 1994.

———. *Cyberia: Life in the Trenches of Cyberspace*. Manchester, UK: Clinamen Press, 2002.

Russell, Peter. *The Global Brain*. Los Angeles: Tarcher, 1983.

Sacher, Howard Morley. *The Course of Modern Jewish History*. New York: Dell Publishing, 1977.

Sardar, Ziauddin. *The Future of Muslim Civilization*. London: Mansell, 1987.

Schachter-Shlomi, Zalman. *Paradigm Shift*. Northvale, NJ: Aronson, 1993.

Schectman, J. B. *On the Wings of Eagles*. New York: Thomas Yoseloff Press, 1961.

Schoem, David. "The Supplementary School." In *What We Know about Jewish Education*, edited by Stuart Kelman. Los Angeles: Torah Aura, 1992.

Scholem, Gershom. *Kabbalah*. New York: Dorset Press, 1974.

Shlain, Leonard. *The Alphabet versus the Goddess*. New York: Viking Press, 1998.

Shostak, Arthur B. *Utopian Thinking in Sociology: Creating the Good Society*. Washington, DC: American Sociological Association, 2001.

Shumsky, Abraham. *The Clash of Cultures in Israel*. New York: Greenwood Press, 1972.

Silver, Abba-Hillel. *Where Judaism Differed*. New York: Macmillan, 1979.

Slaughter, Richard, ed. *The Knowledge Base of Futures Studies*, 3 vols. Victoria, Australia: DDM Media, 1996.

Soleri, Paolo. *Technology and Cosmogenesis*. New York: Paragon House, 1985.

Spady, R., and R. Kirby. *The Leadership of Civilization Building*. Seattle, WA: Forum Foundation, 2002.

Steinsaltz, Adin. *The Thirteen-Petalled Rose*. New York: Basic Books, 1980.

Talmon, J. L. *The Origins of Totalitarian Democracy*. London: Secker and Warburg, 1952.

Tapscott, Don. *Growing Up Digital: The Rise of the Net Generation*. New York: McGraw-Hill, 1998.

Teilhard de Chardin, Pierre. *The Future of Man*. New York: Harper Torchbooks, 1969.

———. *The Phenomenon of Man*. New York: Harper Torchbooks, 1965.

Teutsch, David, ed. *Imagining the Jewish Future*. Albany: State University of New York Press, 1992.

Toffler, Alvin. *Future Shock*. New York: Bantam Books, 1970.

———, ed. *The Futurists*. New York: Random House, 1972.

———. *Power Shift*. New York: Bantam Books, 1991.

———. *The Third Wave*. New York: Bantam Books, 1981.

Tucker, Robert. *Philosophy and Myth in Karl Marx*. Cambridge, MA: Cambridge University Press, 1964.

Vital, David. *The Future of the Jews*. Cambridge, MA: Harvard University Press, 1990.

Weiss-Rosmarin, Trude. *Judaism and Christianity: The Differences*. New York: Jonathan David, 1968.

Wertheim, Margaret. *The Pearly Gates of Cyberspace*. New York: Norton, 1999.

Wilber, Ken. *A Brief History of Everything*. Boston: Shambhala Press, 1996.

———. *Eye to Eye: The Quest for the New Paradigm*. Boston: Shambhala Press, 1996.

Wilson, Edward O. *Consilience: The Unity of Knowledge*. New York: Vintage Books, 1999.

Wine, Sherwin T. *Judaism beyond God*. Farmington Hills, MI: Society for Humanistic Judaism, 1985.

y Gasset, Jose Ortega. *The Dehumanization of Art*. Garden City, NY: Doubleday Anchor, 1956.

Young, Louise B. *The Unfinished Universe*. New York: Simon and Schuster, 1986.

Zaleski, Jeff. *The Soul of Cyberspace: How the New Technology Is Changing Our Spiritual Lives*. San Francisco: Harper Edge, 1997.

Index

Aburdene, Patricia, 221
Advertising, 9–10
Ahad Ha'Am, 165, 218–19
Aliya, 21–22, 24, 38–40, 218
America: confessional identity, 47–48; similarities with Israel, 44–45; similiarities to Jewish culture, 47–48
America, Black: contributions to American culture, 45–46; Exodus metaphor, 45–46
American Declaration of Independence, 3–4
American Jewish Committee's Yearbook, 49
American West, 46
Analytic methodologies: PEST (political, economic, social, and technological), 75; SWOT (strengths, weaknesses, opportunities, and threats), 75
Anti-intellectualism, 11
Antinomianism, 152
Anti-semitism and Zionism, 14
Arab boycott, effects of, 23
"Arab intellectual," 113
Arab population: alienation of, 60; urbanization of, 60
Arafat, Yassir, 68, 113

Aristotle, 15
Arrogance, cultural, 125–26
Art, modern, 10–11
Augstein, Rudolf, 150
Auto-Emancipation (Pinsker), 18, 121

Baalei tshuva, 22
Baby Boomers, 176
Bacon, Francis, 7
Becker, Carl, 137
Ben Gurion, David, 25, 121
Beyond Good and Evil (Nietzsche), 145
Biblical metaphor, 44
Bin Laden, Osama, 72, 73
Bnei Akiva, 123
Bomberg, Daniel, 195

Calvin, John, 152
Capitalism, 7, 9–10
Capra, Fritjof, 2, 192–93
Centennial (Michener), 46
Chauvinism, cultural, 5
Child Power: Keys to the New Learning of the Digital Century (Papert), 208
Civilization, modern, 9–11
CNN, 76
Cold war, Israel-Egyptian-Jordanian, 66–67

Commercial Revolution, 2–3
Computers, impact of, 8–9
Consilience: The Unity of Knowledge (Wilson), 185
Cosmopolis, 80
Cosmopolitanism, rootless, 17
Cosmotheism: Israel, Zionism, Judaism, and Humanity. Towards the 21st Century (Nessyahu), 168
Cultural admixtures, historical context of, 127–29
Cultural attitudes, Israeli: and deculturalization, 126; Levantine elements, 126
Cultural claustrophobia, 127–29
Cultural diversity, 131
Cultural history, Israeli, 129–30
Culture, industrialization of, 11
Cyberia: defined, 184–85; and development of humanity, 184
Cybernetics, 169
Cyber Oral Torah, 206
Cyber Or Project: characteristics of, 201–2; goals of, 202; as knowledge management system, 202
Cyberspace: characteristics of, 173; and civilizing potential, 174–75; cultural implications, 171–73; and Cyberia, 184; defined, 184; definition of, 169; and evolution of humanity, 170; as humanity online, 187; increased rate of change, 170, 186; information superhighway, 171–73; and the Kabbalistic system, 182–86; and materialism, 183–84; need for analytic/critical thinking, 170; and new communal patterns, 220–21; as a new spiritual ecology, 179; and omniconsciousness, 229; opportunities, 174–75; as path to wisdom, 171; personal/planetary transformation, 229; and shared learning, 171; spiritual uniqueness, 184–85; and time, 182–83; as transition to the future, 175; and the uplifting of mankind, 229
Cyberspace/time: celebration of the spirit, 191; and concept of *aliya*, 218; and Diaspora Jewry, 224–25; and human consciousness, 189–91; and the human spirit, 196; impact on education, 202–5; inherent spirituality of, 189–91; and Jewish cybercommunalism, 215–16, 224–25; and Jewish identity/community, 215–16; and Jewish tradition, 194–96; and rules of human interaction, 202; sanctification of time, 222; and spiritual quests, 191–94; and universal cyber consciousness, 189–91
CyberSynagogue: and cyberrabbis, 226–27; and Havurah movement, 228; and Jewish cybercommunalism, 226–27; limitations, 226–27
Cyber-Zionism, 218–19, 223–29

Darwin, Charles, 6
De Chardin, Teilhard, 190, 219
Deism, 3, 5
Democracy, 69–70
Der Spiegel, 150
Determinism/volition, 186–87
Dewey, John, 208
Diaspora, Jewish, 2, 14, 19, 20–21, 24, 25, 39–40, 42, 51, 71–72, 73, 77, 85, 89–90
Diaspora-Israeli relationship: civil service reform, 97–100; and constitutional democracy, 92–93; energy interdependence projects, 94–96; financial contributions, 90, 93–94; focus on civil society, 90–99; future of, 100–101; goals of, 91–92, 100–101; historical success, 90; human resource contributions, 98–99; importance of national projects, 97–100; importance of national-universal projects, 94–97; and majoritarian democracy, 92–93; political context, 91–98; public service reform, 97–100; and survival, 91–93; and totalitarian democracy, 92–93; and Zionism, 100–101
Diaspora Jewry, 159, 161, 176, 179, 218, 224–25
Dreyfus affair, 18
Drucker, Peter, 12
Dubnov, Simon, 148

Ecumenism, 135–41
Education, 10
Emancipation, Jewish, 2–3, 4, 17–18
Energy independence projects, 94–96
English-Speaking Residents' Association (ESRA), 98
Enlightenment, 2–4, 5, 6–7, 9–10
Enlightenment, modernistic, 17
Enlightment/Industrial Revolution, 12
Entropy, 219
Exile, 14, 56
Exodus metaphor, 44–47, 75; and American immigration, 46–47; and the American West, 46; and Black America, 45; and the Mormons, 46; and the Pilgrim forefathers, 44–45; and suburbia, 47

First Wave ideology, 172–73, 216–17
Fourth Wave ideology, 217
Free will. *See* Determinism/volition
French Enlightment and the Jews, The (Hertzberg), 16
Fundamentalism, religious, 4
Futures, alternative, 2

Galilee, demographics of, 59
Gap, social/ethnic, 58–60, 65, 75, 83–84, 103–4, 116–20
Gardner, Howard, 210
Gaza, 61
Generation X, 176
Gibson, William, 169
Ginsburg, Asher. *See* Ahad Ha'Am
Global Brain, The (Russell), 190
Global governance network, 73–74, 83
Global Paradox (Naisbitt), 224
Goldstein, Baruch, 111
Greater Palestine, 113
Green, Arthur, 188
Growing Up Digital: The Rise of the Net Generation (Tapscott), 175–77, 201

Halachic law, 48
Halkin, Hillel, 25
Haredi Jewry: American, 22; anti-Zionist, 21–22; feminist movement, 22–23; national, 21–22; Sephardic, 22; Zionization of, 21–23
Hawking, Steven, 12
Heavenly City of the Eighteenth-Century Philosophers, The (Becker), 137
Hebrew language, regeneration of, 16
Herzberg, Arthur, 25
Herzl, Theodore, 18, 25, 218–19
Herzog, Chaim, 111
Heschel, Abraham, 179
Hess, Moses, 15–16, 25
Hilltop communities, establishment of, 59–60
Holland, 128
Holocaust, 14
Humanism, 3; influence on Jews, 4; Renaissance, 3; secular, 2, 4
Human race, history of, 2
Human rights, Palestinian, 61
Human rights, universal declaration of, 132, 133
Hypertext: as non-linear, 195–96; and the Talmud, 194–96

Immigration and open societies, 127–29
Industrial Revolution, 2–3, 11–12
Industry, labor-intensive, 64–66
Information technology, 222
Inquisition, 3
Institutes, The (Calvin), 152
Intifada, 67–68, 72, 89–90, 104, 110
Islam, 18–20
Islam, Golden Age of, 127
Islamic hostility, 82
Israel, 2; opportunities, 71–72; similarities with America, 44–45; strengths and resources of, 69–70; survival as a democracy, 69–70, 106–14; threats to, 72–74, 82; weaknesses and challenges of, 69–70
Israeli ethnic relations: and breakdown of traditional culture, 122–23; cultural attitudes of, 125–29; cultural pluralism of, 125, 131–33; and cultural prejudice, 124–25; future of, 131–33; historical/cultural context of, 116–20; and music, 129–31; psychological perspective of, 116–18; stan-

dards of progress of, 123–24; and
Zionism, 121–22
Israeli Grand Strategy: Arab acceptance
of, 86; and citizen's rights, 79; and
democracy, 79; and end of international isolation, 86; and the European Union, 78; and globalism, 81;
and Islamic hostility, 82; and Israel as
a city-state, 81–82; and the Israeli
army, 78; and Israeli courts, 79–80;
and Jewish policy, 87; NATO and the
European Union, 80, 86; new policies and programs of, 83–85; and
peace and security, 85–86; primary
goals of, 86; and relationships, 77–78.
See also Jewish Grand Strategy
Israel's future, 131–33

Jesus and the Moneychangers, Jewish
interpretation of, 150–52
Jesus Son of Man (Augstein), 150
Jewish Agency/WZO, 98
Jewish-Arab relations: and corruption,
111–13; economic warfare of, 104–5;
and the European Union, 114; future
policy of, 113–14; and human rights,
109–13; and ideological settlements,
105; and immigration laws, 108–9;
and Israeli Arabs, 109–14; Jewish
symbols of, 106–10; and Law of
Return, 108–9; and militant parliamentary leadership, 113; and moral
superiority, 106–7, 110–11; and
mukhtarism, 112; principles of, 105–6;
and women's rights, 106, 112–13
Jewish culture: and breakdown of secular humanist paradigm, 11; foundations of, 195
Jewish educational aims: and accommo-
dation of multiple intelligences, 210;
and the age of wisdom, 217–18; and
broadcast education, 206–7; and
challenges for educators, 214; and
customized learning, 210; and cyberlearning techniques, 199; and home
learning, 212; and information technology, 199; and interactive learning,
207–8; and the Jewish "Explorato-

rium," 212–13; and learning as fun,
211; and learning to learn, 209; and
learning vs. education, 199–200; as a
lifelong enterprise, 209; a light unto
the nations, 218; and pleasure of
discovery, 208–9; and primary function of education, 214; and reconcep-
tualization of learning, 201; and role
of the teacher, 209; and strategies for
learning, 200–201; and teacher as
facilitator, 211
Jewish-Egypt relations, 113
Jewish emancipation, 17–18
Jewish Grand Strategy: and auto-
emancipation from self-pity, 220–21;
and cultural syntropy, 219–20; defined,
53–55; and futuristic thinking, 56;
historical context of, 56–64; and new
communal patterns, 220–21; positive
view of Jewish future, 220; post-State
settlement policy, 56–64; significance
of the individual, 221–23; threats to,
223; value systems, 55–59, 62–66
Jewish identity: centrality of human
behavior, 157–59; and concept of
Jewish citizenship, 159–63; cultural
traditions, 161; distinctiveness of,
165; and ethical monotheism,
166–68; as evolutionary process,
157–59; historical context, 155–56,
166–68; and idolatry, 160–61; individual moral autonomy, 157; modern
history, 166–67; multifaceted nature
of, 156–57; and nostalgia, 161;
Orthodox Judaism, 167; and pluralistic heterodoxy, 159–62; and the
postmodern world, 167–68; redefinition of, 164–65; and reevaluation of
traditions, 162–64; secular Zionism,
167; space age worldview, 168; and
spiritual pioneers, 167–68; and the
transition generation, 162–64
Jewish industrial proletariat, 64
Jewish metaphor, 44–45
Jewish National Fund, 56
Jewish nationalism, 18
Jewish Net Generation, 205–14; characteristics of, 175–77; and Diaspora

Jewry, 176; "edutainment" as aid to networking, 222; and nonlinear thinking, 177; and Talmudic thinking, 177

Jewish Publication Society Bible, 143

Jewish spirituality: characteristics of, 188–89; in crisis, 191–92; in cyberspace, 179; and Diaspora Jewry, 179; evolution of, 188–89; and globalization, 192; and hypertext, 194–96; and technology, 197

Jewish State, 17, 18

Jewish State (Herzl), 18

Jewish symbols, attacks on, 107–10

Jewish Underground, 111

Jewry: Ashkenazi, 116–20, 122–23, 125, 126–27; Iraqi, 124; North African, 122, 124; Oriental, 121–27; Russian, 124; Spanish, 124

Jews: anti-Israeli, 21; cosmopolitan, 16–17, 18; decline of viable communities, 19–20; and exile, 14; and Jewish integrity, 135; and Jewish nationalism, 18; mediocrity, 25; place in modern world, 1–2, 12, 14, 16–17; relationships with Christian world, 135; self-criticism and Zionism, 17; self-emancipation, 17–18; self-hate, 17; survival, 1, 19, 25–26, 40–41, 49, 52, 53, 106–14, 135; threats to, 135; threats to identity, 148–52; work ethic, 39

Jews, American: and American Jewish identity, 52; challenges to, 48–49; contribution to Jewish future, 51–52; demographics, 48–50; and exile, 48–49; and fundamental Zionism, 43–44; influence on American culture, 47–48; and normality/abnormality of life, 49–51; political power, 56; ties with Israel, 51–52; uniqueness, 44–45

Jews, ultra-Orthodox, 21–22

Jews for Jesus, 140, 146, 147–49

Judaism: Bundism, 5; Conservative, 5; modern, 3; neo-Orthodox, 5; Reform, 5; Yiddishism, 5; Zionism, 5

Judaism and Christianity—The Differences (Weiss-Rosmarin), 146–47, 149

Judaism (magazine), 162–63

"Judaizing the Galilee," 59

Judenrein, Zionist prediction of, 17

Judeo-Christian ethic: and acausal ethics, 146; and anti-Jewishness, 148–49; and belief vs. behavior, 143–46; and Christian missionary strategies, 147–48, 154; and Christian prejudices, 141–50; and Christian worldview, 135–36; comparisons/contrasts of, 136–38; and forgiveness, 145; fundamental differences, 141–50; and good manners, 153–54; and intellectual honesty, 140–41; interpretation of Jesus and the Moneychangers, 150–52; and Jewish legalism, 152–53; and Jewish values, 141–50; and Jewish worldview, 135–36; macroethical principles, 136; meaning of, 138–41; microethical principles, 136; and morality, 144–46; nature of God, 141–44; and New Testament argumentation, 149–50; and responsibility, 143–46; and self-defense, 138–40; shared values of, 154; and stereotypes, 146–53; and superficial ecumenism, 140–41; Talmudic vs. New Testament thinking, 145–54

Judge, Anthony, 173

Kabbalah, 182; characteristics of, 196–97; increased study of, 196–97; and spiritualization of cyberspace, 196–97

Kesse, Zvi, 58

King, Martin Luther, 45

Klatzkin, Jacob, 25

Kook, Rabbi Abraham Isaac, 157, 162; intuitions regarding light, 179–82; and www.orot.com, 181

Kotkin, Joel 218

Labor Party, 57–59

Labor Zionism, 57–59, 64

Land Day, 60

Law: natural, 4–5; rational, 4–5

Law of Return, 108–9
Lazarus, Emma, 47
Letter to an American Jewish Friend
    (Halkin), 25
Levinson, Joseph, 158–59, 188
Liddell Hart, B.H., 53
Lieberman, Joseph, 52
Life in the Trenches of Hyperspace
    (Rushkoff), 184
"Light unto the Nations," 131

Madrid/Oslo process, 104–5
Manifest Destiny, 46
Marx, Karl, 6, 7, 125–26
Mazzini, 15
McLuhan, Marshal, 180–81, 202
Megatrends (Naisbitt), 194
Megatrends 2000 (Naisbitt, John, and
    Patricia Aburdene), 221
Meir, Golda, 58
Messianic Jews, 140, 147–49
Metaphor: Biblical, 44; Exodus as, 44,
    75; information superhighway as,
    171–73; Jesus and the Moneychang-
    ers as, 150–52; light as, 180–82;
    pagan, 44; phoenix as, 75; Pilgrim
    experience as, 44
Michener, James, 46
Mill, John Stuart, 200
Modernism, 6, 9
Mormons, 46
Moshavim, 57–59
Multiculturalism, 5, 7
Mythology: European, 43–44; United
    States, 43–44

Nationalism, Romantic, 17–18
Nazis, 18
Neomodernism, 8–9, 12
Nessyahu, Mordechai, 168; the cosmos
    as a conscious entity, 190; and uni-
    versal consciousness, 219
Neuromancer (Gibson), 169
New Israel Fund, 91–92
"New Jew," 7
"New Middle East," 67
New Testament, 149–50
Newton, Isaac, 5, 6

Nietzsche, Freidrich, 145
Noosphere, 219

Old Newland (Herzl), 25
Open societies: and immigration,
    127–29; metacultural bases, 130
Oslo Accords, 66–67
OstJuden, 17

Pagan metaphor, 44
Palestine Mandate, 61
Papert, Seymour, 208
Paradigm: defined, 2; dominant, 2; of
    Enlightment/Industrial Revolution,
    11–12; inherited, 2; shift, 2–8
Peace, 66–68; Arab view of, 23–24;
    Israeli view of, 23–24; obstacles to,
    62; process of, 103–6; as product of
    power, 70
People of the Book, 204–5
People of the Story, 206
Peres, Shimon, 67
Persian Gulf Oil, 72–73
PEST (political, economic, social, and
    technological) analysis: and Jewish
    Grand Strategy, 75–76; results of,
    76
Phoenix metaphor, 75
Pilgrim metaphor, 44
Pilpul, 149–50
Pink Floyd, 10
Pinsker, Leon, 18
Portnoy's Complaint (Roth), 15
Porush, David, 194
Postmodernism, 4, 6, 7–8, 9
Premodernism, 7
Project Renewal, 91–92

Rabbinical establishment: Ashkenazi,
    123; Oriental-Sephardi, 123
Rabin, Yitzhak, 77–78
Rationalism, 4–6
Renaissance, 2
Rome and Jerusalem (Hess), 15, 25
Roosevelt, Franklin Delano, 150
Roth, Phillip, 15
Rushkoff, Douglas, 184
Russell, Peter, 190, 219

Sacks, Rabbi Jonathan, 171
Sadat, Anwar, 23
Sartre, Jean-Paul, 166
Saudi Arabia, 72
Schoem, David, 200
Science: ethical implications of, 11; as fundamental intellectual superstructure, 7
Scientific Revolution, 2–3, 6, 8–9
Scientism, 7
Second Wave ideology, 10, 172–75, 216–17
Secularization, 6
Self-defense, 138–40
Self-hate, 17
Sephardic accent, 21, 22
Settlement policy, ideological: and anti-Zionism, 63; legality of, 61; political problems with, 62; security issues, 62–63
Settlement policy, post-State, 56–64; and Arab resistance, 56; immigrant absorption, 57–59
Settlement policy, pre-State, 56–58
Seven Commandments of Noah, 144, 153
Shapiro, Rabbi Rami, 177
Shas Party, 122
Sigal, Rabbi Phillip, 162–63, 166
Silicon Wadi, 39
Silver, Rabbi Abba Hille, 146–47
Six-Day War, 57, 75, 90, 129
Skinner, B. F., 7
Smith, Adam, 6, 7
Socialism, 6–7
Spain and obscurantist darkness, 128
Spanish Inquisition, 128
Spielberg, Steven, 202
Strategy (Liddell Hart), 53
SWOT (strengths, weaknesses, opportunities, and threats) analysis, 69, 75
Syntropy, 219–21
Szent-Gyorgyi, Albert, 219

Taliban, 72
Talmon, Yaakov, 92
Talmud: characteristics of, 195–96; and hypertext, 194–96; non-linearity of, 195–96

Talmudic page, 199
Tapscott, Don, 175–77, 206, 211, 213
Ten Lost Tribes, 45
Theology, 5; Deism, 3; natural, 3
Third Wave: civilization, 39; economy, 39; ideology, 8, 10
Third Wave, The (Toffler), 216
Third Wave ideology, 8, 10, 173–75, 216–17
Toffler, Alvin, 216
Totalitarian Democracy (Talmon), 92
Toynbee, Arnold, 148–49
Tribes (Kotkin), 218
Turning Point, The (Capra), 192–93
Twin Towers, 73

United Nations, 70
United Nations Resolution 194, 24, 83, 113
Utopianism, 180

War of Independence, 57
Wasteland, 8
Watson, 7
Waves of civilization, 216–17
Weisel, Eli, 145
Weiss-Rosmarin, Trude, Dr., 146–47
Where Judaism Differed (Silver), 146–47
Wilbur, Ken, 190
Wilson, Edward O., 185

Yiddishkeit, 143–44
Yom Kippur War, 68, 90, 130

Zionism, 2, 6; achievements, 16, 104–5; aims of, 13; and American Jews, 43–44; analysis and the Islamic world, 18–20; analysis of, 13–14; and concept of curing, 14; and contributions to human civilization, 15; as cure to anti-semitism, 14–15; defined, 50–51, 103; and the European Union, 36–37; goals of, 7, 35–36; history of, 31–33; ideological crisis inherent in, 13; and Jewish self-criticism, 17; and Jewish working class, 41; of mediocrity, 24–25; and modernist Enlightment assumptions,

5; and multiculturalism, 15; and new social ideology, 84; outcome of, 26; political program of, 13, 23–24; and power, 41; as proto-postmodernist movement, 18; rejection by Islam, 19; relevance, 13, 26–30; segments and ideology, 59; and self-criticism, 121; and the space age, 38–39; success of, 13, 23–25, 33–35, 41; survival of, 38; and the twenty-first century, 223–29; views on exile, 14

Zionism, post-, 13
Zionist Idea, The (Herzberg), 25
Zionist Project, 5

About the Authors

TSVI BISK is founder and director of the Strategic Educational Planning Institute.

DR. MOSHE DROR is the Media Director and Futurist at the National Teachers Center for the Study of Judaica, Humanities and Society, an arm of the Israeli Ministry of Education.